Abrahan.

American Prince

Abraham Lincoln, American Prince

Ancestry, Ambition and the Anti-Slavery Cause

WAYNE SOINI

McFarland & Company, Inc., Publishers

Jefferson, North Carolina

ISBN (print) 978-1-4766-8812-1
ISBN (ebook) 978-1-4766-4558-2

LIBRARY OF CONGRESS AND BRITISH LIBRARY
CATALOGUING DATA ARE AVAILABLE

Library of Congress Control Number 2022005022

On the cover: Abraham Lincoln immediately prior to Senate nomination,
Chicago, Illinois, Alexander Hesler, 1823–1895, photographer,
February 28, 1857, printed later (Library of Congress)

Printed in the United States of America

*McFarland & Company, Inc., Publishers
Box 611, Jefferson, North Carolina 28640
www.mcfarlandpub.com*

To Professor Charles B. Strozier,
mentor and friend

As to my book, all that I claim for it is that it is truthful
as far as I understand it.
—William "Billy" Herndon (1888)

We are all victims of stories in one way or another,
even if we are not in them, even if we are not born yet.
—Iphigenia in Barry Unworth,
The Songs of the Kings (2002)

Ah, bear in mind the garden was enchanted!
—Edgar Allan Poe, "To Helen" (1848)

Table of Contents

Table of Contents

Acknowledgments

After expressing my gratitude to Professor Charles B. Strozier, *sine qua non*, I fear omitting many other people who helped during my contemplation, research, writing and rewriting of this book. Nobody used more time and energy on behalf of a stranger than Jay Garner of Richmond County, Virginia, whose notes and many illustrations greatly amplify the sense of place in Lincoln's story. Members of BIO's active and lively Cambridge group, including (but not limited to) Patti Bender, Nigel Hamilton, Isabella Jancourtz, Melinda Ponder, and Ray Anthony Shepard, encouraged me when my energies and belief in accomplishing anything flagged. Dr. James Cornelius and the staff of the Abraham Lincoln Presidential Library found materials I requested and very kindly invited my attention to data I never knew existed. To the National Archives I owe much but especially the 1860 Lincoln interview that constitutes unique evidence of the significance of familial influences on Lincoln's development. Tom Emery, an indefatigably careful Illinois journalist, generously opened his sources to me about the Winter of the Deep Snow. With apologies to any inadvertently missed, I also want to acknowledge feedback angels Marsha Blitzer, Kirk Companion, John Galton, Roger Haynes, Ray Hildonen, Betty Ann Maney, Laura Plummer, Maureen Rogers, and Roxana von Kraus. Hats off also to my ever-ready loyal and honest beta readers Shelby Allen, Lise Breen, Kitty Beers, Jackie Fenn, Martin Levin, John Oberteuffer and Laura Ventimiglia. A California artist and weaver, my old classmate from the University of Massachusetts Amherst as well, Nancy Stark Jorgensen, provided an insider's view of the lost art of making linen cloth.

Two gifted public-school teachers in Gloucester, Massachusetts, namely Paul Harling, my fifth grade dynamo, and Thomas Brennan, my high school history teacher, each in turn intrigued generations of Gloucester kids to become history buffs. History-infused and happily histrionic lectures delivered at Suffolk University Law School by the

Acknowledgments

late Professor Herbert Lemelman definitely influenced my style. Behind any felicitous phrases, I hear Professor Lemelman in a deep voice yet unstilled. I was further, and more recently, inspired by Professor Julie Winch's enormously relevant classes (including both Genealogy and Biography) at the University of Massachusetts Boston and by the biographies she researched by overcoming obstacles inherent in the minefield of African American documentation. We can never thank any of our teachers too often.

Last but not least, my considerate family extended itself to make up for a great deal of time during which I was engaged in this project, and physically and/or mentally unavailable to them. Thank you for your love and patience, Anne, Eric, Mai, Heather, Kevin, Derek, Hannah and Jayden.

To anybody I omitted, I sincerely apologize.

Preface

A week-long seminar in Narrative History in 2011 changed my life. It was taught by Professor Charles B. Strozier, the author of *Lincoln's Quest for Union: Public and Private Meanings*, a best-selling bombshell of a book in 1982, the first psychobiography of Abraham Lincoln. Exposed to heady intellectual life daily, assigned a myriad of research and writing exercises, criticized in great detail but constructively, decades after college I found that a passionate fascination with Abraham Lincoln ignited.

Professor Strozier, then at work on the first dual biography of the friendship between Lincoln and a Kentucky enslaver named Joshua Speed, accepted when I volunteered to research and to comment. My next four years was enlivened by a great learning experience. Columbia University Press issued his book, entitled *Your Friend Forever, A. Lincoln: The Enduring Friendship of Abraham Lincoln and Joshua Speed*, in 2016. In the finalist pool for the annual Gilder-Lehman Lincoln Award, this book, another breakthrough, won praise from readers and reviewers nationally.

Could I explore Lincoln on my own?

Audaciously, I decided to try.

But what could I do?

One of Boston's treasures, displayed at the Museum of Fine Arts, is Paul Gauguin's painting, "D'ou Venons Nous/Que Sommes Nous/ Où Allons Nous," or "Where do we come from? What are we? Where are we going?" Applying this to Lincoln, the questions of "Who am I?" or "Where did I come from?" or "What were my highest hopes?" overmatched me in one sense. I could not survey the vast literature and master the context to mount an objective study of these great questions. On the other hand, I thought that it might just be possible for me to document Lincoln's *own* impressions of who he was, where he *thought* he came from, and *his* expressions of his highest hopes.

1

Preface

For such a project, in fact, Professor Strozier's book constituted a ready foundation and guide. Over five years, I worked with archival materials to piece out, check out and cross check solutions to the puzzles of how Lincoln saw himself, of who the people were to whom he felt he owed the most, and of the hopes he burned most intensely to attain.

Given short shrift in almost all biographies (Professor Strozier's excepted), Lincoln's ancestry gradually appeared to me to be the most pivotal and enduring influence in Lincoln's development, education and political agenda. I concluded that when Lincoln looked in the mirror, he saw himself as an American prince. Even though he was limited to hinting because his inheritance came with a family scandal, Lincoln often and publicly hinted at his Revolutionary lineage in speeches, documented as far back as 1838.[1]

The Lincoln I have unearthed was confident of a special destiny from childhood up and his ultimate hope, influenced by his mother and by her father as Lincoln idealized that man, was to immortalize his own name by linking it to the cause of anti-slavery.

Some may look askance at the propositions I unfold. After all, Lincoln knew his mother for less than ten years, as she died young, and he likely never met his maternal grandfather. Readers may be reluctant to accept a book about ancestors whom Lincoln either briefly or never knew—how relevant can they possibly be to his education, his political career, his Presidency and to history?

The book itself must answer for me. I contend that documents gathered here demonstrate that:

Lincoln's mother and her father, a Virginia planter, were frequent, major presences in Lincoln's mind;

"The Virginia planter" evolved from ridiculous in Lincoln's boyhood to revered in his adulthood;

The Declaration of Independence, Thomas Jefferson, George Washington and his grandfather became closely and inseparably associated in Lincoln's mind, as well as honored to a point of veneration;

His mother and her father led Lincoln from nearly the beginning of his life, inspiring and encouraging him to learn, to lead *and* to limit the time of slavery;

Without these two ancestors, Lincoln would likely have learned no more than an average farm boy, aspired to no abstract or noble goals, never felt sufficient confidence to strive for public office, and possessed no special interest in eradicating slavery from the United States.

To the extent that my conclusions differ from Strozier's and extend beyond statements he made in his now classic book, this book is new. I am, I believe, the first person whose theory it is that Lincoln ascended to otherwise impossible heights by way of ancestral allies. In the end, I come not to praise the familiar self-made Lincoln myth but to bury it. Unlike one of my sources, William "Billy" Herndon, who saluted "Lincoln the unaided—uneducated—lone penniless barefoot boy, [who] through holiness and persistency of an honest purpose carved upon the world's history—the character of *Honest Abe*," I see Lincoln's rise as a group effort, at its core most constantly and primarily composed of Lincoln and two ancestors he idolized, hidden allies of whom he paradoxically spoke directly only rarely.

Part One consists of a collection of seven reports and analyses, roughly chronological, about Lincoln and his blood kin. Two chapters are devoted to Lincoln's mother, Nancy Hanks Lincoln, so often scanted and shadowy in other Lincoln biographies, although inestimably significant in her son's life, while the balance reconstructs Lincoln's little-known and difficult to discern relationship with her father, the Virginia planter.

Part Two is a group of nine reflections on Lincoln's identity, more wide-ranging in time, each focused on a single pattern or theme related to Lincoln and his blood kin. Again, in another two chapters, Nancy is brought out as visibly and audibly as archives allow.

Part Three gives a short summary or recapitulation. An afterword, appendices, chapter notes, bibliography and index conclude the book.

A Note on Method
and Sources

Readers may be shocked by the fact that the inferences drawn in this book—new to them—are, first of all, the natural implications of many of Lincoln's own letters and speeches. My major conclusions are drawn from clues in Lincoln's own words, from sources including his first public address, the so-called Lyceum Address of 1838, in which he embraced a Revolutionary ancestry publicly, his speech at Peoria in 1854, notable for the intensity of its focus on Revolutionary blood, his "grandfathers" speech in Chicago in 1858 debate with Stephen Douglas, the 1860 Cooper Union Address, in which he tracked the founders' post–Revolution votes on slavery, and even the Gettysburg Address in 1863, which begins with a "four score and seven years ago" reference (back to 1776) and which is filled with evocative birth-related terms like "brought forth," "conceived," and "new birth." These orations were all peppered with many hints of "the Virginia planter" of whom he almost never spoke directly. The unique exception to Lincoln's public silence, presented and analyzed at length for the first time in this book, is the single interview that Lincoln gave during the 1860 Presidential campaign. In his home, addressing the public through an unnamed "special correspondent," Lincoln said more *expressly* about his grandfather than ever before or after.

What more exists? Because the Lincolns were for a long time poor farming folks living in cabins in sparsely settled regions, their existence went undocumented. "There was very little attention given to books, papers or records," Erastus R. Burba of Hodgenville said of old times in Kentucky. "As the Lincoln family at that day cut no considerable figure, all of these minor incidents (were) lost sight of."[1]

It is thus appropriate to ask Professor Annette Gordon-Reed's question, "Does the lack of certainty mean that no attempt should be made to reconstruct the lives of people who were deliberately forced to

4

the margins in their own time?" Of the enslaved specifically, but relevantly to other marginal populations, Professor Gordon-Reed answered, "There is an urgent moral dimension to this question that goes beyond the stories of the enslaved. One can argue that historians have a duty—for the sake of historical writing itself—to look beyond the presentations of people who deliberately forced obscurity upon others and portrayed the oppressed in a way that justified their rule over them. Privileging their documents has historians playing along with a rigged system, producing history that is indelibly marked by prejudice, a form of fantasy written in fact."[2]

How may historical fantasy be defeated? The question rises here in the shadow of Lincoln the self-made, self-educated, self-motivated man. To dislodge the man from this myth, a conflation deriving from an incomplete record, I scavenged. It was "root, hog, or die," as Lincoln might phrase it. To avoid replicating the "violence of the archives," I gave especially close readings to five documents authored by three problematic people. Standing by Lincoln, the witnesses at the foundation of this book are Lincoln's law partner, William "Billy" Herndon; Christopher Columbus Graham, one of Kentucky's early settlers; and Dennis Hanks, Lincoln's older cousin, who lived in the Lincoln family's Indiana cabin for years.

All three sources come with various red flags. No one can avoid a struggle with fastidiousness over using any one of them. However, on point, in my opinion, after long consideration, these sources ring true and merely flesh out details of Lincoln's maternal grandfather, a man who *must have lived* but who must rest otherwise not only unnamed but entirely featureless. Historical injustice may be overturned by hearing witnesses, men who heard and recalled different vestiges of "the Virginia planter" and the planter's enduring influence. By accepting these three as sequestered witnesses who spoke at different times independently of one another, we sight the Virginia planter's and his daughter's huge historical influence upon Abraham Lincoln and also upon us and our times.

The documents examined and quoted herein are: (1) some of Herndon's letters; (2) the first edition of Herndon's famous biography of Lincoln (especially a section on ancestry deleted from later editions by its authors); (3) sworn affidavits of Christopher Columbus Graham; (4) several of Dennis Hanks's letters to Herndon; and (5) Dennis Hanks's last interview, as reported by newspaperwoman Eleanor Atkinson in a 1908 book.

Without these witnesses, the rigged archives win again. With them, no longer insulated from challenge by rejecting documents that sound a different note, the self-made Lincoln built upon an artificially narrow evidentiary foundation falls. In place of fantasy, we find a more human and less marble figure, a slow learner inspired in his struggles to learn by an ancestor whom he never met, a bloodline that suggested leadership was his birthright, a boy encouraged by the fireside Revolutionary stories of his heroic and Jeffersonian mother to finish the work of the founders, the nation-building generation that prominently included his own grandfather.

Source Abbreviations

Several books are so frequently quoted that, after a first full citation, abbreviations are used. They are:

Atkinson	Eleanor Atkinson, *The Boyhood of Lincoln* (New York: Doubleday, Page & Co., 1908)
CW	Roy P. Basler, ed., *The Collected Works of Abraham Lincoln* (New Brunswick, NJ: Rutgers University Press, 1953)
Brookhiser	Richard Brookhiser, *Founder's Son* (New York: Basic Books, 2014)
Frank	Arthur W. Frank, *Letting Stories Breathe* (University of Chicago Press, 2010)
Harrison	Lowell H. Harrison, *Lincoln of Kentucky* (Lexington: University Press of Kentucky, 2009)
HI	Douglas L. Wilson and Rodney O. Davis, eds., *Herndon's Informants: Letters, Interviews, and Statements About Abraham Lincoln* (Chicago: University of Illinois Press, 1998)
HL	Douglas L. Wilson and Rodney O. Davis, eds., *Herndon's Lincoln, Life of Lincoln, The True Story of a Great American Life* (Chicago: University of Illinois Press, 2016)
Kaplan	Fred Kaplan, *Lincoln: The Biography of a Writer* (New York: HarperCollins, 2008)
LL	Douglas L. Wilson and Rodney O. Davis, eds., *Herndon on Lincoln, Letters* (Chicago: University of Illinois Press, 2016)

Source Abbreviations

Miller	Richard Lawrence Miller, *Lincoln and His World: The Early Years, Birth to Illinois Legislature* (Mechanicsville, PA: Stackpole Books, 2006)
Strozier	Charles B. Strozier, *Lincoln's Quest for Union: Public and Private Meanings* (Chicago: University of Illinois Press, 1982; 2nd ed., Philadelphia: Paul Dry Books, 2001)

PART ONE

Reports

1

Nancy Hanks,
Backwoods Debater
(*circa* 1800)

SOURCE: Christopher Columbus Graham, physician and herbalist
FIRST WRITTEN: Sworn affidavit, 1884

> Abe Lincoln the Liberator was made in his mother's
> womb and his father's brain and in the prayers of Sally
> Bush; by the talks and sermons of Jesse Head, the
> Methodist circuit-rider, assistant county judge, printer-
> editor, and cabinet-maker. Little Abe grew up to serve as
> a cabinet-maker himself two Presidential terms.
> —Christopher Columbus Graham

Preface

Charles B. Strozier began his definitive psychobiography of Lincoln by quoting Lincoln: "God bless my mother. All that I am or ever hope to be I owe to her."[1]

This book is built upon two premises: that Lincoln's mother told him a secret and that that secret mattered very much to him, to his education, to his confidence and, ultimately, to American history. Before reaching the moment when Nancy Hanks Lincoln felt compelled to tell her son her deepest secret (for the secret was hers before it was his), you ought to know something about Nancy, her life and about her mother and her father.

None of this makes sense yet, I know. What is all this about secrets, and people from literally hundreds of years ago, ancient history, right? We all know that scandals, especially old scandals, and one as common as pre-marital sex, do not matter much for very long even to the people most directly involved. Scandals and secrets and sex, oh my. Nothing to see here, right?

1. Nancy Hanks, Backwoods Debater (circa 1800)

Wrong.

This secret mattered. What Nancy Hanks Lincoln told her son shaped his life and, in shaping his life, shaped our country. Slavery ended in the United States in part because of the secret shared by a mother with her son in a log cabin that the boy's father built himself. Humble words between humble folks in humble surroundings. Even if you had been a witness and overheard what was said, you would never have predicted the reverberations that followed.

But Lincoln knew and, as we shall see, after exacting a pledge of secrecy during his own lifetime, Lincoln shared the powerful secret with his law partner, who eventually published it (in 1889). At the same time, Lincoln made the remark that his mother had made him everything that he was and ever hoped to be.

Our book begins with Nancy as a vocal teenager, about five years before she married Tom Lincoln, as observed by a man passing through Elizabethtown, Kentucky, in about 1800. The eyewitness who reported it in a signed affidavit was named Christopher Columbus Graham. But for Dr. Graham, we would not know anything about Nancy's thinking as a young woman. Through Dr. Graham, we know that she already carried and spoke about ideas and attitudes suitable for the mother of a man who would oppose slavery in America.

Thinking the way she thought, but then holding a secret close to her chest, Nancy was smart and outspoken enough for Dr. Graham to make note of what he heard as she talked with her friends.

Nancy Hanks Lincoln, Intellectual

Lincoln's mother was a verbal wizard. No writer, she exhibited a quality of thinking on her feet, of fashioning an argument and of hammering out her points with confidence, if not flair. Nancy held audiences, even of one person, rapt. From her talk, Nancy's neighbors inferred a brilliant mind. They awarded her a label rarely given in rural areas, and even more rarely to women—intellectual. Because she could not have risen so high by indulging in gossip, she must have spoken seriously in conversations that far surpassed the mundane.

Nancy's reputation for superior intelligence was so solid that it long survived her death in Indiana in 1818. Six weeks after Lincoln's assassination, or almost thirty years after his mother's death, when John Hanks first sat down to be interviewed by Herndon's research assistant, John

Miles, he told Miles that Nancy "had a clear intellectual mind." The following year, Hanks was all the more emphatic. To Herndon himself, he said, "She was beyond all doubt an intellectual woman—rather Extraordinary if anything." Another cousin who when orphaned had lived in the Lincoln cabin for years, Dennis Hanks—albeit a notorious exaggerator, whose frequently inconsistent recollections must always be scrutinized—described Nancy likewise as "keen—shrewd—smart & I do say highly intellectual by nature." William Wood, one of Indiana's first settlers, who sat up with Nancy during her final illness, described his neighbor as "very smart, intelligent and intellectual."[2]

Despite a welter of contradictory recollections of how she looked—fair, dark, of various heights and weights—others who knew her less well or who recalled less were unanimous about her mind. Nat Grigsby, whose brother married Nancy's daughter, Sally, knew both mother and daughter well. When he described Sally as "an intellectual & intelligent woman" he added immediately, "(h)owever, not so much as her mother." Nat praised Nancy's "extraordinary strength of mind" specifically and called her "brilliant."[3]

When Women Had No Vote, Nancy Hanks Had Her Voice

Although almost all of her words are lost and irrecoverable, one document echoes Nancy, early and vocal on the ramparts, refining and defending cutting-edge positions on current issues that mattered. Our source on point is Christopher Columbus Graham (1784–1885), a long-lived and much-traveled frontier Kentuckian. An eccentric, self-sufficient physician and herbalist, in his old age Graham committed his memories to paper, swore to their truth and signed them. One can doubt neither his seriousness of purpose nor his desire to share what he remembered with precision. Notably, he did not quote Nancy in his affidavit. Not pretending to recall what she said fully, he modestly reported his fading memories.

(Graham's narrow focus veers toward the hilarious. For example, he happened to be in the right place at the right time to attend Tom Lincoln and Nancy Hanks's 1806 wedding feast. About the bride and groom, he said next to nothing, though he remembered and recounted in great detail the spread of food at their reception.)

In an unembroidered way, Graham described Tom (Lincoln's

father), Nancy (his mother), and Sally Bush (eventually, Lincoln's stepmother). As the three chummed together in the vicinity of their homes in Elizabethtown, Graham said, they revealed themselves as "just steeped full of [the Rev.] Jesse Head's notions about the wrong of slavery and the rights of man as explained by Thomas Jefferson and Thomas Paine."[4]

Graham, who spent too much of his time alone, deep in the backwoods foraging for medicinal roots and herbs, not to be all ears for novelty when passing through a village or town, obviously stood rooted to stake in the spectacle of young women engaging as peers in debate with an older man. Most shockingly, the sounds that stopped him in his tracks were assertions that slavery was wrong.

Through Graham, we witness Tom, Nancy and Sally in a *politically interested* huddle. Graham heard not a chorus but a conversation. Their voices may have been calm and quiet—we lack any basis to reconstruct their decibel level or excitement—but their politics were literally revolutionary. Plainly and prophetically, they were arguing among themselves about slavery and the promise of equality contained in Jefferson's war-time Declaration of Independence, a promise which pointedly and painfully went unfulfilled in the Constitution that was ratified after the war.[5]

Graham did not distinguish the male from the female speakers, but we can logically sort them and the core elements of his report may be quickly abstracted. Graham entered key words into the historical record. He heard topics including "slavery," "wrong," "Thomas Jefferson," "Thomas Paine," and the "rights of man" (or, possibly, *Rights of Man*, Paine's popular 1791 book), and, by assumption, the Bible. From these topics and authorities, a dominant voice may be tentatively or circumstantially identified.

Of the three, Tom was illiterate and uneducated. Nobody later recalled Tom as a speaker on political issues. (Some recalled Tom as a *raconteur* who told comical stories and spun yarns. To others he was a slow and silent man. In general, political debate seems to have been unwelcome noise to Tom.) Accordingly, even though Tom was the group's senior member at age 24—and the only eligible voter in those days of an all-male electorate—it is not likely he was the lead spokesman or chair of an informal discussion about slavery. With Tom, the girls were of varying interest. Bold Nancy was closer to him in age, but little Sally Bush was closer to his heart.[6]

Nobody ever characterized pretty Sally, 13 or 14 in 1800 and Tom's "first flame," as a provocative thinker. Then on the cusp of adolescence and likely glad for respite away from oppressive parents, she had a personal reason not to be caught saying anything against slavery. Her father, a searcher paid to find fugitives from slavery, was a patrol captain who profited from the institution. Sally's level of schooling is unknown, although she seems not to have been literate. (In adulthood, she liked being read to from books, including Sinbad the Sailor.) In her old age, she talked disparagingly about "what little mind" she had.

Basically, Sally then was a charming and fashion-conscious village girl who liked to dress up. But she and Nancy did not—or at least they did not always—discuss fabrics, dresses and fashions. When Tom, older than Nancy, a carpenter-cabinetmaker, came around to join them, his eye was mainly on Sally. As a trio, they may have attended church, or gone to dances, and done other things together. Their cheap and commonly reliable entertainment seems to have been talking about current issues, however, although for young Sally, bold political talk was something to listen to rather than to take part in.[7]

By default, the intellectual powerhouse was Nancy Hanks. Inferences permit us to approach her a bit closer. She seems to have excelled in plain speaking—in her mid-teens, she had managed to reach someone who did not speak her language when she retaught her cousin English.[8]

A Kentucky drawl or backwoods dialect would be natural to impute to this intellectual who lived from age two to 32 in rural Kentucky. Her youthful voice seems to have been particularly pleasant. According to one Elizabethtown, Kentucky, neighbor, whose uncle was a Baptist preacher, she was a "good singer" who sang in church alongside the minister. She was not too shy to sing or take part in discussions.[9]

Odds are good that it was Nancy's clear, pleasant voice that caught Graham's attention and that hers were also the ideas and the authorities that Graham recalled.

The Pull of Paine

Marooned in the backwoods, Nancy took part in the anti-slavery movement, at least nudged to do so in church by the Rev. Jesse Head. Nancy and Tom's admiration of anti-slavery the Reverend Head may be inferred from the fact that he solemnized their wedding in 1806. Graham's identification of Paine and Jefferson is intriguing because it pushes back by one generation the known link between Lincoln and both founders. Nancy's son emulated Paine's style. When Roy Basler edited the *Collected Works of Abraham Lincoln,* he declared that only Thomas Jefferson stood ahead of Tom Paine in the rational and logical writers who influenced Lincoln's *thinking.* And, as the model for Lincoln's *eloquence,* Basler placed "Paine above all others."[10]

Paine remained Lincoln's model and possibly shaped his religious beliefs as a Deist, specifically non–Christian. In New Salem, one of Lincoln's horrified neighbors burned Lincoln's anti–Christian essay. Other Paine-inspired formulations took popular root. Every important speech and policy letter that Lincoln wrote owed something to Paine. If Nancy's admiration of Paine precipitated her son's, when we admire Lincoln's lucid prose, we admire the influence of his mother. By Graham's account, Lincoln's first teacher of rhetoric was someone who loved the works of Tom Paine.[11]

Graham's allusion to Paine's *Rights of Man* may be correct. It was a popular book. If Nancy read books, Paine's were a logical choice. Novice readers could follow Paine. He wrote to be easily understood while frequently adding flourishes like, "Independence is my happiness, the world is my country and my religion is to do good," and "Whatever is my right as a man is also the right of another; and it becomes my duty to guarantee as well as to possess."[12]

Paine's widely available *Common Sense* employed short words to great effect. It famously began, "These are the times that try men's souls. The summer soldier and the sunshine patriot will, in this crisis, shrink from the service of their country; but he that stands by it now, deserves the love and thanks of man and woman." The pamphlet could be used as a child's primer. Possibly, it was so used when Nancy brought up her children.[13]

Besides his lucid simplicity, Paine in his writings glamorized the future. Eric Foner summarized Paine in a superb sentence, "Through this new language he communicated a new vision—a utopian image of an egalitarian, republican society."

It is hard not to imagine the impact and appeal of that vision on a social atom, a girl on the margin of society, a poor relation not well educated. If she read Paine, Nancy probably read the print off his pages. Or, if someone read Paine to her, Nancy certainly retained what she heard. Graham's report implies that she spoke along with others about a glorious future, a world without slavery. Intensity of conviction crackled in the air as Graham listened to what he called somewhat dismissively "notions" about the wrong of slavery and the rights of man as described by Jefferson and Paine.[14]

Later Ripples

Tom and Nancy obviously continued to talk about the wrong of slavery. Lincoln recalled the move to Indiana as having been "chiefly" motivated by disputed land titles but also "partly on account of slavery." Lincoln made this point in his sketchy autobiographical outline without sorting out which of his parents said what. Either Tom or Nancy or both might have conceived of crossing over the Ohio to live in the free state of Indiana, but which parent likely pulled the strongest verbal oar? Nancy was the intellectual, always better able than Tom to air views about human equality and the wrong of slavery.[15]

While it may be too much to visualize that Nancy quoted to her children the Reverend Head, Jefferson and Paine on the wrong of slavery, when Lincoln recalled forty years later that they moved "partly on account of slavery," Lincoln remembered *someone's* declarations before they set out, explaining that they were leaving Kentucky for a moral reason. Nancy is the parent whose words he likely remembered. Why should Nancy not speak out just as she had as a teenager?

A Pause Before Concluding

We have not weighed quite all of the evidence. Anyone lingering over the original handwritten manuscript of Lincoln's autobiography will notice that initially Lincoln had not included the sentence about "partly on account of slavery." These words were *inserted*. Omission suggests hesitation. He was running for national office and political correctness compelled caution. Finally, only these clipped words passed Lincoln's censor.

What more might Lincoln have said?

It is speculative but we have a basis to infer that Nancy probably articulated a reason beyond common for their sufferings and sacrifices, crossing the broad Ohio at hazard of capsizing, to take on a harsh wilderness, concomitant with losing friends, familiar sights and—most devastatingly for the children—any schooling. Somehow, it was likely she who cast the Lincolns in a starring role within the national

1. Nancy Hanks, Backwoods Debater (circa 1800)

Farnham Creek is an offshoot of the broad and navigable Rappahannock, famous for troop movements on it and along its banks during the Civil War. Waterways like the Rappahannock permitted easy and cheap transport of perishable agricultural goods that would be delayed or prohibitively expensive over land (courtesy Jay Garner, Richmond County historian).

movement for equality. Coming from his outspoken mother, her son likely heard something inspiring—and too perilous for a presidential candidate to quote. Too bad.[16]

We have a reasonable right to think that Lincoln's opposition to slavery started with Nancy. Thoughts and feelings crackling electrically in the Kentucky backwoods air around 1800 would in time strike a baby yet unborn. When Lincoln said, and later wrote, that he could not *remember* a time when he did not oppose slavery, he was referring back to his early boyhood. Who will seriously argue that those thoughts and feelings about slavery came to him unaided and independently of his mother's own?[17]

As dim as the light is and difficult to discern, a heroic woman may stand behind moving to free soil rather than to yet another Kentucky home and, equally significantly, behind explaining why, the same woman who Lincoln would say had everything to do with what he was and all that he ever hoped to be.[18]

2

The Weaving Shed Story
(1817 or 1818)

SOURCE: Dennis Hanks, Lincoln's cousin
FIRST WRITTEN: Letter, 1866

> "I cannot wish the fault undone, the issue
> of it being so proper."—Kent, *King Lear*

Preface

We skip through the next twenty years, during which Nancy Hanks and Tom Lincoln married, had two children who survived, and the four of them, "partly on account of slavery," emigrated across the Ohio River, leaving Kentucky for Indiana.

In the wilderness where the panther still screamed, Tom, who did carpentry and cabinet making when he was not farming, designed and built a rugged cabin, a carpentry shop, a smokehouse and, for Nancy, at least a weaving shed. After storytelling, Bible reading and hymn singing by Nancy, the chief teacher of Sally and Lincoln when Spencer County as yet had no schools, the day came that Lincoln thought up a joke. Perhaps surprisingly, perhaps predictably, the little boy's joke related to his mother's deepest secret.

Lincoln's Nightmarish Boyhood

When the Lincoln family crossed the Ohio, settling inland in Little Pigeon Creek, on the periphery of Spencer County, it was as if they had fallen outside of civilization. Kentucky had schools that Lincoln and his sister attended, and the children had friends. Here, brush so thick barred the way that they had had to cut a path to reach their home site. Living in an

A replica of the log cabin in which two adults and two children lived, now at the Lincoln Living Historical Farm, part of the Lincoln Boyhood National Memorial (Rene Sturgell, 2012, CC BY-SA 3.0).

open lean-to for months, hearing the screams of panthers in the night, Lincoln would have been unusual if he was not homesick, or even terrified. In morose autobiographical words he penned over forty years later, in Indiana he discerned "absolutely nothing to excite ambition for education."[1]

During the next two years, the last years of his mother's life, no one opened a school in Spencer County. For those years, the Lincolns' isolated family farm was Lincoln's entire world. His days were filled with work, helping his father. The family was near no road. No passersby afoot or on horseback regularly appeared. A mile around their cabin and several outbuildings, a bramble-festooned, untrimmed, and pathless forest ran on and on. Around them, as Lincoln later flatly recalled, was "a wild region, with many bears and other wild animals still in the woods." With few neighbors and no books or music, young Lincoln grew bored. Eventually, he asked a horse breeder to notify him whenever a stallion was to cover mares, as something interesting to watch.[2]

In this intellectual desert, before he could read, Dennis witnessed Nancy with the Bible "repeating it to Abe and his sister when very young." He said, "Lincoln was often & much moved" by the stories. It turned out that the boy was getting ready to grind out his own.[3]

Playing Paternity for a Laugh

The great difference between Lincoln's parents was legitimacy. Lincoln's father was the youngest of three sons born to Elizabeth and Abraham Lincoln, a self-sufficient owner of great tracts of virgin land in Kentucky and a friend of Daniel Boone. Being "land rich and cash poor," the original Abraham Lincoln did much of the labor on his farm by himself. He could thus be numbered among Virginia's "second families." By contrast, Lincoln's mother was the child of a poorly-reputed, teenaged single mother—and, supposedly, a brilliant and dashing Virginia planter whose name can now only be guessed.[4]

Mount Rushmore. Lincoln heard from his mother that his blood was "as good as Washington's," and, as First Family of Virginia descendant, Lincoln had a lineage that included Washington, although distantly. He felt that he was blood kin to the Virginia planter Presidents (Pixabay.com).

2. The Weaving Shed Story (1817 or 1818)

It was Nancy's secret to share; she was the bastard. When Lincoln was about eight or nine, at the latest, Nancy seems to have decided that it was time. If, as appears likely, she spoke to her children after they were together, isolated, bonded together closer than ever physically and emotionally, Lincoln was given food for thought. The concepts of paternity and bastardy, new to him, Nancy necessarily explained so that he could understand. In time, Lincoln, so often a questioner, was ready to pop a fabulous question.

Working with humble materials, a father who was no father, and tales of Bible characters, Lincoln cobbled together a trick question, a joke. The joke simultaneously preserves the first Lincoln quote and the *only* extended glimpse of the boy's interactions with his mother.

Lincoln's homemade joke—recounted below—like a fly in amber, reveals a familial obsession with legitimacy; second, his mother's receptivity to Lincoln's wit; and, third, a link between Lincoln's lineage and his education.

Zebedee

How did Lincoln encounter Zebedee? When Lincoln could not read the Bible himself, he relied on oral sources. With a precociousness beyond his youthful years, whatever he was told or overheard was retained. Witnesses recalled how he repeated sermons verbatim, gestures and all. It was said that he never forgot what he heard, and that Lincoln mulled over what he heard. Obsessive thinking was a core trait of his remarkable mind. Within his seething melting pot, Zebedee and illegitimacy morphed together.[5]

Zebedee is an actual figure in the Bible. Zebedee appears in the call scene famous for Jesus's quote, "I will make you fishers of men," which opens as Jesus sees "two brethren, James the son of Zebedee, and John his brother, in a ship with Zebedee their father, mending their nets; and he called them." The mending reference would have offered Nancy, an avid weaver and fabric-conscious, an added kick.[6]

Most of all, though, Nancy had father issues and the Biblical Zebedee was a "father." The quintessential father figure in the Bible, of all men in the Bible, only Zebedee is characterized simply as a father. Father Zebedee's economic status—just as wealth was manifest in the South— is reflected by the noting that he had servants. Luke wrote succinctly of James and John following Jesus after "leaving their father Zebedee in

Horse and rider, Williamsburg, evoking the image of a rich, prominent Virginia planter of the 1770s and 1780s (courtesy Jay Garner, Richmond County historian).

the boat with the hired men." Zebedee, a rich mute man with servants, stayed behind.[7]

The parents' reactions were distinctly different. The disciples' mother took steps to strengthen the family's position within the Christian community. Unnamed, she joined them in worship and asked a favor of Jesus. "When Jesus asked what she wanted,/ She saith unto him, 'Grant that these my two sons may sit, the one on thy right hand, and the other on the left, in thy kingdom.'" This active and vocal mother stands in stark contrast against the disciples' perpetually indifferent father. Lincoln mulled over the particulars until, in this rich but impassive father, he found a caricature that embodied the story of his mother's life.

Lincoln patently had no wish to annoy his mother. In Zebedee, Lincoln simply found a comic means to hit back at her derelict father. Zebedee allowed Lincoln, with a great grin, to take a swipe at the illegitimacy that dogged his dear mother. If Lincoln had asked his mother to name her father, he had gotten nowhere. But by using as proxy this long-ago father figure of the Bible, the imaginative boy was empowered to ridicule the grandfather who had long ago abandoned his beloved mother. As "Zebedee," his grandfather fell far from being a revered and prominent patriarch and was, instead, held up and berated as a sorry excuse of a father.

The Joke

The day came, showtime. Lincoln probably solicited Dennis to join him. The barefoot boy in his linen shirt and home-sewn jeans was taking a risk and, when going out on a limb, company can be a comfort. Besides, the bigger the audience, the better and Dennis wanted to see the fun. Dennis would have gone shoulder to shoulder along the sides of fields or followed Lincoln through less-cleared land up and into the open doorway of Nancy's weaving shed.[8]

When the boys reached the shed, they could have walked right in. Its door would have been propped open for light enough to work and for ventilation. (Tom Lincoln, a skilled man with hammers, saws and drills, built more than a cabin for his family. He was a carpenter for whom building well and large was natural. The snug cabin was a large one with a loft and a good-sized hearth for cooking and light. Nobody ever complained of being cramped even as the numbers of inhabitants doubled for four to eight. Tom certainly built a privy, a barn, a smokehouse and at least two work sheds, one for his carpentry and cabinetmaking and another fair-weather shelter for his wife—likely with a wide trapdoor on each shed's roof, and an identical broad front door. Nancy thus had a place of her own to use in making fabric on her loom or to sit and sew or otherwise work in relative quiet and comfort.)[9]

Nancy may have looked up and spoken first. If so, Dennis left any greeting unreported. With Dennis in easy earshot, Lincoln delivered his immortal one-liner:

"Who was the father of Zebedee's children?"

He likely spoke it in a quick jumble, though he was capable of fancier performances. He may have shifted into a minister's singsong voice—he liked to imitate the preacher's earnest shout—sounding roughly like, "Who's t'fadder uv Ze-buh-DEE'S chillun?"

Besides getting her son's joke, Nancy the intellectual may have noted not Zebedee but a sophisticated abstraction, namely, the "father of Zebedee's children." This construct was a puckish way of asking if Zebedee were *really* the father of "his" children. Key to the boy's joke was background that his mother shared with his sister and him at table, a Bible story. The story of Zebedee was needed to make it work. Namely, would the father of sons who were flesh of his flesh and blood of his blood actually sit silently as they ran off, without a word of protest, grief or wishing well? No? Then, their father was *not* Zebedee and there is no answer to the question but laughter.

The curtain came down. Woe. "You nasty little pup, you," his mother said, possibly with a grab for the "pup." But Nancy's protest was feigned. Per Dennis Hanks, the scene ended with laughter all around, after all. The intellectual in her could not object to or be offended by her son finding his way forward to becoming a regular little Tom Paine.[10]

Zebedee Reformed

Lincoln had good grounds to forget his maternal grandfather. A rich, emotionally undemonstrative, passive father concerned with his property, his boat, his nets, his servants, indifferent to his children, Lincoln's Zebedee was a highly subversive and disturbing image. His Zebedee fell short of the nineteenth century ideal. Moreover, his mother's childhood miseries followed her father's abandonment. Then, why did Lincoln cling so to Zebedee, this personification of an absent father?

The answer is: Lincoln did not, not for long. After his mother—his *teacher*—died, her boy lost himself in thought. According to Dennis Hanks, Lincoln once tried the joke again, on a clergyman. Although a minister might be expected to know the gospels, the joke misfired. Upon approaching one of the itinerant Baptist ministers his stepmother received as guests, Dennis said, "Abe asked him who was the father of Zebedee's children, blamed if he could tell."[11]

Lincoln found that he could not revive or relive his merry moment with anyone else in his mother's place. Nonetheless, in a setting so bereft of appealing subjects, nothing drifted into his mind more frequently than the Virginia planter, for Lincoln was an obsessive thinker who once warned a friend against "that intensity of thought, which will sometimes wear the sweetest idea threadbare and turn it to the bitterness of death."[12]

What other use could he make of mute Zebedee? The more the young boy thought, the more the Virginia planter changed. Stepping out of that boat in the Bible, immersed now in history, a background figure in stories of Washington and the Revolution, no longer Zebedee, the unnamed rogue was recast as one of the Men of '76. He became, if not a founder, at least a friend of the founders, a patriot and supporter among other Virginia planters. Washed in the blood of the Revolution, the planter stood cleansed of sin and stood fit to serve as a heroic ideal of whom his grandson could be at least privately proud.[13]

3

Two Scary Grandfathers
(Lincoln's Boyhood)

PRIMARY SOURCE: John W. Scripps
FIRST PUBLISHED: 1865 (in letter)

> (W)e know that the true beginnings of an event
> lie half hidden in earlier movement, so that the
> visible starting point is in fact a culmination of
> forces which pre-dated its appearance.
> —Rosemary Ashton, *One Hot Summer, Dickens,*
> *Darwin, Disraeli and the Great Stink of 1858* (2018)

Preface

Lonely, isolated Lincoln spent a lot of time with two men he never met. One was his namesake grandfather, the original Abraham Lincoln, and the other was a man whose name he did not know, referred to in the family as "the Virginia planter." Neither brought their grandson any pleasure in his boyhood, when he had reasons to be afraid of each man. The following report establishes "ground zero" in his relationship with his grandfathers, before he was proud of either of them, especially before one of them would step up via idealization into being a virtual combination of George Washington, Thomas Jefferson and all the Virginia planters of the Revolutionary era.

Ancestors Mattered to Lincoln

David Donald famously began his gold standard biography of Lincoln not with ancestors but by stating absolutely, "Abraham Lincoln was not interested in his ancestry." This is surely wrong and, as the twig was bent the branch has grown, generally unfortunate. Borne within a biography otherwise so nearly flawless, the implications of Donald's error have spread. Michael Birmingham, echoing the substance of Donald's comment in his ambitious chapter, "The Most Ambitious Man in the World," concluded that the "origins of Lincoln's ambition are obscure." Burlingame quoted Lincoln's long-time Springfield neighbor and banker, John W. Bunn, who declared, "He no doubt had his personal ambitions but no man then or now can say what they were or how they originated. He never gave his confidence to any living person about what was strictly private and personal to himself."[1]

Bunn was wrong. Although Lincoln famously discouraged John Scripps, his first biographer, from reconstructing the influences of his youth, to him Lincoln "communicated some facts concerning his ancestry, which he did not wish to have published."[2]

Contrary to Donald's impression of indifference, Lincoln cared infinitely about his ancestry. Contrary to Bunn, little in his early environment influenced him more. Scripps summarized for Herndon that

Mars Hill, Richmond County, prime farmland once owned by Griffin Murdock Fauntleroy, a Revolutionary War veteran and prominent member of a wealthy family. Fauntleroy, then a bachelor, who in his will indicated a surviving illegitimate child, has been identified as a possible father of Nancy Hanks (courtesy Jay Garner, Richmond County historian).

Lincoln decried "the utter absence of all romantic and heroic elements" from his youth. That *ancestry* compensated for that absence is obvious.

However, Lincoln was not promiscuously intrigued by anyone to whom he was related. He was selective. He made choices. That, by his choice—although probably guided by his mother—his maternal grandfather, a Virginia planter, *became* his romantic hero is obvious. Lincoln's reserve about his ancestry was extreme, but (as would stun Bunn) on one occasion he listed his "ambition" as inherited—from the Virginia planter.[3]

Ancestry mattered to Lincoln. Peculiar to Lincoln was the agony of having an ancestor important to him whose name he did not know. Among American leaders, Lincoln's dilemma was a singular one that he solved by hinting about his ancestors. Lincoln closed the door but opened windows in speech after speech, hinting about the origins of his good mind, his ambition, his skills, and his hopes. He both told us and did not tell us about his grandfather, the Virginia planter, merged as one of the Men of '76.[4]

The Grandfather He Was Supposed to Follow

When Lincoln's parents chose a source for their firstborn son's name, they picked no intellectual. Tom's hand is obvious in requiring his father's name to be given to the baby. Named as he was, situated as he was later in Indiana, this 1809 Abraham Lincoln was aimed like an arrow by the constant, sheer influence of his name to grow up as a fearless American pioneer. For the Kentucky-born lad to go West, sleep under the stars, his rifle at his side, alert for the snap of a twig, appeared to be his destiny from birth.

Lincoln's name came from a rugged, Indian-fighting, land-clearing pioneer. His father had once stood under the shadow of a raised tomahawk. Nobody knew how many Indians Lincoln's uncle killed. Dennis Hanks told Eleanor Atkinson that Nancy described the original Abraham Lincoln to her son more as a brainy and brave man "who came out to Kentucky with Daniel Boone. He was mighty smart and wasn't afraid of anything, that's what a man has to be out here to make anything of himself."[5]

Following his namesake grandfather, making tracks over the continent, scaling mountains, and surveying the country seemed likely to be this boy's destiny. Many young boys did not long in vain for such adventures; to become an explorer of the Western wilderness was a viable career. Kit Carson was born in the same year as Lincoln. Men like Jim Bowie (of "Bowie knife" fame), John Colter, Jedidiah Smith, Jim Bridger, James Beckwourth, John Charles Fremont, and many others showed how mountain men, trappers and frontiersmen could win both fame and fortune.

Moreover, Lincoln was not a homebody but a lad who readily dipped his toe into danger. A trip down the Mississippi at 19 almost got him killed—a band of enslaved people hit him repeatedly with clubs, leaving a scar over one eye. During the brief Black Hawk War, he served as captain of volunteers (an election that delighted him more than any later office), although Lincoln's only boasts of personal heroism in that conflict were mocking.

In spite of the name given him and the many factors noted, Lincoln's dreams were not informed by his name nor by anybody on his father's side of the family. In plain truth, the first Abraham Lincoln was horror movie fare. His gory death, although not Custer's Last Stand, bears a small-scale resemblance to it. In a scene vividly played and replayed in the boy's mind, a silent movie flickered of an innocent pioneer set upon by stealthy savages.

Like a saint in stained-glass, the image of the first Abraham Lincoln was bloody and flat. Trapped for all time in the moment of his death, this Abraham Lincoln died violently and continuously. Lincoln heard eyewitness accounts. When the martyr's oldest son, Mordecai, "Uncle Mord," visited, as he did often, the two brothers talked about their father's murder. Immediately after the slaughter of his father, Tom—then a boy of seven—was screaming "Don't kill me! Take me prisoner!" At that moment, he was saved and the Indian was killed by a long rifle shot. The sniper behind that single shot was—Uncle Mord, then 16.[6]

Even though Lincoln never said how he *felt* about any of these stories, it is impossible to believe that he was unmoved. He was the second *Abraham Lincoln* living in former Indian territory, in an isolated cabin in the wilds of Spencer County, named after Lieutenant Spencer, killed at the Battle of Tippecanoe. Did Lincoln ever hunger for revenge? When he wrote to relatives, he said only that his *mind* was strongly imprinted with what he heard without acknowledging any correspondingly strong *feelings* or nightmares.[7]

The image of the bloody original Abraham Lincoln may have haunted him, boy and man, nonetheless. Herndon reported that his senior law partner worried aloud about some vague but destined

The road not followed: Lincoln's grandfather, Abraham Lincoln, his name-sake, was killed by Indians. Lincoln's uncle, Mordecai Lincoln, was a famous "Indian killer" in turn. Lincoln personally took arms against Native Americans only during the Black Hawk War (Schoepski.com).

"terrible end," without venturing to state a cause for his panic. Could his namesake have spawned his terror?[8]

Ultimately, in any case, Lincoln marched to a different drummer: the grandfather he followed was his mother's father, after remaking him into a paradigm indistinguishable from Washington and Jefferson.[9]

The Scary Nameless

Lincoln's planter grandfather embodied a horror peculiar to Lincoln. Dennis Hanks noted the boy's dominant obsession. As a child, Lincoln worked out anxiety over his identity by ceaselessly writing his name on any surface with the ends of burnt sticks. Whether the cabin was too small to escape observing it or his judgment was sharper than usual, Dennis told Atkinson, "His name was mighty important to him. He wrote it over and over."[10]

3. Two Scary Grandfathers (Lincoln's Boyhood)

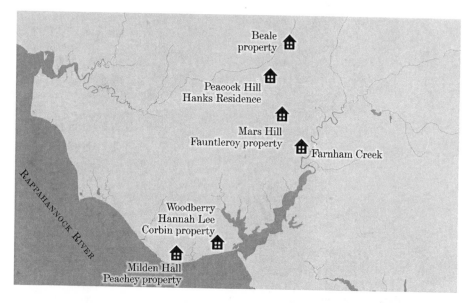

Richmond County map. The sites of Joseph Hanks's homestead and farm and the plantations of the Beales and Fauntleroys in proximity to Hanks's are indicated. The Hanks, Beale and Fauntleroy estates were within walking distance in a half-hour of one another, quicker on horseback, if the horse was healthy (courtesy Jay Garner, Richmond County historian).

The boy's fear had a name. To the Greeks, the fear of being obscure and forgotten after death was *athazagoraphobia*. In Lincoln, *athazagoraphobia* raged as a fire never banked. His fear was partly rational. Lincoln witnessed both of his heroes fall into oblivion. His gifted Virginia planter grandfather, once prominent, was prominent no more. Lincoln's beloved intellectual mother, who died when he was nine, was buried under a stone that did not bear her name. Time carried his ancestors terrifyingly away.

To defeat fleeting Time, this subsistence farmer's son in an isolated cabin practiced making his mark *literally*. Then, in the first products of his pen, he celebrated himself, his name, and his chief battle: against time itself. When he was about age twelve, he wrote this in a homemade notebook:

> Abraham Lincoln his hand and pen he will be good
> but god knows When Time What an emty vaper
> tis and days how swift they are swift as an indian arr[ow]
> Meter

31

fly on like a shooting star the presant moment Just [is here]
then slides away in h[as]te that we [can] never say they ['re ours]
but [only say] th[ey]'re past
Abraham Lincoln is my nam[e]
And with my pen I wrote the same
I wrote in both hast and speed
and left it here for fools to read[11]

The sense that nothing lasts long pervades his doggerel. He might sportively razz the "fools" who were to gawk at it, but his name was too important to get wrong. In Lincoln's thinking even as an adult, one must take care about one's name. A lasting and legible *name* was a mortal's only possibility of immortality. If anyone was unable to write his or her name well—famously, his father Tom did so only "bunglingly"—the usually kind and tolerant Lincoln was cruelly scornful. Lincoln wanted people to remember Abraham Lincoln, and not for the horrible way he died but for his words and deeds. In Lincoln's world, anyone unremembered, as if he never lived, was worse than damned. The Virginia planter was so obscured, in perpetual namelessness.[12]

The planter's grandson worried himself sick over being remembered. When he was stricken by such severe depression in 1841 that he barely spoke above a whisper, bedridden Lincoln disclosed what scared

Some of the acreage once tilled by its owner before 1800, Richard Beale. Beale, although married, is considered a possible father of Nancy Hanks (courtesy Jay Garner, Richmond County historian).

him. He told his best friend, Joshua Speed, that he feared *being forgotten*—not death but *being forgotten* "as if he never were."[13]

Speed, recollecting that conversation, told Herndon in a letter, "He said to me that he had done nothing to make any human being remember that he had lived." Lincoln was in his thirties when this neurotic anxiety nearly overwhelmed him. Speed, who watched over Lincoln, took away his razor. He wrote that Lincoln had been "so much depressed that he almost contemplated suicide."[14]

Who has such thoughts? Who is so disturbed about *posthumous* memory? Lincoln. To understand his worst fear is to understand Lincoln. In reverse, his greatest *hope* was eternal fame. Speed wrote how his friend, teetering on the brink of insanity or death, confided "that to connect his name with the events transpiring in his day & generation and so impress himself upon them as to link his name with something that would redound to the interest of his fellow man was what he desired to live for."[15]

Although the grammar of Speed's statement is a bit twisty, Lincoln seems to have conveyed the astonishing meaning that he only "desired to live" *if* this ambition might be satisfied. Lincoln did not merely mildly wish that other people might know his name. It was his most profound concern, the fire that burned at the core of his being. But this begs the question of its source. Was his extreme *athazagoraphobia* and of his ambition to be remembered forever a consequence of unremembered ancestors?

Prominence by Proxy

A connection may be proposed. If one is looking for anomaly, some way in which Lincoln was different from most people, then Lincoln's complicated relationship with grandfathers he never met, especially the relationship between Lincoln and the Virginia planter, invite attention.

We know from Dennis Hanks that Lincoln was directed by his mother to look to his lineage for encouragement. She may have known the value of this from experience; her father's idealized image may have inspired her in her own younger and less confident years, a time when her neighbors had dismissed both her and her roots. One of her old Kentucky neighbors, John B. Helm, after speaking of "Miss Hanks," about whom he rambled negatively, sniffed that "she was very obscure and was not of noble blood."[16]

Helm's derogation of Nancy as "very obscure" is interesting, and what was that about her ancestry? When Helm declared that she was "not of noble blood" was he rebutting rumors to the contrary? Did Helm decry her deficiency in noble blood because Miss Hanks comported herself with *hauteur* as if she were a rich planter's daughter? Any airs she was pleased to assume, and intellectual posturing she may have indulged, would have offended burghers like John B. Helm. Her detractors and Nancy seem to have both been ancestor focused.

By contrast, Lincoln was self-focused and intent upon his own eternal fame. In fact, regardless of cause and whether his grandfathers triggered his rare and painful condition or not,

Lincoln, from *The Abraham Lincoln Portfolio of Photogravures from the Famous McClure Collection*. Within about five years, on returning from Washington after his term as a Congressman, Lincoln shared with his law partner, William "Billy" Herndon, the secret of his ancestor, the Virginia planter. He had Billy swear to keep it secret during Lincoln's lifetime. Herndon did not make it public until 1889 (Library of Congress).

Lincoln occupied the front ranks of mortals most in need of the assurance of immortality. He must be remembered for that if for nothing else.

Let's Hear It for Our Grandfathers

Until July 10, 1858, Lincoln celebrated his grandfathers only in deep privacy. Then, on that day, in Chicago, from the same stage where

3. Two Scary Grandfathers (Lincoln's Boyhood)

Stephen Douglas had spoken the previous day, he went public in a big way. Lincoln uttered with emphasis the plural "grandfathers" for the first time in any speech. He overcame any need for wariness by a rhetorical trick: he smuggled *his* grandfathers for a raucous reception by referring to *all* grandfathers. His paean erupted just after he said casually, "we fix upon something that happened away back, as in some way or other being connected with this rise of prosperity."[17]

Although he normally spoke extemporaneously without even an outline of his remarks, Lincoln then reached for what was obviously his premeditated climax by saying, "We find a race of men living in that day whom we claim as our fathers and grandfathers; they were iron men, they fought for the principle that they were contending for; and we understood that by what they then did it has followed that the degree of prosperity that we now enjoy has come to us."[18]

This is Lincoln as we rarely envision him. Buoyant and charming, he urged us to be "in better humor with ourselves" and to attach to one another *and* to become more firmly bound to our country.[19]

Bringing native and foreign-born Americans together, Lincoln added, "besides these men—descended by blood from our ancestors ... men that have come from Europe themselves, or whose ancestors have come hither and settled here, (find) themselves our equals in all things."[20]

Lincoln immediately quoted from the Declaration of Independence, "We hold these truths to be self-evident, that all men are created equal," along with his proposition that all of the men hearing him possessed "a right to claim it as though they were blood of the blood, and flesh of the flesh of the men who wrote that Declaration,"—interrupted here by "loud and long continued applause"—before he finished up, declaring, "and so they are."[21]

Lincoln was on a roll. Having begun with all grandfathers, and after declaring a fraternity by blood or by sentiment, he concluded but a short step from announcing the corollary aloud that, all men having been created equal, therefore, the evil of slavery must end. This final point, however, he left obvious, logical and tacit.

From this public exaltation of his and all "grandfathers" simultaneously in the only public appreciation of both of his own that he ever dared, one infers that Lincoln, consciously "blood of the blood and flesh of the flesh" of the Virginia planter, spent considerable mental time with his Revolutionary ancestors, and that when he did, he felt borne up by exhilarating connections. Associations may be discerned between

Warsaw Tavern, built about 1750 (destroyed by fire in 1898), would have been a likely resting place if Lincoln visited Richmond County while he lived in Washington as a Congressman, 1848–49 (courtesy Richmond County Museum).

high spirits and the recollection of his grandfathers, an exuberance that quickly spread to all Americans, and to the country.

Blood and High Hopes

While Lincoln offered the crowd in Chicago their (and his) "grandfathers" for an ovation, he did not reveal something else explicitly: his highest hopes. When five of the first six Presidents had been Virginia planters, Lincoln might logically aspire to follow Washington and Jefferson, given his descent from a "nobleman so-called" of Virginia. These "grandfathers," founders, and signers or supporters of the Declaration of Independence, excited his hopes because so many of them were his possible (although distant) blood kin.[22]

Ironically, Lincoln had been more candid as a boy. When he addressed his brothers by "flesh and blood" or sentiment in 1858, he had been thinking about the White House for about forty years. He was aware of his goal when he set out on his great and monumental effort in self-education. The boy told his Indiana neighbors like the Crawfords, as he daubed their cabin chinks with clay, and maybe he told his mother— if *she* did not tell *him* first—that he was going to be President.[23]

Lincoln later confided this personal history to Ward Hill Lamon. Lamon, himself a native Virginian and a long-time friend and political ally who rode with Lincoln as a lawyer on circuit in Illinois, though not a witness to Lincoln's boyhood, recalled Lincoln reminding him after he was President, "You know better than any man living that from my boyhood up my ambition was to be President." The most solid grounds he had to stand on was the birthright he inherited from the Virginia planter.[24]

4.

Lincoln Investigates His Grandfathers (1848 and 1854)

SOURCE: Hon. Abraham Lincoln, Congressman
FIRST WRITTEN: 1848

> There is a goddess of Memory, Mnemosyne;
> but none of Forgetting. Yet there should be,
> as they are twin sisters, twin powers, and walk
> on either side of us, disputing sovereignty
> over us and who we are, all the way to death.
> —Richard Holmes, *This Long Pursuit, Reflections
> of a Romantic Biographer* (2017)

Preface

They were in his mind early and often but only in his late thirties did Lincoln document a word about either of his grandfathers. When he first arrived in Congress, he began to pump out letters regarding Abraham Lincoln, his namesake grandfather. He was replying to letters forwarded by other Congressmen whose constituents had inquired whether they might be related to the new Congressman. Through his fallen grandfather, the answer was yes, they shared the same blood.

Unlikely but still not impossibly—evidenced only in a terribly garbled and vestigial way—Lincoln may have engaged an attorney, begun an investigation, or made a visit to his mother's birthplace, taking a look for the Virginia planter or vestiges of him around and about Richmond County, the site of the liaison and original scandal that set so much in motion, beginning with the conception of his mother.

The Lookback of '48

For Lincoln in 1848, populating his family tree was no hobby. He had to look back before he could move on. The rising politician was driven by political necessity when, for the first time, Lincoln wrote "grandfather" in any writing that survives. He was 39 years old, in Congress, and he wrote the word thereafter a dozen times in thirty days. He dropped almost everything else to respond to two relatives, Solomon Lincoln and David Lincoln, who wrote to their Congressmen inquiring about him.[1]

One surmises that his prompt letters were sent in waves in 1848, and again in 1854, and finally even in 1860 to make certain that the original Abraham Lincoln was a worthy ancestor. Receiving assurances, in his outline for Scripps, Lincoln spent 32 lines on his father's side of the family and 4 lines on his mother's side before beginning the chronicle of his own activities.[2]

By then, Lincoln knew the political disadvantages of standing alone without family. He had stumbled when, in the first handbill he circulated for election, he maintained, "I have no wealthy or popular relations to recommend me." He lost.[3]

Although pulled in many directions in early 1848, freshman Congressman Lincoln devoted hours writing to find out more about his grandfather. Lincoln sent out at least five within his first thirty days in Washington, all addressed to Lincolns who lived in Virginia. Any hope that his paternal grandfather was a friend of Thomas Jefferson or knew George Washington went unfulfilled. Replies confirmed what he knew, that his grandfather died when shot by passing Indians.

The Hanks Side Ignored?

There is almost no evidence that Lincoln identified and sent similar letters to descendants of his maternal grandfather, although apathy about his mother's father would have been odd, given a desire to know his roots. His political or personal interests were the same on both sides of his family tree—but he was hindered by the absence of this grandfather's *name*.

That is almost all that may be said about Lincoln's inquiring mind and the Virginia planter. Almost. A single curious, possibly unrelated and garbled story suggests Lincoln made a search for his *maternal* grandfather. This evidence (or supposed "evidence" in quotation marks) is tucked into the papers of Caroline Dall today stored by the Massachusetts Historical Society.

A journalist whom Herndon hosted, when she stayed at his home as a guest, he freely allowed Dall to read his Lincoln materials. A clingy contact, when Dall hounded Herndon for items after she left, Herndon complied by sending her, for example, his only copy of an early speech by Lincoln, the now-famous Lyceum Address. The woman could not get enough. Dall is suspected of perpetrating a priceless archival theft: Herndon had separated some of his most sensitive material into two small memorandum books, books that vanished when Dall left Springfield.[4]

Did Dall find them too sensational to let go? The memo books have never resurfaced, but fragments may have survived, along with other Dall documents. As a scholarly sleuth, Helen R. Deese, researched her vivid biography of the mercurial Dall, she transcribed a reconstructed journal that Dall made. Dall's enigmatically-sourced journal includes the following note:

> When he was elected—he was determined if possible not to enter the White House—in the name of Lincoln—and saw no legal obstacle to another, if he could establish his right to it. He wrote to lawyers in Kentucky and Western Virginia—and told them what he wanted.... The legal investigation showed that Lincoln was probably the son of a more educated man named Bloomfield.[5]

On its face, this entry is nonsense. It is lunacy to take literally a report that Lincoln desired to change his name or prove that Thomas Lincoln was not his father in 1860. What remains after discounting the superficial, however, is an unusually well-placed journalist's mixed-up impression that Lincoln engaged lawyers about his lineage and discovered an "educated" man whose name was different from his own. Was it his non–Lincoln *grandfather* whom lawyers found?

In other words, in 1848, did Lincoln write other letters which have not survived? Nobody can access the source which *may be* the missing, Herndon's two infamous memo books. The Massachusetts Historical Association's document transcribed by Deese faintly suggests the possibility that a detective was engaged or even (in a leap) that a visit was made by Lincoln or by an agent in his behalf to interview people in Richmond County. Such a visit on Lincoln's part in 1848 or 1849, if successful, would go far to explain Lincoln's haste to tell his story to Herndon in about 1851.

Lincoln's Possible *Visit to Richmond County*

A visit was feasible at that time. In Washington, Lincoln was nearer to Richmond County than ever before in his life. Nearer by water than over land, the county was a day away by steamboat and several days by horseback. George Washington, in the next county, took five days to ride to Williamsburg and the roads and mileage between Richmond County and Washington were little different. Without Mary and the children holding him back, Lincoln may have found the temptation to visit his mother's birthplace eminently practical in 1848.

However, if he visited, Lincoln was likely disappointed. He may have seen "Menokin," once the two-story elegant home of Francis Light-foot Lee, a signer of the Declaration of Independence, then owned for decades by the Lomax family. But his great-grandfather Joseph Hanks's

Milden Hall, Richmond County, Virginia, the homestead of the Peachey family in the 1780s. Joseph Hanks was plantation overseer for Col. William Peachey from 1761 until just prior to the Revolution. Joseph also took over as road surveyor from William Peachey's brother, Leroy Peachey in 1773; therefore, the Hanks and Peachey families knew each other well. Note: 52 years old in 1782, Col. Peachey cannot be ruled out among suspect planters as Lincoln's maternal grandfather (courtesy Jay Garner, Richmond County historian).

Menokin, under reconstruction. During the Revolution, one must visualize this partial ruin as the elegant mansion of Francis Lightfoot Lee, a signer of the Declaration of Independence. Trustees have plans for a unique glass-swathed dreamlike reproduction of the house as it was (courtesy Jay Garner, Richmond County historian).

acreage by Farnham Creek probably stood untilled, if not overgrown, as farming was barely profitable. Virginia's economy, including Richmond County's primarily agricultural base, had tanked during the extended trade interruption of the War of 1812. For years, its farms changed hands frequently.[6]

Elisha Hall had sold Woodberry, where hellfire Baptist preaching may have turned Joseph Hanks and his family against slavery before they started out anew in Kentucky, the Peachey family sold Milden Hall and the son of Griffin Murdock Fauntleroy (who has been proposed as possibly "the Virginia planter," Lincoln's maternal grandfather), after the old Revolutionary's death, sold the Fauntleroy homestead on Mars Hill. Resolutely bucking this trend—the sale of colonial era's fine houses was the story in Richmond County for about fifty years—the Carters maintained Sabine Hall and the Tayloes their home on Mount Airy but, even so, the "Men of '76," the county's planters of the 1780s, were gone, and the new owners of their mansions would probably not have known anything of interest to Lincoln.[7]

Woodberry, in a mansion long torn down, owned by Hannah Lee Corbin, was the site of Baptist meetings and impassioned sermons opposing slavery. Some attending (including one of the Carter family) were moved to act, abandon their claims on enslaved people and legally recognize them as free. It is undocumented but *possible* that among those converted to oppose slavery were plantation overseer Joseph Hanks, and his family, before they moved from Richmond County (courtesy Jay Garner, Richmond County historian).

At best, Lincoln may have gone inside some of the homes and warily shared something of what he knew—he may have had a name to ask about or other details his mother told him—but we do not know, and his errand likely turned up nothing.

After Lincoln's investigations, both the certain and the merely hypothetical, he felt safe to label his grandparents on both sides as "second families," i.e., families lacking resources, making moot any question of their having been enslavers. That Lincoln knew better is clear—but his planter grandfather was a *secret* nobody knew but Herndon, and Herndon had pledged not to disclose what he knew while Lincoln lived. For Lincoln to cut the distinguished family of the "nabob" down to a "second family" was only good politics.

The Revolutionary Generation's Influence on Lincoln

The letters turned up nothing new (or disturbing) and, if he made a visit to Richmond County, neither did that possible journey seem to have changed anything. Lincoln was left with a Revolutionary generation. Of their revolutionary or radical view on slavery he was constantly conscious. This was the generation whose Jeffersonian "all men are created equal" clause, applied broadly, became his *mantra*.

Ten years later, on September 15, 1858, in Jonesboro, Illinois, just after Douglas concluded, to three cheers, "Why should we not act as our fathers who made the government? There was no sectional strife in Washington's army. They were all brethren of a common confederacy, they fought under a common flag that they might bestow upon their posterity a common destiny, and to this end they poured out their blood in common streams and shared in some instances a common grave," Lincoln rose to speak.[8]

Dirt road to Peacock Hill, Richmond County, Virginia. Peacock Hill was the site of the farm and home of Joseph Hanks and his large family, including his oldest child, his maverick daughter Lucy Hanks (courtesy Jay Garner, Richmond County historian).

Farnham Creek, central to the business and traffic of Richmond County from colonial times to the Civil War. Joseph Hanks (Lincoln's great-grandfather) operated a farm near the creek. He also served as an overseer for other nearby planters before moving his family, including two-year-old Nancy, to western Virginia and to Kentucky (courtesy Jay Garner, Richmond County historian).

Given the triggering words "Washington," "posterity," and "blood," Lincoln could hardly avoid being powerfully stirred to talk about the Revolutionary generation. Saying nothing directly of the Virginia planter, Lincoln loudly touted the Revolutionary origins of the positions he espoused. He opened up with the question "Why can't we let it stand as our fathers placed it?"[9]

He placed, in essence, his grandfather's views rather than his own before his audience:

I say in the way our fathers originally left the slavery question, the institution was in the course of ultimate extinction, and the public mind rested in the belief that it *was* in the course of ultimate extinction. I say when this government was first established it was the policy of its founders to prohibit the spread of slavery into the new Territories of the United States, where it had not existed. But Judge Douglas and his friends have broken up that policy and placed it upon a new basis by which it is to become national and perpetual. All I have asked or desired anywhere is that it should be placed back again upon the basis that the fathers of our government originally placed it upon. I have no doubt that it *would* become extinct, for all time to come, if we but re-adopted the policy of the fathers by restricting it to the limits it has already covered—restricting it from the new Territories.[10]

In Jonesboro in 1858 Lincoln spoke as one with authority, defending a truth handed down to him, without sharing its all-too-startling provenance with his listeners: the grandfather he kept to himself. As he understood the Virginia planter, that gentleman was "broad minded." His Jeffersonian mother and her heroic stories of Washington's army, his connection by blood, all urged him to complete the unfinished business of the Revolution by redeeming the Declaration of Independence's promise of human equality.[11]

5

What Lincoln Told
Billy Herndon (*circa* 1851)

SOURCE: William H. Herndon, Esq.
FIRST PUBLISHED: 1889

> I can only answer the question "What am I to do?"
> if I can answer the prior question "Of what story
> or stories do I find myself a part?"
> —Alasdair MacIntyre, *After Virtue* (1981)

Preface

This fifth report requires a drumbeat because just here the rubber hits the road. In this report, Lincoln shared the secret he had withheld from everybody until then and, to top it off, required secrecy during his lifetime (which is extraordinary for several reasons, gone into here).

In advance of reading it, though, consider that Lincoln was a cerebral type. As Herndon once wrote, "Lincoln lived in his head and conscience—not much in the heart." On this day of telling his mother's secret Lincoln was what Herndon described him as being, and more specifically, "a man of profound judgments" or sagacity.

Given this bias or left-brain dominance as the proper context, when Lincoln offers to trace the sources of his power of analysis, logic, mental acuity and even his ambition, as he did that day and only that day, one must lean forward to listen closely because Lincoln *was* his mind, he identified his best self with his thoughts, his analyses, his logic, his mental acuity and his ambition, aptly known as the "little engine that knew no rest." In these elements one has the essence of Lincoln. When he purported to tell where *these* qualities came from, Lincoln proposed to spell out what or who had to do with his very self.[1]

Resistance and Reluctance

Billy Herndon had many good traits, but he was also opinionated and stubborn. Perhaps these reason-resistant factors in Herndon's make-up led Lincoln to hesitate before introducing himself to his law partner as the proud descendant of a brilliant Revolutionary. Hints aside, it was a story that he had never told anyone. We see now that Lincoln intended to communicate his high hopes and gratitude, while Herndon, on intuition and facial expressions, viewed Lincoln as hopeless and his story as a shameful family scandal.

Lincoln made his disclosures as they were riding together in Lincoln's small one-horse buggy on the outskirts of Springfield some ten years before he was President. Herndon associated the time of Lincoln's disclosures with the "Compromise of 1850," a notorious series of bills that passed only at the very end of 1850.[2]

Lincoln's hesitation sounds odd. Nancy Hanks Lincoln praised her father. Why may a daughter's praise of her father not be shouted from the rooftops? Only slowly does it become clear that Nancy, too, probably hesitated. Motivated to encourage her boy more than anything else, Nancy plainly steeled herself until, with both humility and bravery, she said that she had been born a bastard. One day in her early thirties she would have been tempted to reveal that her father was rich, prominent, intellectual, and the possessor of several other heroic qualities.

Admission of bastardy was the price of speaking and, to her eternal credit, that price Lincoln's devoted mother was willing to pay. Her priority was not herself but her children. To instill a glowing image of inherited brilliance, to boost confidence when her children had so little else to "excite the ambition for education," was Nancy's goal and gift.[3]

Nancy's gift outlived her, especially in her son. He famously compared his mind to a steel plate, hard to scratch but, once scratched, scratched forever. Scratched, Lincoln carried more vividly than anything else of his boyhood his mother's tales of his grandfathers, and of Washington and of the Revolution.[4]

Lincoln, who could not pass a day without hearing the name of a pioneer gunned down in his cornfield—the man whose name was his name, too—had another grandfather, a nameless one. That grandfather was with him in the buggy with Herndon that day of disclosures. That day, his thoughts ran toward his mother and to her father.

The Odd Couple

The two men could have been taken for father and son. Lincoln, tall and imposing, turned 42 in 1851 but looked older. Assuming that the "hoss" of Lincoln & Herndon was dressed as he commonly dressed for court, on the day of his disclosures he wore a black broadcloth suit of medium fineness, a frock-tail coat, but no cravat or stock or necktie. As Herndon saw him, his "flesh was dark—wrinkled and folded: it looked dry and leathery, tough and everlasting." Never handsome, "his eyes were small and grey—head small and forehead receding" and his hair was remarkably wild and unkempt. A portrait painter wrote later of his "broad brow, surmounted by rough, unmanageable hair." In better days, Lincoln joked that his hair sought ways to rise as high as possible.[5]

In contrast to his long-legged, gaunt partner, Herndon was short and plumpish with facial features that were oddly angular, almost ratty. High cheekbones afforded him sharp eyes that, though they seemed half-closed, were quite alert. Herndon, 32 but looking younger, wore stylishly long, sometimes bushy hair. He also sported a neatly clipped chin fringe of curly, bushy beard that distinguished him from his then clean-shaven, gaunt senior partner.[6]

The odd couple differed in behavior and politics as they did in looks. Herndon, lively and more emotional, tended to enjoy a drink while Lincoln was a teetotaler. An impassioned abolitionist, Herndon was vocally impatient with Lincoln's Constitution–based legalities. Douglas Wilson wrote in summary, "William Herndon was very different from his partner. Outgoing and exuberant by nature, he was as communicative and unbuttoned as Abraham Lincoln was guarded and reserved." However, Lincoln's general "shut-mouthed" deportment did not preclude annoying noise. Lincoln read the daily newspaper aloud as Herndon tried to work in their office. The habit drove Herndon crazy, though he could never get Lincoln to stop it. For sanity's sake, Herndon would sometimes grab his hat and stomp out of the office.[7]

Like people back then, scholars now wrestle with the mystery of how these two ever stayed together for some fifteen years, or until Lincoln left for the White House. The short answer is that they got used to one another—that, and, when he was not reading his newspapers aloud, complex, quirky Lincoln absolutely fascinated Herndon. He was such an odd duck he compelled Herndon's attention. Although they kept a satisfactorily dusty office on Sixth and Adams Street, near the State House, they were often on the road traveling together as well. They probably saw one another more than they saw their wives and children. Few people ever knew Lincoln better than Herndon knew him. On this day in the early 1850s, Lincoln greatly expanded Herndon's knowledge of him, expanded it even more than Herndon himself ever grasped.

An Unscheduled Stop

They were expected in court that day in adjacent Menard County. They would have met up at about 7 a.m. to be in court by mid-morning. Both men were familiar with their destination because Lincoln had lived in Menard County as a young, unmarried man, in New Salem, while Herndon had resided in the region spreading outward from Springfield since he was two years old. Carrying bags packed with handwritten pleadings, a law book or two, pens, ink and paper, they were headed to a hearing, part of a complicated divorce, a case that had clogged (and would continue to clog) the Menard docket for years. That day, they were to argue about the "hereditary qualities of mind." Herndon later thought that Lincoln was stimulated by that topic in play to expose his own family secrets.[8]

Lincoln probably drove in order that, when he wanted to slow or stop, they would. Probably pulled by Lincoln's trusty horse, plodding old "Bob," the two jolted along for about half an hour, probably in silence. As Herndon once wrote, "Lincoln was a poor conversationalist; he was a poor listener in the social line, too." Complete silence offended neither of them. Lincoln surely did not hurry Bob, literally on his last legs. Bob was a nag that hailed from New Salem and had been no colt when Lincoln bought him 8 or 9 years earlier. When they came to the top of the hill, Lincoln slowed, if he did not stop, at what seems to have been a traditional rest area for Bob to catch his breath.[9]

Having loosely guided the reins for almost three miles—Bob knew the way as well as he did—Lincoln showed his hand. He decided to tell Herndon *conditionally.* The scene burned into Herndon's memory. Thirty years later both where it happened and how his senior partner began remained vivid. Having reached the top of "a hill overlooking Spring Creek on the road to Petersburg 2½ miles west of the city," Herndon recalled, Lincoln turned and said, "Herndon, I'll tell you something, but keep it a secret while I live."[10]

Why Share Then, and Conditionally?

Lifelong secrecy? An astonishing beginning. Herndon, the younger man, was offered secrets he might disclose *after Lincoln was dead.* Instead of preparing Herndon to address a judge in Menard County, Lincoln was preparing his partner to address posterity. A bell ought to have gone off, but Herndon made nothing of this crucial clue. This was deeply ironic because Herndon whined many times in different words that Lincoln was an infinitely silent man who "was thoroughly and deeply secretive, uncommunicative and close-minded as to his plans, wishes, hopes and fears." Then, when Lincoln offered revelations, the hints sailed over his partner's bushy head.[11]

Formally, of course, his audience was Herndon. But, from his opening question, Lincoln was using Herndon as an agent charged to speak after Lincoln's death. Lincoln's determination to withhold all information about his mother and her father wavered suddenly. He was casting a spell over his afterlife.

Superficially sharing a second-hand parental reminiscence from the 1780s, Lincoln was taking a step forward, beyond his own life. He wanted the ancestral causes of foreseen future success to be published. The honored dead from whom he took inspiration were to be remembered around his bier. Lincoln, a fatalist to the core, believed in a sequential unfolding of events that individuals were powerless to retard or to advance. He wanted it known that he had been fated to succeed as a child forming in the womb.[12]

Apparently by a quick nod or gesture, with no hesitation, Herndon agreed. In his trademark staccato notes—separated by dashes—idiosyncratically capitalized and at least once substituting "good" for "God"—Herndon wrote that Lincoln told him about his family's origins and how much two specific ancestors meant to him. Lincoln said, "My mother was a bastard—was the daughter of a nobleman—so called of Virginia. My mother's mother was poor and credulous &c. and she was shamefully taken advantage of by the man. My mother inherited his qualities and I hers. All that I am or ever hope to be I get from my mother—God bless her."[13]

Notwithstanding the key words "ever hope to be," reflecting *high* hopes, Herndon did not grasp that Lincoln "got" what he hoped to be from his mother—to be a liberator in some way—and that Lincoln wanted to be known as the grandson of a Virginia planter because a connection somehow existed between that ancestor and those high hopes.

Lincoln may be faulted for vagueness. He did not quote his mother. He did not clarify the role of his grandfather apart from biological components. Only from other evidence—presented in the first report, by Christopher Columbus Graham—do we know that Nancy was an ardent Jeffersonian and an anti-slavery egalitarian who was vocally concerned about human rights. Nonetheless, nobody would exact a pledge of life-long secrecy to say that their *mother* made them who they were and all they hoped to be. No, Lincoln's secrecy concerned *her father's* influence, which he "got" from her. All that he ever hoped to be Lincoln also associated his grandfather, the Virginia planter.

An Idealized Ancestor

Yet how could an enslaver—for the economics of a Virginia planter, rich and prominent in the 1780s, a nabob, a "nobleman so-called," required enslaved labor—inspire *opposition* to slavery? What is going on here?

One word may be suggested, idealization, or, in three words, idealization by association. Lincoln viewed his grandfather as more paradigm than prodigal. Something had smoothed the rogue's sharp edges like beach glass, whether in Nancy's original affectionate telling, from the passage of time, by Lincoln's logic and imagination, or all of these together. By 1851, Lincoln resented nothing about his wayward grandfather. The old gentleman seemed instead to be formed of Washington's best parts and Jefferson's finest aspects.

Lincoln's admiration became clear from what may have been a second private conversation between the two men, after the buggy ride confidences. Herndon apparently somehow got his usually silent partner to describe the Virginia planter, when Lincoln really poured on the praise. The qualities Lincoln praised of the most revered of his blood kin were, *not* incidentally, Lincoln's *own* most prized qualities. According to Herndon, Lincoln "argued" his grandfather's impact on him in describing the planter as the *source* of his "power of analysis, logic, mental acuity, ambition" and the other unstated qualities that distinguished him.

"Ambition"? That last word is especially intriguing. Lincoln's highest hopes were influenced by a Virginia planter whom he never met—logically, how can that possibly be argued?

One solution is derivative. Nancy may have embodied an ambition to fix the wrong of slavery that Lincoln adopted (more than inherited).

Much evidence survives that Nancy, the intellectual, thought and was concerned about matters far beyond her personal situation. Although she left no record and her son was "mum" about his mother, Christopher Columbus Graham listed the ideas that moved her to speak. If his mother spoke like that, with her father's mind, as Lincoln held, did she not express her "broad-minded" father's and Jefferson's notions about the cause of equality? The old Revolutionary's posited ambition was Lincoln's ambition, too. Lincoln felt that his mother and his grandfather preceded him.[14]

Lincoln's presumed embodiment of his mother's mind, which derived from the planter, is central to this proposed solution—as it was to Lincoln's stories that day. Herndon, who missed some of the finer points, fully understood this one. "Mr. Lincoln's own mother was a woman of very strong mind; it was not only strong but it was quick," he wrote in 1867, before saying, "She was a child of some *high blood rake* in Virginia—not from a common man." Above all, Herndon was cogently aware that Lincoln was conveying the source of his brainpower. "When Lincoln spoke to me as he did, he had reference to his mother's *mind*—nothing else."[15]

Consistently with that mental heritage, Lincoln wrote and spoke publicly and unapologetically, often and eloquently of the ambitions of the founders. Their agenda was his agenda. That much is public record and newspaper headlines. Behind his speeches and writings stands a shadowy figure to whom the speaker was related. From Herndon's reference to "ambition," we know that whenever Lincoln thought, spoke, and acted to realize the promise of equality featured in the Declaration of Independence with which the Revolution began, he rallied behind his grandfather's (and latterly his mother's) ambitions. In his mind's eye, Lincoln was a walking Revolutionary, 1776 to the present in a straight line.

A Glance at Washington

A counterargument beckons. The planter was prominent, rich and brilliant. But—was he actually ambitious to end slavery? The argument that Lincoln inherited this ambition, the idea that he associated his ambition to end slavery with his bloodline, seems ludicrous on its face. One might interpret instead the cogent phrase "all that he ever hoped to be" as an allusion strictly to Lincoln's highest *personal* aims.

If so, what were Lincoln's highest personal hopes in 1851?

He had already *been* a Congressman (and a four-term state legislator and, of course, a trial lawyer), so—to which office not yet occupied by him did he aspire? The Senate or the Presidency? Despite setbacks, virtually humiliated and in exile from the national seat of power, Lincoln could see hopeful signs if he looked at the sitting President.

In 1851, that was Millard Fillmore, a Whig. Like Fillmore, a New York trial lawyer and politician who succeeded as President when Zachary Taylor died, Lincoln was (1) a trial lawyer; (2) a staunch Whig; (3) a former state legislator; and (4) a former Congressman. For another lawyer-legislator-Congressman Whig from north of the Mason-Dixon line to become President had precedent.

Into the mix, if omens matter—and Lincoln was superstitious—all three Whig Presidents before Fillmore had been born in *Virginia*, and had been *planters*. Lincoln's grandfather had risked everything for the American experiment. As a "first family of Virginia" scion, rich and prominent, the "nobleman so-called" bet everything, including his life, on the cause of Washington and Jefferson. The Declaration of Independence, 1776 and his grandfather were all one to Lincoln. The Virginia planter's blood in his own veins was "as good as Washington's." That Virginia planter was in the right place at the right time to be elevated by the highest gift in the possession of his fellow countrymen. Conclusion: The Presidential ambition unrealized earlier by his forbear Lincoln might realize in his own time.[16]

The Interrogatory Story

Signaling a shift, Lincoln went interrogatory. Having largely exonerated the man, Lincoln, as a good grandson, handled his grandmother gently. His grandmother's story was embodied in but two short questions. He asked Herndon:

"Did you ever notice that bastards are generally smarter—shrewder and more intellectual than others? Is it because it is stolen?"[17]

By two questions, Lincoln upended his original version of events. "Stolen" leaps out as the odd, even extraordinary, word. His grandmother, Lucy Hanks, conned the gifted planter. The classic seduction and abandonment story, which Lincoln initially told, reflected theft *from* the maiden who loses her "virgin patent." But in his follow-up, teasing questions, *the mind of the Virginia planter* and *his* qualities were "stolen." *She* led *him* to impregnate *her*.

54

Stepping away from the "poor and credulous" cover Lincoln had granted Lucy in his first version, she rises instead as a plucky—and successful—trickster. His grandmother, ardent with purpose, stole for posterity. Although her "noble man so-called" abandoned her, wily, pregnant Lucy had the last laugh: she carried away his bloodline. With his sly questions, her grandson, never a puritan, ballyhooed her unconventional triumph. (As Herndon said, "His idea was that a woman had the same right to play with her tail that a man had and no more nor less.")[18]

In Lincoln's final version of his mother's conception, his grandmother, a seeming simpleton herself, managed to bear a daughter well above average. Lucy by this scenario was a gutsy rebel who flouted rules and ignored prohibitions of her time to bring the blessing or boon of brilliance into her family, including Lincoln. By this version, the fire that lit the minds of Nancy Hanks and her son, the rightful property of the planter, was a Promethean treasure that Lucy copped.

The Rest Is Silence

In Lincoln's chest beat a rataplan to advance. Although in vain and heard but not clearly understood by Herndon, Lincoln had vouched for the supportive lineage that justified his noblest hopes. Herndon heard no ancestral drumbeat. Lincoln broke off abruptly, not so much conclude as simply ceasing to speak after the word "stolen."

As Herndon put it, Lincoln "lapsed into silence." The two men rode on thereafter "without exchanging a word." Although Herndon said that Lincoln was customarily "a poor conversationalist" and "a very poor listener," the ensuing degree of tension between the partners must have been unusually palpable. By some body language that Herndon interpreted as inviolate, Lincoln "drew around him a barrier" that Herndon said that he literally feared to penetrate.[19]

The blanket that descended like a curtain supports speculation, both then and now. Herndon guessed that Lincoln withdrew "musing over the disclosure he had just made" but Lincoln was more likely musing over a great disappointment. Lincoln seems to have deduced a flat failure to communicate: his startling disclosures had not aroused his *audience*.[20]

Lincoln's judgment was spot on. Despite dots, Herndon drew no connections. He continued to think that he sat beside a desperate man.

Even at the time, in the buggy, "a flood of light burst on me," Herndon said, thinking "that Lincoln meant more than he said out and out."[21]

In short, Lincoln had spoken to the first of the biographers who would discount his remarks. When Herndon wrote his Lincoln biography, he presented Lincoln's disclosures in the context of political hopes never lower. Back in Illinois practicing law, former Congressman Lincoln stood repudiated. That impression possessed Herndon, who judged that the sweeping Compromise of 1850—which only bought time for a divided nation—might forever sideline moderate progressives like Lincoln.

On the contrary, Lincoln *was* hopeful. Herndon only imagined his stoic partner's desperation and, yet more ludicrously, conceived that Lincoln was ashamed of his *own* illegitimacy. Herndon wrote of it histrionically as the "fiery shirt" that Lincoln wore. In Herndon's resulting unintentionally ironic book, Lincoln remained both hopeless and ashamed.[22]

Herndon had it backward but, much worse than this, he did not write in vain. His errors caught on, he found an audience for the self-made Lincoln, the lone phoenix who rose from ashes. Herndon's facile gloss on Lincoln's disclosures took deeper root than his partner's profound revelations. In part distracted by Herndon's simultaneous commentary on Lincoln's hopeless political situation, in part thrown off by Lincoln's indirect and partial form of disclosures, several generations of scholars now have discounted or at least not discerned his ancestors' huge significance.

Until now, most people have, like Herndon, taken Lincoln's epochal celebration of his gifted planter grandfather's legacy *and* of his trickster grandmother's splendid theft as stories of no consequence either to Lincoln's life or of any impact in American history. (In response to public and critical condemnation of indiscreet revelations, Lincoln's disclosures were actually *removed* from the second edition!)[23]

But these developments lay far ahead on that day in the buggy in 1851. Lincoln had sufficient grounds to consider that if Herndon, his friend and law partner, did not understand, if *he* did not grasp the implications of what Lincoln said, perhaps no one ever would. The natural question for Lincoln to ponder not only during the rest of their ride but for the rest of his life was: whether he ought to speak of the Virginia planter ever again. He answered in the negative—until one evening in 1860.[24]

6

What Lincoln Told the "Special Correspondent" (1860)

SOURCE: Anonymous, "Special Correspondent"
FIRST PUBLISHED: 1860

> One must picture everything in the world as an enigma, and live in the world as if in a vast museum of strangeness.—Giorgio de Chirico

Preface

Do you wonder whether "Honest Abe" told the truth about his ancestry to the American people? A partly affirmative answer arises from one article that appeared in newspapers in August 1860, the only interview Lincoln gave to anybody during the campaign, in which he also made no speeches. He did not tell everything. He told less than he told Herndon. As with what Lincoln told Herndon, there are some surprising aspects and implications in what he said, and in what he did not say. (Thanks to the National Archives for unearthing the clippings of these unique articles.)

Breaking Silence

After accepting his party's nomination for President, Lincoln went mute. The Republican candidate delivered no speeches, debated nobody and gave no interviews. He did not ride outside of Springfield. He approved the publication of transcripts of his 1858 debates with Stephen Douglas and wrote a few letters "not for publication." That was all.

Then, on the evening of Monday, August 7, as the Lincoln family relaxed at their two-story clapboard house on the corner of 8th and Edward Streets, a man walking down their shadowy street, suddenly turned, climbed up the home's several wooden front steps and, when he knocked, he was admitted. This gentleman, never named, clearly expected an interview, for Lincoln instantly took part in the most candid he ever gave. After Herndon in 1851, Lincoln talked with no one for publication about his ancestors. That evening, with the unnamed gentleman, he talked about his grandfathers.[1]

Lincoln's exceptionally trusted interviewer published anonymously. Who, of Lincoln's circle of friends, was dubbed a "Special Correspondent" by the *New York Herald*'s editor and publisher, James Gordon Bennett, over an article published six days later? Young John Hay, a local who later served as one of the President's secretaries in the White House, is one possible author. However, Michael Burlingame's book of over 400 pages, entitled *Lincoln's Journalist*, drawn out of Hay's many other anonymous articles during the years 1860–65, did not include this

Lincoln's home in Springfield, the site of the only interview he gave during the Presidential campaign of 1860. During that interview, he spoke of coming from "good Revolutionary stock," and a grandfather—whom he did not name, but described as both lively and brilliant (Pixabay.com).

one. Norman B. Judd is another possible author, a Chicago lawyer then riding especially high in Lincoln's confidence. Judd was a savvy political ally whom Lincoln later excluded from his cabinet choices with great reluctance. Herndon might be considered. Lincoln sat with whoever it was either in the Lincolns' cozy downstairs parlor or in the adjacent family room, which featured tables and chairs, toys and a stereopticon, a spot where Lincoln in his shirtsleeves sometimes sprawled out full-length on the carpet to roughhouse with his "cubs."[2]

The people present that evening were listed. They included Lincoln's two lively sons, Mary Todd Lincoln, Adeline Judd (spouse of Norman B. Judd), and Congressman E.B. Washburne. This time, when Lincoln spoke fluently about his family and even made a sensational remark about the South and slavery, he was among his nearest and dearest. The resulting remarkable article ran in the *Herald* on August 13, 1860, and in an edited, shorter form in the *Chicago Press & Tribune* on August 15, 1860. Lincoln never challenged its authenticity or accuracy.

A Wide-Open Interview

Lincoln was drawn to express memories of his mother, usually taboo. As Herndon put it in a memorable meme, Lincoln was "mum about his mother." In his autobiographical sketch or outline for Scripps, Lincoln gave his mother's name and wrote nothing at all about his maternal grandfather. Yet in his home on this one evening, Lincoln positively bubbled on about his mother *and* her father. He edged nearly up to what he told Herndon. One may compare and contrast, "My mother inherited (her father's) qualities and I hers. All that I am or hope ever to be I get from my mother—God bless her," against, "His mother was the daughter of a man of nerve and energy, and she herself possessed those distinctive characteristics which have since rendered her son a man of mark in our country."[3]

More notably, after first speaking of the grandfather whose name he bore, who "perished beneath the tomahawk of the savage," Lincoln spoke of his *other* grandfather's understood or implied part in the Revolution. From what Lincoln said—who honorifically deemed Lincoln a "Colonel" for his military service during the Black Hawk War—the "Special Correspondent" was moved to write that "Colonel Lincoln came from the best among our Revolutionary stock."[4]

After this unprecedented celebration of "the best among our

Revolutionary stock," Lincoln came as close as he ever did to saying that his Virginia grandfather opposed slavery.

The French Connection

Lincoln said that many Southerners secretly abhorred slavery. The connection to his grandfather was subtle. Lincoln opined that "many people in the South" were obliged publicly to sustain slavery, "although they secretly abhorred the institution."

This statement invites close analysis. By "many people in the South," did Lincoln mean a good portion of citizens who lived south of the Mason-Dixon line or many of the educated and articulate public men of the South? The latter possibility is contextually supported because, at this point in his interview, Lincoln offered a historical example. Speaking of leaders of the French Revolution, Lincoln referred to a recent historian's account of the execution of Louis XVI. From it, Lincoln said, he gleaned that "although the leading revolutionists were publicly obliged to declare in favor of that deed, they were privately opposed to it." The erstwhile correspondent quoted Lincoln as saying to him that evening, "Public opinion is not always private opinion."[5]

Scholar William C. Harris, who unearthed and analyzed the unique *Herald* article and highlighted this quotation, surmised that Lincoln had no basis to make this claim of "secret abhorrence" of slavery within the institution's defenders. Harris concluded expressly that Lincoln held "a false understanding of white Southern opinion on slavery." However, Harris did not detect that Lincoln may have been alluding to a *familial* abhorrence and opposition to slavery, an opposition to slavery that he had been taught as he sat in the Lincoln cabin at his mother's knee.[6]

Though Lincoln said nothing directly that evening or ever about *ancestral* opposition to slavery, his lineage was the topic just before he spoke about "secret abhorrence." Having the ancestors he had may go far to explain why Lincoln never demonized the South.[7]

Notwithstanding, Lincoln was realistic about the balance of the Southern population. Toward the end of his interview, Lincoln adverted to them. After he "said he should like to go South and talk to the Southerners" about slavery, he admitted that what stopped him was that "the minds of some" were so inflamed that they might lynch him.[8]

7

Lincoln's "Great Cause" (1863)

SOURCE: Various
FIRST PUBLISHED: Beginning 1866

> If our nation had done nothing more in its whole history
> than to create just two documents, its contribution to
> civilization would be imperishable. The first of these
> documents is the Declaration of Independence and the
> other is ... the Emancipation Proclamation.
> —Dr. Martin Luther King, Jr. (September 12, 1962)

Preface

What was Lincoln thinking when he realized his highest hopes? Lincoln made no address on the occasion of signing the Emancipation Proclamation. So far as the few witnesses were aware, he was caught up in worrying over how his signature would look. The absence of an address stymies us from knowing his thoughts—but, fortuitously, a few weeks later, Lincoln wrote a letter, a thank you note, to a group of working men and their families in Manchester, England. Belatedly, he exposed what he was thinking.

He adverted to the founders, the promise of the Declaration of Independence, the concept that all men are created equal. One could almost transpose from Dr. Graham's report of Nancy Hanks discussing notions about the wrong of slavery and the rights of man as explained by Thomas Jefferson and Thomas Paine, as if it were a list of Lincoln's thoughts as he penned his other grandfather's name on his proclamation for all time.

As with the six other reports, the picture is not fully developed although a pattern is apparent when dots are connected—and that

61

pattern is one increasingly familiar to us. Although Lincoln made no reference to his mother or her father's role in his life on January 1, 1863, or even in his letter to the British working men and their families, their Revolutionary ideas, as he understood them, and his idealized ancestors seem to have been flashing in Lincoln's head when he signed the Emancipation Proclamation.

The Proclamation

On the first day of 1863, President Lincoln was highly conscious that he would be signing an unquotable document that was nonetheless designed to outlive him. Above a sea of dense legalese, only its large, black letter title—Emancipation Proclamation—and, below the block of fine print, his signature would compel attention. Facsimiles would be made and even framed. He knew that he was making his mark for all time. In viewing it, people yet unborn would wonder at "Abraham Lincoln."

Even so, after 2 o'clock on that first afternoon of the year, Lincoln was a man in trouble. For three hours, he had shaken hands at the President's New Year's reception. With anxiety increasing by the handshake, in hellish thralldom as the country's Greeter-in-Chief, Lincoln grasped thousands of outstretched hands, many of them wringing and clinging to the war-time leader as if for their salvation. After the ordeal, his abused right hand throbbed with pain.

Signatures, Names and Significance

Throughout his life, Lincoln's signature was a kind of wonder to him. In part, this was because he had come late to writing. Lincoln had learned to sign his name about age ten. His mother had died, his father was away, he had been left in the lackadaisical care of an older cousin, Dennis Hanks. Exuberantly scrawling his name with creel, or chalk on flat surfaces of the paperless Lincoln cabin, the boy cried aloud to Dennis, "That stands for me."

For Lincoln, no conventional Christian, to live in the hearts and minds of people was the only eternity. Lincoln made this tic emphatic on February 22, 1842. Addressing a crowd assembled in a church in Springfield on Washington's birthday, Lincoln told them, "Washington

IN THIS TEMPLE
AS IN THE HEARTS OF THE PEOPLE
FOR WHOM HE SAVED THE UNION
THE MEMORY OF ABRAHAM LINCOLN
IS ENSHRINED FOREVER

The Lincoln Memorial in Washington, D.C. Lincoln had a lifelong horror of being forgotten (known as athazagoraphobia in Greek). His planter grandfather's name was unknown to Lincoln, a nightmare scenario. Above everything, Lincoln's quest for immortality motivated him, for a memorial and perpetual recollection that he had lived (Pixabay.com).

is the mightiest name of earth—*long since* mightiest in the cause of civil liberty; *still* mightiest in moral reformation. On that name, an eulogy is expected. It cannot be. To add brightness to the sun, or glory to the name of Washington, is alike impossible. Let none attempt it. In solemn awe pronounce the name, and in its naked deathless splendor, leave it shining on."[1]

What was good for Washington was vital to Lincoln. He believed in name immortality and he feared nothing so much as extinction out of mind. Lying depressed in bed in early 1841, he confessed this private worst terror to a friend, Joshua Speed. To him, Lincoln whimpered that he had done nothing to make any human being remember that he had lived. What he desired to live for, Lincoln whispered at ornate Victorian length, was "to connect his name with the events transpiring in his day and generation and so impress himself upon them as to link his name with something that would redound to the interest of his fellow man."

Lincoln's words about being forgotten were long remembered.

63

When Speed visited the White House in late 1862, Lincoln sounded him out: did Speed recall his rasped remark? Speed said that he did.

At the time of Speed's visit, Lincoln had issued the preliminary notice of emancipation. To his Kentucky friend, Lincoln vouched for its personal significance.

"I believe," Lincoln told Speed months prior to signing this official draft on January 1, 1863, "that in this measure my fondest hopes will be realized."

When Lincoln addressed the Congressmen of the border states in July 1862, seeking their support for state laws of compensated emancipation, predictably, he had told them that such a noble act would vindicate their common country's history, cherished memories and future happiness. But then he touched them with his personal grand prize of an eternal name: "To you, more than to any others, the privilege is given, to assure that happiness, and swell that grandeur, and to link your own names therewith forever."[2]

January 1, 1863, marked the belated ritual of his initiation into the founders of the country. His proclamation was a war-time affirmation of Jefferson's promise of equality, a promise renewed on his say so and unilateral authority in a military order, the Commander in Chief acting in the capacity of Commander in Chief. Lincoln was forever linking the war with the Revolution. At the dedication of a Union military cemetery in Gettysburg later that year, the famous phrase "four score and seven years ago" at the beginning of his Address meant 1776.

The 1776 document had been a dense block of highly legalistic jargon. Generations of Americans had studied facsimile copies to make out the names: a group of immortals whose signatures flowed around and under the flamboyant and generous first one by John Hancock. That document's author, the Virginia planter Thomas Jefferson, a less flashy penman than Hancock, signed legibly and firmly. On his ticket to immortality, Lincoln did not want his hand to shake.

In the Name of His Grandfathers

Lincoln took a seat. He held up a steel-point pen to dip into a brass inkwell. He wanted to sign legibly and firmly, like Jefferson, but his hand trembled. Decisively, he set the pen back down. How he would be *remembered* was at stake. He took a minute or two to calm himself.

Always hyperconscious about how people signed their names, he mentioned in his autobiography the unflattering fact that his father signed his name "bunglingly," and today Lincoln worried that his hand would jerk and signal hesitation when he signed. The more he thought about it, the more concerned he grew, and the small entourage that had followed the man into his office heard him speak of nothing else.

Wording differs, he probably made more than one statement; by all accounts, the President said something about shakiness and close future scrutiny of his signature. One dignitary recalled that Lincoln said comically that three hours of hand shaking was not good for performing chirurgy (surgery). Another remembered and quoted a longer and more pointed remark, "If my name ever goes into history it will be for this act, and my whole soul is in it. If my hand trembles when I sign the Procla-mation, all who examine the document hereafter will say, 'He hesitated.'" He probably both joked and worried aloud while he rubbed his hands together, pressed them atop the desk firmly, or in some other way settled his nerves, although no one was so indiscreet as to note such exercises.

At last, he was ready. He had steeled himself. There, in the center of his desk, an engrossed original of the Emancipation Proclamation was open and complete but for his signature. Those assembled witnessed Lincoln slowly and carefully inscribe the letters of his name. Anyone who examines the result today will discern his success. "Abraham Lin-coln" appears to have been neatly and carefully written, each letter indi-vidually legible. To this day, it is a signature that reflects a determined man who signed without doubt.

He did subscribe his title, as he sometimes did, "Pres'd't." To the right and only later, William H. Seward, Secretary of State, dressed things up officially, adding "By the President" but, until Seward's fussing, one unadorned name stood alone as if in a spotlight:

Abraham Lincoln.

Satisfied, Lincoln looked around to all those assembled, and, smil-ing, declared, "That will do."

Abraham Lincoln would be remembered now. The President who had signed with the name he shared with one of his grandfathers, whose other grandfather's name was unknown, said nothing about his grand-fathers or about anything else, but his personal gratification may be inferred from what he told the border state congressmen and Joshua Speed. His highest hopes realized, within the events transpiring in his day and generation, his name was now linked with something that would, as he once put it, "redound to the interest of his fellow man."

His signature would do, without a word.

The British Thank You Note

Had Lincoln not soon written a remarkably worded thank you note, we would not have a basis to infer what he was thinking when he issued the proclamation. However, from that letter, two o'clock in the afternoon of January 1, 1863, might best be understood as the finest hour of the relationship between Lincoln and the Virginia planter.

The evidence lies among President Lincoln's few letters to British subjects. Jobless workers of textile mills of the industrial city of Manchester, England, whose factories closed because of the Northern blockade of Southern cotton ships, rallied around the Emancipation Proclamation. They wrote and passed a resolution that said, "We joyfully honor you, as the President, and the Congress with you, for the many decisive steps towards practically exemplifying your belief in the words of your great founders, 'All men are created free and equal.'"[3]

Because *they* saw him in the light of 1776, he had to respond. Lincoln, whose sacrificing parents took him at age seven to a primitive Indiana wilderness "partly on account of slavery," wrote workingmen who, along with their wives and children, were enduring a like degree of suffering—partly on account of slavery.

To these innocent civilians caught in economic crossfire, Lincoln wrote on January 19, 1863,

> I know and deeply deplore the sufferings which the workingmen at Manchester and in all Europe are called to endure in this crisis.... Through the actions of our disloyal citizens the workingmen of Europe have been subjected to a severe trial, for the purpose of forcing their sanction to that attempt. Under these circumstances, I cannot but regard your decisive utterance upon the question as an instance of sublime Christian heroism which has not been surpassed in any age or in any country.[4]

It is the very last sentences that repays close attention. At first, it might seem that Lincoln spotted their heroism in "severe trial" for the cause of equality; however, analysis of Lincoln's precise and careful words reveals instead that the British families' *suffering* was not the *locus* of their heroism. Lincoln's wording is extraordinarily angled: he celebrated their *resolutions*. Lincoln found *unsurpassed* heroism in these workingmen's "decisive utterance."

To his way of thinking, they spoke, wrote, voted and signed resolutions in support of the proposition that "all men are created equal." *This* equation fairly invites, if it does not require us, to track their heroism not surpassed but the *equal* of any other age or country back.

That is, which *other* age, and which *other* country might be his original referent?

Of course, the obvious surfaces: the *founders* spoke, wrote, voted and signed resolutions in support of the proposition that "all men are created equal," risking their lives, fortunes and sacred liberties. Their decisive utterance was, indeed, literally echoed in the workingmen's resolution. When Lincoln praised British citizens, it was for having heroically and effectively *re-enacted* the "decisive utterance" of the Declaration of Independence in 1776 by their support.

Logically, by this exact measure, although Lincoln's silent partner went unsung, his grandfather was heroic, too, The Proclamation's materialization as the fruit of a long partnership with his grandfather went unacknowledged. It bore one name, his, reflecting one author acting singularly in his own time. The greetings from Britons who saw through Lincoln's mask so directly to the founders moved him to write back with his own phantom reference to the sublime Christian heroism of other ages and countries. A conclusion that Lincoln thought of the founders, and specifically of the Virginia planter, on January 1, 1863, would not be misplaced or unreasonable.

PART TWO

Reflections

8

Lincoln's Mother, Lincoln's Hero

A hero is someone who has given his or her life
to something bigger than oneself.—Joseph Campbell

From Christopher Columbus Graham's report of Nancy Hanks standing as an outspoken opponent of slavery among her community, to the sole surviving account of interaction between Nancy and her son in Indiana—which evoked Lincoln's ambiguous feelings about the Virginia planter—to the attention Lincoln paid to his grandfathers both during his childhood and in his adulthood, the foundation of Lincoln's understanding of his heritage is laid.

He finally shared his ancestral stories with Herndon in about 1851, but thereafter maintained his silence until the only interview that he gave in the 1860 campaign, when he took some risk to say what he did. Finally, from Lincoln's concern and close attention to getting his signature right on the Emancipation Proclamation along with the letter to Manchester workingmen, we connected 1776 to 1863, equality promised to equality proclaimed.

After this tour of significant scenes in Lincoln's relationship with his ancestors, Nancy hovers about indistinct and vague just when her importance is obvious and, likewise, Lincoln's sister, Sally, and Nancy's mother, Lucy. Reflections are offered that differ from reports in being less anchored in time and more focused on theme. Two chapters about Nancy before she married precede a lamentably short chapter about tragic sister Sally, another brilliant descendant of the Virginia planter, followed by a chapter on the planter-boosted education of Lincoln, sketching obstacles that he overcame, then a speculative explanation of Lincoln's seeming rebirth after year-long stagnation, ending with four reflections: one on the missing grandparent, the Virginia planter's lover, Lucy Hanks; the untold, or what Lincoln left out from what he told

Herndon and the special correspondent; Lincoln's interest in his grand-father's occupation, farming, or his protested lack therein; and, lastly, a quote-rich study of Lincoln and his ancestors caught up in the crossfire of Stephen Douglas.

"Hero" Characterized

During the rare moments that Lincoln talked about his mother, his law partner was fully alert. On the day that he disclosed his mother's bastardy and his Virginia planter grandfather, sandwiched between references to his mother's intellect and his own inherited mind, Lincoln described her as *heroic*. Herndon meticulously recalled Lincoln saying that his mother "was an intellectual woman—a heroic woman—that his mind he got from his mother &c." Another time Lincoln characterized her as "cool and heroic." It is necessary to explore what Lincoln may have meant by "heroic" because Lincoln said no more to anybody about his mother's heroism and he never defined "heroism."[1]

A word search of *The Collected Works of Abraham Lincoln* immediately turns up an anomaly: the Civil War was a war without heroes; Lincoln ceased using the word "hero" altogether. During the war, President Lincoln called no man or woman a *hero* and only a handful of times did he write the words "heroism" or "heroic," most significantly in two thank you notes, both of them to civilians.

As noted in the previous chapter, the first followed the Emancipation Proclamation and was written when Lincoln was moved by people's daily, stoical endurance for the cause of equality. If this is heroism, why would Lincoln not likewise see his mother as heroic in exactly the same light? She endeavored to ameliorate a multitude of daily hardships after taking a principled position outside of slavery, settling in the wilderness of Indiana. Thus, his mother's uncomplaining endurance of toil and privation like hunger and discomfort "partly on account of slavery" qualified her as heroic.

And yet, of course, a counterargument remains open: Lincoln never so specified. Is there any reasonable basis to think that Nancy in her *youth* inspired him to speak of her as both cool and heroic? For this purpose, a close study of her earliest struggles is justified.

As Lincoln understood and told Herndon, Nancy Hanks was born outside of wedlock to a single mother. Beyond this, as Lincoln likely knew from her lips, she passed through many hands in her childhood, girlhood and early teen years. She lived among various Hankses. Lincoln is known to have viewed the Hanks clan as dysfunctional or, in his exact words, "lascivious—lecherous—not to be trusted." By that cutting phrase, Lincoln established that his mother in her youth was surrounded by bad examples, if not by bad influences and possibly by bullies. More than most children, Nancy faced pressures toward waywardness, exploitation and ignorance. While Nancy lived among relatives who notoriously skirted the edge of decorum, she may have faced more obstacles than she did as a married woman pioneer in Indiana. The cool heroism her son admired may date back to Nancy Hanks's early years.[2]

Within her unenviable early environment, Nancy was extraordinary. She displayed compassion and patient teaching skills beyond her years, educating a cousin under circumstances shortly to be described. She was standing on her feet and vocal in political discussions by her mid-teens. By her late teens, Nancy was an accomplished seamstress and made fabrics as a weaver. To do any of these things, Nancy had to overcome dysfunctional households absent adult resources or examples of decent and mature relatives. She was remarkable.[3]

A Missed Opportunity

Lincoln in adulthood was serious and emotionally detached. His first law partner, John Todd Stuart, labeled him "a vegetable." Because Lincoln never similarly praised his father, one might think that he always saw himself as his cool and heroic mother's son, never as his father's son. But one document disproves that hypothesis. It simultaneously reflects a missed opportunity. Speaking to volunteers from Indiana, the President somewhat grotesquely invoked Tom Lincoln to whip up courage in the fight to bring about equality and a level playing field for all human beings. He said to the Hoosiers[4]:

I happen temporarily to occupy this big White House. I am a living witness that any one of your children may look to come here as my father's child has. It is in order that each of you may have through this free government which we have enjoyed, an open field and a fair chance for your industry, enterprise and intelligence; that you may all have equal privileges in the race of life, with all its desirable human aspirations. It is for this the struggle should be maintained, that we may not lose our birthright—not only for one, but for two or three years. The nation is worth fighting for, to secure such an inestimable jewel.[5]

Disappointingly, Lincoln failed to tell the Indiana soldiers about his mother or his Virginia planter grandfather even though we know that it was in Indiana that his mother told him about his blood being "as good as Washington's." As for what he called "this struggle," partly on account of slavery, Nancy had doughtily crossed the Ohio in 1816 and stoically undertook a straitened lifestyle. Lincoln really came into the Presidency not as his "father's child" but as the descendant of the two ancestors whose importance Lincoln had disclosed and emphasized to Herndon in 1851. In Lincoln's words exactly to the soldiers, the struggle *was* over a birthright, but it was one maintained in his mind not to lose his *mother's* and *her* Revolutionary father's "inestimable jewel."

Lincoln might have done better to say that to the young men of Indiana. Had he told them about his mother, if not his grandfather, the Virginia planter, in a burst of unprecedented candor, much work may have been saved. The occasion of talking to the Indianans reflects a missed opportunity.

The Hankses Reprised

What might Lincoln have told them, had he attempted it? Probably that a "cool and heroic" woman had made sacrifices and brought him up to oppose slavery and to be dedicated to the proposition that all men are created equal. He might have alluded to her Virginia nativity. In an unprecedented burst of candor, he could have disclosed the circumstances more fully, as Washington's army broke up, before the Constitution was a glimmer in anybody's eye, while Jefferson's promise floated above the republic as its guiding words, just then a "well-bred" and "broad-minded" Virginia planter took a fancy to his grandfather. Imagine the outcry. Lincoln probably did imagine the outcry and decided against presenting himself publicly as anything but his "father's child."[6]

But Nancy stirred to life in a woman named Hanks whose first name, Lucy, was the same as others in the Virginia and Kentucky Hanks clans. Lincoln altogether avoided naming or describing her. In his 1860 interview during his campaign for President, Lincoln spoke of his mother's father but said nothing of her mother. Lincoln traced Nancy's best traits (and his) emphatically to her *father*. Lucy did not shine.[7]

Lucy's regional home, Richmond County, on Virginia's Northern Neck, deserves description. It was no isolated mountaintop. A strip of fertile land along the banks of the wide and navigable Rappahannock, accessible year-round by boat at a time that waterways were the country's major highways, the long-settled county was home to gentry like Francis Lightfoot Lee, a signer of the Declaration of Independence born in 1734 (who had no children following his 1772 marriage). It was a county of plantations with sufficient agricultural production and commerce to be a wheel of larger adjacent Lancaster County. George Washington was born in the adjacent county in a house that stood a half-day's leisurely ride from the center of Richmond County. An active place where folks kept up with the times, in the 1780s Richmond County was a patriotic hotbed in more ways than one.

A fair consensus supports her birth to her teenaged mother on February 5, 1784. Counting back from this date within the normative gestation period of 247 to 284 days, the baby's conception occurred in about late April through early June 1783. On April 19, 1783, General George Washington announced England's official cessation of all hostilities and began down-sizing the Continental Army. Whole regiments were furloughed, supervised by their officers to march home. In uniform, with muskets and equipment that Washington allowed the veterans to keep, handsome, gloriously victorious soldiers who had saved the country were on the move when and where Nancy was conceived.[8]

The war was not technically over but farming had its own schedule, and most of the men were farmers. In northern Virginia, cotton was planted between late April and mid–May. Young Lucy Hanks, around seventeen years old, lived in northern Virginia, in Richmond County. Nancy's father may have been a soldier, though not a professional military man. Lincoln described him as a "planter" rather than a soldier or veteran. Potentially a fellow resident of Nancy's native Richmond County, which was full of planters, he may have been either among the first veterans to reach home or he may never have left home during the Revolution. Perhaps he served in the local militia. This possibility cannot be verified or denied; there is no way to check muster rolls without a name.[9]

Whether by Lucy's voluntary decision or reluctantly yielding to her parents' judgment, soon after her birth (or weaning?), Lucy relinquished Nancy to them. Whether she departed alone or rode off in bad company, she left the baby but not her desires. Lucy became a mother again as her unfortunate but fruitful encounters with men continued. They may have been strict and watched her closely, lest they raise another Lucy.

One last little mouth to feed, one more body to bathe and to clothe, made no difference to Lucy's parents who, in their late sixties, were still raising Lucy's eight younger siblings. Joseph Hanks was a tenant farmer and plantation overseer in demand in Richmond County. Lucy's little baby was thereafter the squalling youngest in his houseful of children, all older, all already walking and talking.[10]

Accordingly, although born in Virginia, Nancy's grandparents moved and resettled in Kentucky before she was two, so that Nancy grew up in and around Rolling Fork. When she was nine, her grandfather died, his household commenced to break up, and the estate was divided among the children, except that Lucy was left nothing. The older Hanks children—young Nancy's surrogate siblings—scattered and Nancy, possibly by sheer default of any other takers, went to live with Lucy, then perhaps 26 or 27. Nancy's childhood ended in Harrodsburg, Kentucky, where her mother lived, Lucy having in the interim married impecunious Henry Sparrow.

(After Nancy was born and consigned to care of Lucy's parents, Lucy, at possibly 19 or 20 [?], gave birth to a second daughter, Sarah, again outside of marriage. Lucy either came with her family to Kentucky in about 1790 or joined them soon afterwards. From thin official paperwork, between lines penned by frontier bureaucrats, promiscuity continued. Even by frontier community standards, Lucy's behavior was too wild. A grand jury indicted her for fornication. Prosecutors only left the maverick alone after she married Henry Sparrow, when she was *about* age 23 or so.)

Into the Fire

The fact that Lucy had no further run-ins with the law does not prove that she lived the life of a nun. It is hard to envision Lucy, with her background, as a sedate woman, the iconic matron knitting in a rocking chair. The serial motherhood by different men suggests that Lucy was extroverted and vocal.

For Nancy, nine uninterrupted years with her grandparents and older siblings, where she had been "the baby in the family," suddenly ended. Upon relocation to her mother's impoverished cabin, the little girl was suddenly the *oldest* child, the one looked to to help her mother, to change diapers, to wash dishes, to clean up messes, to feed chickens and gather eggs, to do the innumerable chores of any house filled with infants and children, to do tasks that the adults did not want to do.

Likewise, Nancy had a stepfather, a stranger to her who had

somehow been lured to marry a woman accused of fornication. That he married Lucy despite her notoriety marked a marriage that began in an unusual light, overseeing a house in which children kept coming.

The dynamics of Lucy and Henry's daily interactions with Nancy can hardly have run smoothly or by Nancy's preferences. Nancy may have withdrawn emotionally; by some accounts, she was a sad and serious adult, and constant moodiness in adulthood typically goes back to one's youth. Or the bright girl's curiosity could have annoyed Lucy, who may have had less playful affection to offer nine-year-old Nancy than most daughters of that age enjoyed.

Yet one bright light shined in Nancy's life. Amidst chaos, a vision offered hope. No matter what Nancy had been told or overheard, she had a great father of whom she could be proud. He resembled Jefferson, whose words Nancy treasured speaking and hearing. She bore blood as good as Washington's. Nancy idealized her father as a brilliant, prominent man, a rich Virginia planter. Possibly simultaneously, she romanticized Lucy's fall into a clever "theft" of the gentleman's greatest treasures, including his brilliant mind and his soaring "ambition."[11]

Up to the Berrys

Nancy's stop with her mother was a bump in the road. The arrangement of parachuting into the cabin of her benighted mother and impoverished stepfather, with younger children underfoot, did not work out. One imagines a house boiling with resentment, tension, arguments or incidents, rancor and maybe violence. Some academics speculate that her sojourn with her mother lasted for two or three years. Others, perhaps more realistic or from larger families, think it endured for a much shorter time. Certainly by no later than age twelve, Nancy was bounced to her Aunt Elizabeth, newly-married, with no criminal record and no children.[12]

Still, who can say, Nancy's early adolescence *may* have been fun, a regular merry-go-round. Her homes were all near one another, within a few Kentucky miles, a mere walk in those days. Throughout this period, she passed through at least three pairs of parental figures (her mother being likely the least parental of all) but she was never stuck. And one document implies successes that could have gratified her. Mrs. C.S.H. Vawter, in a letter published by the *Louisville Courier* (February 20, 1874), described Nancy as adept at spinning flax, winning spinning competitions against all others. "Tradition says that Nancy Hanks generally bore the palm, her spools yielding the longest and finest thread," Mrs. Vawter wrote.[13]

This period remains foggy. Such a kind child as Nancy would have been predictably easily bruised in a rough world. Nancy was not the type to target a person for their foibles. Indeed, Lincoln cherished his mother for her compassion. "Mr. Lincoln told me that his mother was a kind of genius—a great hearted & a big headed woman. He further stated to me that she was oversouled with goodness—tenderness & sympathy," Herndon wrote. If Nancy aspired and fought to stay on perpetually in the same family, she lost the struggle. Put in reverse, if she aspired to change families with whom she resided, she won her fights. Or it may also be that she drifted passively, taking up opportunities as they occurred, moving as circumstances required, one door closing, another door opening.[14]

Ultimately, Nancy kept moving and her son later was implacably and inexplicably hostile to his mother's family. For fear of offending Lincoln, Herndon took care "not to speak the name Hanks in his presence." No state records or social worker's notes exist to illuminate her condition. In those days, the state stopped at the cabin's door. A neglected, ill-fed or abused child had nowhere to go to complain.[15]

Clearly, from what Lincoln said to Herndon, his mother presented herself proudly as a planter's daughter. Per Lincoln, he was a "nobleman—so-called," an ambiguous phrase that his intellectual mother may have spoken first. Her father was, and was not, noble. She also told her children stories of Washington and said that in her and in them blood ran that was "as good as Washington's."[16]

Overall, moving may not have bothered Nancy as much as we imagine. Nonetheless, at some point finally she resisted that shuffling, apparently after she realized that she was not going to prosper with either her mother or her aunt. About in her mid-teens, adolescent Nancy was ready to fly from whatever nest of Sparrows or Hankses she was living in or working for to a more remote branch of the family tree, the Richard Berrys.

Good but Not Good Looking

The Berrys did not pick Nancy for her good looks. Unquestionably, Nancy was no classic beauty. Her nephew, John Hanks, recalled that "her face was sharp and angular, forehead high," before describing black hair and eyes. (Nobody really knows Nancy's hair color, eye color or complexion, descriptions impossibly diverge and contradict. Hanks varied between interviews; "dark hair, hazel eyes" somehow turned into "black hair & eyes," for example.)[17]

"She was rather coarse-featured, had the appearance of a laboring woman, but nevertheless was a good-looking woman," another old-timer, with a broad definition of "good-looking," named Henry Brooner remembered. Of a dozen informants, none called Nancy Hanks beautiful. Neither did her son. *The Collected Works of Abraham Lincoln* exemplify a phenomenon of inhibition that may be psychological. Lincoln shied away from the word "beautiful." Although he applied that term to *language* several times, he only once referred to a "beautiful" face—his own, mockingly. ("I have made my appearance now only to afford you an opportunity of seeing, as clearly as may be, my beautiful countenance!")[18]

Nancy as she appeared at the Berrys' doorstep was no small and petite girl, but rather a gangly one. The closest witness to Nancy as a teenager is of Nancy in her late twenties. Her nephew, John Hanks, a part-time carpenter familiar with measuring, whose father was one of Nancy's uncle "brothers" of the Joseph Hanks household, knew her in Kentucky when he was a boy and recalled her standing an exact 5 foot, 7 inches high. This still struck him as "tall." This impression rose in part because she was thin. He spoke of her "spare delicate frame." Her hair color, eyes and other features blurred, but people all remembered Nancy as thin. Surely, Nancy had not been overfed. Almost everybody spoke about her boniness in one way or another. Neighbors recalled Nancy being a slender woman.[19]

One wonders in vain what events precisely precipitated her move to the Berrys. After so many households, did waves of adolescent moodiness drive her away as *persona non grata*? Did she rebel or catatonically withdraw? Certainly, the compassionate Berrys may have volunteered to help a troubled young girl. Or a wailing baby may have crowded Nancy out of her bed, when a new boarder arrived at about this moment: Aunt Elizabeth undertook to raise the newest illegitimate Hanks child (the same Dennis Hanks who later provided many tales, both truthful and untruthful, of his famous cousin). However it happened, by whomever initiated, from rougher surroundings Nancy landed next in the well-appointed house of a generous and loving couple and their great match is the essential point. The Berry cousins became Nancy's last stop before adulthood, courtship and marriage.

Kindly and deserving Nancy found a real home at last. She bonded strongly with the couple. She worked as hard as ever, and this time she thrived. During the most stable and rewarding decade of her life, Nancy was probably never happier than she was between about 1797 and 1806.

The sympathetic Berrys made the young and probably fragile-appearing woman welcome in their home. With no legal formality, one Richard Berry stepped forward as the young girl's unofficial "guardian." His wife was a distant cousin of Nancy's mother. Nancy must have been happy with the arrangement because at her age she could run away and she was never far from any number of familiar homes. But she only moved upon her marriage. On her wedding day, though it was not legally required, she sought her informal guardian father's blessing. Nancy had Berry sign her marriage certificate. Doubtless both asked and given out of affection, Berry signed as her "Guardian."[20]

Presumably, the bargain was in Richard Berry's and his wife's favor. Nancy helped around the house. She performed the usual duties of a kitchen maid, though probably not of a cook. On the other hand, she was especially good with fabrics. She made dresses and mended clothes. She wove linen. She spun wool. As a result of her mastery of these skills, an event of huge and enduring significance unfolded at the Berry home.

Progress Note

We may by now make an informed guess to solve two puzzles: why Lincoln called his mother "heroic" without explaining her heroism *and* why he did not talk much about her.

Perhaps she achieved heroism under circumstances that were somehow painful or embarrassing to discuss or to reveal. We know now that, among her benighted Hanks relatives, not least Lucy, and possibly with *no* formal schooling, Nancy grew into a feisty contender in life. As noted previously, she "won the palm" in spinning contests as an extremely young competitor. As will be noted in the next section, she displayed compassion and natural teaching skills likewise beyond her years, educating a cousin in domestic arts and language. By her teens, she was an accomplished weaver and seamstress. She also had ideas and spoke as one with authority, holding her own while discussing current events, quoting sources and debating politics with her peers. In a word, Nancy managed heroically.[21]

To achieve so much, Nancy used her imagination. The planter took shameful advantage of Lucy, but what tone did Nancy use when she told her children? How did she utter that key word "shameful"? Seriously or mockingly, solemnly or giddily? If she said "shameful" (or "shameless"), did she roll her eyes? All we really know is that Nancy made such judgment calls and that she had a mind that could shift gears.

Long years before, she turned her mother's shame into her own highest point of pride. Nancy presented herself to her son as a planter's daughter and claimed an aristocratic heritage for herself and him both. Nancy surely stopped short of labeling her father dishonorable because her son later called him a "nobleman—so-called," a marginal and teasingly ironic phrase Nancy may well have spoken first. Her father was, and he was not, noble. By default of anyone better in the families around Nancy, he became her flawless father. To her children, she implicitly hinted or expressly said that he served in the ranks of George Washington's soldiers.

To establish any of this, Nancy first had to admit that she had been born a bastard. For her, that was a small price to pay. Her son paid it readily later. It was the first thing that he told Herndon on that amazingly candid morning in 1851.[22]

Accordingly, Nancy was her son's hero but Nancy's hero was her father. She told her children stories of Washington and, most likely, of Jefferson as well. She made First Family Virginians "family" for her boy. Her father, his grandfather, the Virginia planter, was an "aristocrat," a "nabob," not merely a contemporary colleague of Virginians like Washington and Jefferson but a branch of their extended, intermingled family trees. And in her son ran that same precious blood.

Nancy Hanks, Teacher

Nancy undertook what proved to be to her the convivial role of teacher. The period of years during which Nancy taught Sarah Mitchell weaving and English forms a high point not only of her decade with the Berrys but in the saga of her entire life. Never was more creativity required of her, never were the stakes higher. The origin of this development was extremely unusual, though not unique.

At about 13, Nancy faced someone even more lost than she was. From a first report written almost fifty years after Nancy's death, and a few fragments, more is unknown than known. Although Nancy's time with the Berrys was probably identical with her time teaching Sarah, it is impossible to know for certain. Whether Sarah Mitchell arrived first, and the call went out for Nancy, or Nancy was present to welcome Sarah from the beginning, cannot be reconstructed now. Nancy may even have begun teaching Sarah before she lived with the Berrys and joined the household later.

Sarah Mitchell, 16, Nancy's slightly older cousin, had been an Indian captive. By a 1795 treaty, captives were released back to white culture. Although Sarah had assimilated Indian ways, no one asked the girl, five years in a tribe and bearing a Native American name, who had married a brave and may have had children, who spoke a Native American tongue, what she wanted. Suddenly placed in white society again, she needed training and basic teaching in English, no longer understanding the language.[23]

Because Sarah's parents were dead, the Berrys had stepped forward as next of kin. A daily school opened at their home. Someone (Nancy herself?) thought that Nancy might teach weaving to the new member of the household. In fairness, Nancy's proficiency in weaving rather than her intellect probably led to her assumption of responsibility but, no matter, Nancy did better. The girl who helped around the house thrived in teaching. Whenever she was not peeling and cutting fruits and vegetables, she found the patience—her cool and calm manner was remarkable and remarked on by relatives—to pass on her weaving skill and to serve as an articulate and vocal *ad hoc* teacher of language.

Nancy's teenaged tendency to empathize, evidenced by Dr. Graham, who found her speaking out about the wrong of slavery, was surely engaged. In teaching a young woman slightly older, who had been a captive, Nancy as a sensitive assistant with strong empathy listened as much or more than she talked. In her sole student, Nancy soon discovered a good friend. She would have taught English by immersion, conversing constantly with Sarah, who could share, if she would, so much with less-traveled Nancy. To inexperienced Nancy, this married woman from another culture offered an exotic interviewee. Predictably, they clicked. Over weaving and words, the two initially puzzling and puzzled cousins bonded, becoming a pair who were "as intimate as sisters."[24]

The Implications of Weaving

Nancy's proficiency in weaving generates four implications:
First, the fact of her proficiency offers circumstantial confirmation

to those informants who recalled Nancy's easy-going, patient side. Any good weaver has to exercise exceptional patience constantly. Sometimes one of the warp strings breaks and needs to be traced back to the point of breakage so the two ends can be joined with a "weaver's knot" to resume weaving. The risk is greater with thin, fine thread and Nancy's thread was notably thin and fine. She devoted herself to the ultimate goal of producing palpably outstanding, fine-textured cloth. The thinner the spun thread for the warp and weft, the finer the resulting linen.)

Secondly, weaving requires coordination, agility, good vision and strength. A young woman who consistently excelled in weaving, as prodigious Nancy seems to have when but a young teen, would have possessed such a combination beyond the norm.

Thirdly, spinning and weaving indicate, without being conclusive, good eyesight. This allows scholars who opine that Nancy was literate at least to exclude poor eyesight, that may have precluded reading.

Lastly, Nancy, loved weaving: not least, she was likely drawn to it initially as a very therapeutic activity, keeping up the alternating rhythm of throwing the shuttles filled with the weft back and forth, and watching her creative project grow as she worked the treadles with ever-increasing facility. Spinning and weaving helped her get through lonely time while, ironically, affording her occasional prominence among women at spinning parties, and wherever her linen was shown or worn.[25]

The process of making linen is labor-intensive at all steps. It was (and still is) most often done by teams or groups. Before weaving, Nancy probably would have taken part in the earlier stages, beginning with gathering and preparing the flax, working with other women. The raw material of linen is the rotting stems of flax plants, which smells awful. Hydrogen sulfur gas comes up off the mess being beaten into fibers that can be spun. Spinning is required before any weaving can be done because yarn must be available to dress the loom before weaving may begin.

Nancy would have used a spinning wheel to spin fibers into yarns. Most spinning wheels then featured a spindle on the end opposite the seated spinner, to hold the accruing bundle of prepared linen fibers. Nancy would have drawn out a single continuous strand, then twisted it into long yarns for dressing the loom, the next step, a very tedious job that starts with cutting each warp string to measure the same length. These identical warp strings are strung the length of the loom through eyes on so-called heddles, after which the weft, yarn filler of spun linen, is strung back and forth in alternating sheds or spaces between the series of lifted and depressed warp strings. This latter step is like threading many stationary needles alternately along two or more frameworks called "harnesses." (Harnesses allow for varying patterns of fabric according to the sequence in which they are threaded.)

On the loom, once fully "dressed," spun yarn is woven into cloth. Yarns attached to the harnesses by a wire or strong rope to the heddles on the loom are lifted alternately by treadling. In this literal step, ideally, the feet of an experienced weaver deftly and gracefully press the loom's pedals at a steady (and usually fast) speed.

A last and optional step was usually done on the next sunny day—after advising children in the vicinity to steer clear—by setting out the finished woven linen to bleach white. In this phase, finished fabric was stretched out flat in the sun. One can imagine the amiable cousins taking on this open-air task as a celebratory frolic on a good day, viewing the product of their work together while executing a choreograph of a sort to accomplish the task, and then to gather and fold the bleached white linen into baskets as the sun set.[26]

In Sum

Nancy was clearly a survivor who got along on very slim pickings in her childhood and youth. After age nine, if not earlier, her environment was chaotic for years. Despite far above-average intelligence, she likely got little education in homes in which she was the proverbial child left on the doorstep. As a poor relation relegated to scrubbing and hauling chores, Nancy's mental acuity, later her trademark, would have languished unused.

(It is unlikely that she was taught to read before she was fifteen and she never learned to write. At the Berry home, and perhaps not much before, Nancy learned to read.)

Gawky but smart, maybe deporting herself differently as a planter's daughter, Nancy doubtless had to deal with rejection and ridicule. Then she bonded with Sarah Mitchell, and Richard Berry was a surrogate father. Richard Berry's signature on the marriage certificate as "Guardian" is suggestive of his approval, but had he advanced matters earlier than the wedding day? The Lincolns were married in the Berry home at the Berrys' charge, but had their parlor been the courting place earlier as well? These are unanswerable, teasing questions.

Part Two—Reflections

Lastly, what about the old Virginian? At the stable Berry house, did Nancy forget him, her "nabob," her personal link to the First Families of Virginia, whose good mind and noble blood she bore? No, he was her claim to fame. Nothing could change that. We have Graham's account of her enthusiasm for Jeffersonian equality and high-mindedness in general. It follows that her inspiration, her absent father, abided by her side. Moreover, when Nancy had children, she shared this boon with them.

Lincoln clearly did not hear about the Virginia planter from his father. Ancestry meant nothing to Tom Lincoln. Orphaned at age eight, Tom shuffled around the hills of Kentucky, house to house, a wandering laboring boy. He picked up carpentry skills and earned his way until he could farm on his own. His children heard nothing from him about old times in Virginia. On point of ancestral stories from Tom, Lincoln was categorical that he got *none*.[27]

9

Nancy Hanks at and Outside of the Berrys'

What you seek is seeking you.—Rumi

Nancy Outside of the House

Although Nancy was valued as a spinner, weaver, and teacher, the Berrys likely used her primarily as a maid-of-all-work. Fabric filled her life only when she was not teaching or paring apples. She was supposedly paring apples in a shed outside of the main house when Tom Lincoln came by to pay court. Though he said it was after a dream of meeting her there just so, he could as easily have been directed at the house where to find her, and made up a romance. This was later, however, because for years Tom did not loom large in Nancy's life outside the Berrys' home.[1]

As Sarah Mitchell was courting and on the way to marrying and moving away in 1800, Nancy outside the house socialized with a neighbor girl younger than she was, Sally Bush, and with Tom Lincoln. Apparently, Sally drew Tom to these chatting teens. Nancy was closer to Tom's age but buxom Sarah was closer to Tom's heart. Tom eventually proposed to Sally but she married another man in 1804. Tom's courtship of Nancy does not seem to have begun in earnest until then, after Sally's marriage, as he apparently only then gave up all hope of winning the younger lass.[2]

Premarital Possibilities

In light of Lucy's example, her fall or genetic "theft," did Nancy follow suit? Some loose talk about Nancy being a loose woman survives.

Was bony, angular-faced, intellectual Nancy pregnant when she wed? And, if so, by whom?

A man unequivocally tagged her *"encient"* when she married Tom, but the same man at the same time had her *encient* with her famous *son.* (In fact, her son came second and Sarah, known as "Sally," was the first child.) Another rumor circulated that the biological father paid Tom Lincoln to marry Nancy, a tale complete with the exact figure ($160). But a quirky (smart) bride and her slow groom, as near friendless as poverty could make them, were easy targets for malicious gossips. Critics sniffed at the couple with "very little to commence keeping house with." Any qualities they might possess were doubted, discounted, or scoffed at.[3]

Herndon floated an interesting idea—that jealousy lay behind such calumny—writing, "Mrs. Lincoln is charged with unchastity and the like. Do not these charges come from the fact, among women—her neighbors, that she was a bold—reckless—courageous, daring, self-reflecting and self-reliant woman—one with an idea of her own."[4]

Nonetheless, did Nancy and Tom brazenly or inadvertently re-enact the 1780s courtship between Lucy Hanks and the "nabob"? Perhaps, at 22, Nancy had been impatient. She may have been eager to snare even a poor sort like Tom Lincoln. The documented key data is the time span from the wedding to the birth of their brilliant Sally.

That period was eight months. A short-term pregnancy? Such short-term babies were not viable in the early 1800s. Did Tom want to be certain that she was capable of bearing children before they wed? Did Nancy actually favor premarital conception? (After all, Lincoln's question of Herndon was, "Did you never notice that bastards are generally smarter, shrewder and more intellectual than others?" Could this reflect an original superstition of his mother, or grandmother?)[5]

In any case, after a possibly brief courtship—or ratcheting up of their long and chaste friendship, as some think—Tom and brainy Nancy wed. The ceremony took place in the parlor of the spacious two-story Berry house. The Berrys offset any ridicule. For once in her life, Nancy was the Southern belle. It was a wedding all guests, including the guests of honor, would long remember. The well-known Methodist preacher Jesse Head officiated. Invitations were sent out for a virtual open house on June 12, 1806, after which a huge, meat-rich reception followed. One imagines, with good reason, that the bride made her own dress. The honeymoon purchases that Tom made at Elizabethtown's chief emporium, the Blearey & Montgomery store, show his awareness of

Nancy's love of fabrics and dressmaking. The store's surviving shopbook reveals that Tom bought not only necessities, knives and forks, but also skeins of silk for his new bride.[6]

A Slow Child and an Ancestral Answer

Tom and Nancy Lincoln's first-born, Sally, was clearly sharp, while their second child was dull. Tom had no problem with his slow child—many witnesses described Tom himself as slow—but Nancy grew concerned. The boy's attention span and his ability to concentrate were phenomenal, but he was slow. He needed extra time, and many questions, before he understood. To deal with this, Nancy employed her stories. Unlike Tom, who never spoke about his family or childhood, Nancy was a font of ancestral stories, even of Tom's "smart and brave" father, the original Abraham Lincoln, the pioneer whom she celebrated as having come to Kentucky with Daniel Boone. She also offered stories of George Washington, and of the men of 1776 as a form of *faux* family history, too. In a phrase, she, and her storyteller son later, practiced the same magic.[7]

Nancy sought to encourage Lincoln by way of his *lineage*, which simultaneously suggests (without proving) that lineage had worked for *her*. She was an intellectual who had necessarily snatched up learning quickly at any opportunity under unstable, backwoods conditions. Her inspiring, brilliant father was her boy's grandfather; her blood was his.[8]

What made Lincoln learn? Wrong question.

The question is: *who* made Lincoln learn? Not his smug father, nearly illiterate, capable at the zenith of his writing skills of "signing his name bunglingly." Tom, who bore no open, questioning mind, often cuffed his son for asking questions. Mostly kept at home, working, Lincoln doubted that he spent even a total of one year inside elementary classrooms, more than half coming after he turned thirteen.[9]

Nancy tried to jump start and ramp up her son's confidence. Previous scholars who understood that Nancy told Bible stories and taught hymns to her children, including one who shrewdly traced Lincoln's earliest copybook verses back to "Watts Hymns," underestimated the Bible's significance to Lincoln's education. Seen narrowly as a dry division of piety, Nancy's efforts have been given polite and passing attention at best.[10]

Such scholars failed to visualize Nancy, one on one, telling tales to her son. Nancy, a bright intellect, engaged, lively, playful, laughing, innovative, clearly brought the past to life for her children, yet nobody but Dennis Hanks identified Bible tales as an especially exciting time in Lincoln's boyhood. Nobody deduced from Lincoln's memory of a hymn the original fun it likely involved when his mother taught it to him. Bible lessons and singing together amounted to his and his sister's "quality time" with his mother.

Lincoln was thus pricelessly advantaged by years in the close presence of an articulate and imaginative. Many Bible verses, hymns from church and sermon stories were part of her—and her son's—mental storehouse. In their isolation, a mile from any neighbor when they first settled in Indiana, his mother actively stimulated her boy's curiosity, exercised his resistant mind, and got him to generate his own questions, witticisms and stories.

The Bible and history-focused children's hour led by Nancy manifestly did not include Tom. No informant reported Tom sitting at the table when the Bible was read aloud, or hymns were sung. Obliged to mediate and expand Bible stories herself, Nancy seems to have spun homemade versions. While Tom was out hunting, weeding, or something else ("nothing great"), Lincoln's mother was drawing out the best in herself as teacher and in her children. They benefited because their mother was good at spinning stories.[11]

Dennis recalled the arguments between Tom (whose side Dennis actually favored) and Nancy. Tom possibly thought that his son was learning disabled. Of education, "Tom said it was a waste of time, and I reckon he was right. But Nancy kept urging Abe to study. 'Abe,' she'd say, 'you learn all you can, and be some account,' and she'd tell him stories about George Washington, and say that Abe had just as good Virginia blood in him as Washington. Maybe she stretched things some, but it done Abe good." Although Dennis heard these arguments in Indiana, there is no reason to believe that the arguing and Nancy's ancestral boasts had not begun earlier, in Kentucky.[12]

Lincoln was young and impressionable when his mother told him that his blood was "as good as Washington's." To be a blood relation to a luminary *like Washington* was no small thing, then or now. For Lincoln, it was life changing. Although no connection between the weaving shed story and Lincoln's education is obvious, after telling it to Herndon in his letter Dennis moved from Zebedee to Lincoln's education by free association. Immediately after the anecdote, Dennis next wrote, "About Abe's early education and his sister's education let me say this—"[13]

It makes sense to infer that when Nancy offered her children hints of ancestral glory, her son believed. By his forties, he boasted to Herndon of his planter's mind as his major legacy. Through its operation, though slow, he was sure that he could accumulate indelibly all of the learning that he would need. His mother told him so.

A Mother Who Conversed Better Than She Cooked

"Mrs. Lincoln was a good thinker rather than a good house & child cleaner," Herndon concluded from what Lincoln told him and the informants he interviewed. Her later skill suggests early experience in fantasizing. In childhood, she had little to stimulate her. For one astonishing example, a potato was a novelty to her in her thirties.

From the evidence of this potato, one realizes the barrenness of Nancy's Elizabethtown days. For over twenty years, nobody introduced her to a potato, let alone showed her how to cook one. She *was* taught how to peel and core apples, and obediently did so, but she did not know that potatoes were best cooked before they were served.

Though the skinny girl's culinary awareness was limited, she shined in making fabrics and, by logical extension, possibly in dressmaking, but her high art was verbal. She retaught her cousin to speak English. She spoke aloud on issues of the day. She probably told herself stories of heroes as she resisted being swallowed up by her chaotic environment.[14]

Circumstantial evidence suggests the fun and playful manner of engaging with the Bible that Nancy encouraged. Nancy's Bible-based faith was real. The figures of the Bible and a Providential God were dear companions. But she eschewed any reverential or solemn reading of a literalist's Bible. No, instead Nancy laughed with her children as odd thoughts struck them about Zebedee or whomever they were reading about. Her son, when in his teens and twenties, critiqued and adeptly parodied Scripture. It is likely that Nancy was Lincoln's model for approaching the Bible with questions. She learned skepticism from Tom Paine, and her son learned skepticism from her. What her Bible stories taught was not religious ritual but openness to thinking.

Nancy and Her Son's Psychodrama

Tom and Nancy had led superficially similar lives. Nancy had been the poor relation on many different doorsteps and, finally, a relatively contented servant in the Berrys' house. Tom was alone for years, a wandering boy living by heavy, unskilled labor, until he landed in Joseph Hanks's workshop and learned carpentry and cabinetmaking. The difference between them was that Nancy played a role in a drama, life as the daughter of a Virginia planter. Tom dreamed of opening a shed door and finding the love of his life paring apples. Nancy's horizons, both day and night, were far broader. Her expectations were higher. From her Lincoln learned about Virginia planters like George Washington and Thomas Jefferson as relatives, as family, and soon he was involved in the Revolutionary drama—that was not over yet.

Thus, Nancy played a role in a drama, enjoying a rich mental life as the daughter of a Virginia planter, a vessel carrying precious blood. Lincoln was brought up to know that he, too, was involved, as the grandson of the Virginia planter. For an unimaginably isolated and lonely boy in a cabin deep in the Indiana woods, to be a blood relation to a luminary *like* Washington was no small thing.

But before Lincoln turned ten, this great influence expired. Herndon wrote that "Mrs. Lincoln died as said by some with the milk sickness, some with a galloping quick consumption," i.e., a wasting disease, or tuberculosis. In other words, Nancy died from the "milk sickness" but not so much in a sudden and fatal reaction to toxins as by the straw that broke the back of an already sick woman. Later medical experts have opined that Nancy was afflicted by an inherited marfanoid body habitus. If so, this condition rendered her vulnerable to cancer. Before she died possibly from cancer, itself another wasting disease, as she thinned, increasing weakness would have preceded her death.[15]

Lincoln wrote what is the most horrifying image of his suffering mother. Weirdly, it is the sole physical description that Lincoln ever wrote of her. In a letter, he described her "withered features" and wrinkles, as well as "want of teeth" and a "weather-beaten appearance in general." Almost the only explanation for this *grotesquerie* is perhaps this was his impression as a boy when his mother was so sick.[16]

After Nancy was gone, any literate passerby was a wonder. To listen to Lincoln, nobody was smart but transients passing through. Any half-sophisticated stranger brought him to attention. As he put it, "If a straggler supposed to understand Latin happened to sojourn in the neighborhood, he was looked upon as a wizard." (The joke was that Hoosiers understood this visitor, probably a Catholic, to be *casting spells*.) Plainly, he felt, as he was, like a motherless child.[17]

He overcame his grief and alienation by getting into the role of descendant of a Revolutionary with both feet. The evidence of his first extended speech suggests how deeply Lincoln cherished his Revolutionary roots in his twenties and how his mother's stories stirred memorably within him still. In his address, Lincoln mingled "memory," the Bible, stories of the Revolution, and the pervasive influence of such stories on "passions" for the "noblest" of causes, while simultaneously redirecting hatred or "revenge" away from any fellow American.[18]

The Lyceum Address

His first formal speech was supposed to be about the perpetuation of American institutions, but Lincoln chose to deviate and talk at greater length about their *origins.* The past drew him, especially 1776. He lamented that memories of the Revolution were fading. In 1838, almost thirty, Lincoln stood on a stage in Springfield defining influences of the Revolution.

Lincoln claimed to know that influences faded with the death of their original bearers. In context of the period of Romantic literature then reigning, this was rather an extraordinary conclusion. A world of prose and poetry at that time was peddling the old, the antique, the ancient, the ruined. Paddling upstream of mainstream, Lincoln was possibly being personal. As if unaware of this trend, Lincoln touted "scenes of the revolution."

He spoke of "the powerful influence which the interesting scenes of the revolution had upon the passions of the people as distinguished from their judgment." These "scenes" were the images and vicarious or shared memories of incidents of brutality, repression, and sufferings under British rule and in war with the King.[19]

By the time he concluded, a Revolutionary ancestor burned within Lincoln more brightly than in any of his audience. He dubbed all of them "descendants" of Revolutionaries, along with himself. He said, "They *were* the pillars of the temple of liberty; and now, that they have crumbled away, that temple must fall, unless we, their descendants, supply their places."[20]

Of course, Lincoln knew better than anybody in his audience—and never forgot—that his lineage went back to Richmond County, Virginia, during the Revolution, before the Constitution, a close-knit community of plantations, small farms and a growing cluster of mercantile establishments built along Farnham Creek, an offshoot of the well-trafficked Rappahannock River.

His homespun psychological analysis that night reveals more about Lincoln than it does about human psychology. He suggested that the story of the Revolution came with a moral lesson. Readers of his quote are forewarned to look for it: Lincoln equated adherence to a noble cause with ennobling those struggling, not only soldiers but people at home.

He told his audience,

> By this influence, the jealousy, envy, and avarice, incident to our nature, and so common to a state of peace, prosperity, and conscious strength, were, for the time, in a great measure smothered and rendered inactive; while the deep-rooted principles of hate, and the powerful motive of revenge, instead of being turned against each other, were directed exclusively against the British nation. And thus, from the force of circumstances, the basest principles of our nature, were either made to lie dormant, or to become the active agents in the advancement of the noblest of causes—that of establishing and maintaining civil and religious liberty.[21]

When he lamented the loss of this state of feeling, he suggested that at least a partial cure existed: it was the same one that his mother administered to her children in their isolated Indiana cabin. Informed as we are, it is impossible not to hear Nancy reading the Bible and telling stories of George Washington to her children behind his suggestion. The scenes of the Revolution must fade, Lincoln cautioned his fellow Revolutionary descendants, but then he offered his reasons for tempered hope, inviting his audience to join him in that hope: "In history, we hope, they will be read of, and recounted, so long as the bible shall be read."[22]

10

First Fruits:
Sally, the Lincolns' Firstborn

A sister is both your mirror
and your opposite.—Elizabeth Fishel

Unearthing Sally

Orange flags that flutter on long flexible poles above huts in the Himalayas are in place to indicate the presence of a living person if the hut is ever buried by an avalanche. Like an orange flag fluttering just above snow level, this section is a signal that—until Lincoln was seventeen—he grew up alongside an older sister, Sarah or "Sally," now buried under the flow of events since her passing. This chapter is an orange flag, more of a bookmark than a biographical sketch. Sally was more significant than documentation proves, her sluggish brother's earliest model of active intellect next only after his mother. Sally's death left Lincoln as the last known living descendant of the Virginia planter.

Lincoln froze her in death. He penned one letter in 1846 in which he mentioned a visit to Indiana where both his mother and his "only sister" were buried and, in his 1860 autobiography, Lincoln in describing his family referred to an older sister who, grown and married, died "many years ago." Before these brief nods, in life Sally was an important presence until she died, when Lincoln was 18. Never knowing the extended family that was so common then, Lincoln and Sally grew up in a home where their father and mother and they constituted the entire household. (Although a second son was born to the Lincolns in about 1815, he was sickly and died after three days.)[1]

In that claustrophobic context, how could Sally not have exerted an influence upon him? For her brother, Sally was someone to look up to. In Kentucky, when Sally was sent to school to learn her letters, her little brother tagged along. Lincoln was "slow," the tail of the educational kite. However, as Sally showed herself to be smart and succeeded in her lessons, Lincoln had reason to think: so could he. Meanwhile, lively Sally, both tall and smart, for several years overshadowed Lincoln.[2]

Ordinary Days and Then Dysfunction

Because school sessions ran only eight or ten weeks a year, any sibling rivalry was muted. By gendered roles of the time, they were not competitors. Rather, Tom took Lincoln aside to learn farming skills by putting an axe into his hands, although he was a somewhat dreamy, meditative boy, while Nancy would have brought more energetic Sally up to cook, weave, sew and deal with other so-called domestic arts or household economy.[3]

Although nothing survives describing Sally before her mother died, a description of her as a young adult (she died at age 20) serves well, especially because its author knew both Sally and Lincoln and he compared the two siblings. Nathaniel Grigsby, whose brother married Sally, recalled her for mental speed and physical energy. He told Herndon that Sally was "a quick minded woman & of extraordinary Mind—She was industrious—more so than Abraham—Abe worked almost alone from the head—whilst she labored both." She also seems to have inherited her mother's affability and good nature. "Her good humored laugh I can see now," Grigsby said, implying a marked bodily component to whatever her laugh sounded like. She could, he said, "meet & greet a person with the very Kindest greeting in the world."[4]

The "weaving shed story" indicates that Sally did not always accompany her mother to weave or sew, and it shows how her brother ran about unsupervised for hours. Who was most attached to whom? Dennis Hanks distinctly described the Lincoln family's arrangement, when journeying to Indiana on two horses ("not a wagon"), as "Abe rode with his mother & Sally with her father."[5]

No matter, her mother's death was hard to bear. Sally seems to have lost all vigor. Her sudden losses included not only her mother but also the stability of the core group of four who had comprised the Lincoln family all of her life. After her mother's death, months followed of cooking, cleaning, making clothes and performing or just looking at other tasks. With less expertise and no help, twelve-year-old Sally withdrew, overwhelmed.

10. First Fruits: Sally, the Lincolns' Firstborn

For six to eight weeks in late 1819, Tom Lincoln left Sally and her brother under care of Dennis Hanks. Dysfunction reigned for a time. Apparently in a funk, Sally did a forgivably bad job of running the house while her father was away. He went to propose and to bring back a widow, Sarah Bush Johnson. Their new stepmother arrived to find two filthy and unkempt children living in messy conditions. She took charge immediately.[6]

This sad, raw, wild period was replaced in a thunderclap by a new, mostly orderly and huge-seeming household of eight people. Pity Sally, the reserved or shy resident lost in the newly-structured household, and cabin immediately enlarged to fit its residents including her father, her brother, herself, Dennis Hanks, her stepmother (who was "some pumpkins," in Dennis Hanks' phrase for a forceful presence), her oldest daughter, Elizabeth, and two younger children, a stepbrother, John, and a stepsister, Matilda or "Tildy."

Sally had reason to be jealous of Tildy, something of a mischievous cut-up. The so-called baby of the house seemed to have quickly become her brother's pet. When Lincoln returned to school, it was without Sally. Sally's place at the bigger table may have seemed marginal. With whom could the grieving girl relate? Half of the folks in the cabin were new to her, and children who had never lost *their* mother.[7]

Fragmentary Facts

The following stunted summary is an unsatisfactory reflection of a woman who led a life as complex and multifaceted as any of our lives, but one that is thinly documented. Sally was:

- 2 years old when Lincoln was born;
- 5 (or so) when her second brother, Thomas, Jr., died days after his birth;
- 6 (or so) when she began school to learn her letters;
- 7 (or so) when she attended a second school, close to home with her brother;
- 9 when the Lincolns moved from Kentucky to Indiana;
- 11 acting as the Lincoln cabin's surrogate mother after Nancy died;
- 12 when her brother was "thought dead for a time" after being kicked by a mule;

- 14 (or so) when Lincoln learned to read books and write legibly (without necessarily being able to do so herself, or help him learn) (her schooling seems to have stopped after the family's move to Indiana);
- 19 when she married and became pregnant;
- 20 when she died in labor along with her baby son.

Also, extrapolating from Lincoln's disclosures to Herndon, Sally would have gladly believed that she, too, would someday bear the brilliant blood kin of Virginia's first families. Pathetically, this expectation came to naught but a double tragedy when a baby boy died without a name and Sally died in labor.[8]

Supposing that the Grigsbys had not sent for the doctor in time, Sally's enraged brother took to his fists, punching her husband. Less rationally, it is also suggested that Lincoln blamed him because the doctor, though sent for, had arrived drunk and useless. Either way, Lincoln no longer had Sally.

Logical Inferences

Lincoln's rage faded to grief. As he put it once, he lived in the tombs. Lincoln often recited, and sometimes composed poetry about the dead. Perhaps he thought often his lost sister, but he never told Herndon that Sally inspired his ambitions or hopes. We only know that, logically, she must have, as his erstwhile schoolmate, sitting next to him, shoulder to shoulder, back in Kentucky and by the fireside when they both heard and responded to their mother's stories.

Sally's curiosity was possibly less than Lincoln's. (In fairness to Sally, who on earth could compete with Lincoln's imaginative receptivity to his ancestor, the Virginia planter?) In Kentucky, Sally was not one to park herself on the fence by the road like her brother, waiting to hail passing drivers. She was smart enough to keep her questions to herself or ask her brilliant mother. She and Nancy seem to have been the sharp ones while Tom and the slow boy, well. When Lincoln did this fence-straddling quizzing, his father reacted violently. If the small boy was out looking for a certain Virginian, or anybody who had heard of him, Tom would have slapped that nonsense out of him.

For Lincoln, the death of his mother, of his sister, of the baby who

10. First Fruits: Sally, the Lincolns' Firstborn

was briefly another living vessel of the blood of the Virginia planter, like his short-lived brother, Thomas Lincoln, Jr., who drew breath for only three days, may have all crowded upon his consciousness. Sooner or later, the thought would have come that he was the last of the line—and that *everything* was now up to *him.*

11

The Great Educational Debate

Some great victories have no monuments.—Anonymous

A Family Divided

The topic frustrated Herndon, who delivered five highly publicized and successful lectures, one less than he originally planned. The fish that got away was to be about Lincoln's "infant and boyhood education—the means—methods and struggles of it—his mind—to know and develop itself." Lincoln's resistance to rustication is mystifying. His sister Sally did not fight her fate as a farm girl.[1]

We view the boy anachronistically as President of the United States in training but his education divided his family. It was an economic question. With more mouths to feed than ever, all hands were needed in 1820, when the first school opened in Spencer County. Tom's view of education was that "time in school was doubly wasted." Neighbor John B. Helm understood Tom exactly. "His father being a day laborer and without education looked upon bone and muscle as sufficient to make the man."[2]

Possibly, if Nancy had lived, no debate would have ensued. Nancy, the vocal intellectual, was enthusiastic for the education of both of her children. Both children would have likely attended just as she had shepherded both to schools in Kentucky. But she died and then, upon Tom's marriage to Sarah Bush Johnston, eight people lived in the Lincoln cabin on what the farm brought in.[3]

Not only are the dynamics in play difficult to piece together, so also is Lincoln's compulsion to learn. His motivation may have stymied Herndon. How could he talk about the means, methods and struggles of education and omit motivation? After Lincoln learned his letters and some "ciphering" in "blab school" in Kentucky, he was satisfactorily educated by farm standards. Living where the panther screamed by day and the wolves howled at night, survival skills, woodlore, practical farming tips were sorely needed but literacy, poetry, and arithmetic books, not so much. Lincoln had no examples of learned men or women in the vicinity. His recalled how his father put an axe into his hands but not whether Tom taught him how to use it, along with other carpentry tools.

Ironically, Herndon had heard the answer, and from Lincoln himself. Lincoln praised his mother for what he was and all he ever hoped to be. Through her, he got the qualities of the brilliant Virginia planter. Yet Herndon never connected Lincoln's ancestry to his intense drive for education. Nor, after Herndon, did anybody else. Effectively begging the question, Lincoln lamely wrote of being motivated to learn by what he nebulously called "the pressure of necessity."[4]

Lincoln did not attend school when one finally opened in 1820. Beginning before the winter of 1821–22, the education issue was argued in the cabin because schools were not mandatory and not all children attended. The question was which, if any, of the children (in 1822, Elizabeth, 15, Sally, 15, Abraham, 13, John, 11, and Tildy, 8) would be released from farm work to attend school?

Ultimately, one child attended, Lincoln. Dennis identified 1821 as the year that "Abe was getting hungry for books" and was soon a "stubborn reader." Dennis told Eleanor Atkinson, "seems to me now I never seen Abe after he was twelve 'at he didn't have a book." Thus, Lincoln probably resumed school after over five years away, in about the winter of 1821–22, or even 1822–23, at age 12 or 13.[5]

Toxic feelings live between the lines of their reminiscences. Remember that Lincoln said, in speaking of Spencer County, that "there was absolutely nothing to excite ambition for education." Tom Lincoln, in contempt of education, was grammatically and theoretically included.[6]

However, Lincoln attended three schools in Indiana, for several months of sessions. He unquestionably made tremendous progress. He came to read books, to know the history of his country, to memorize parts of the Bible and chunks of Shakespeare. By 16 or 17, his writing was published in a newspaper, and praised for its excellence.[7]

So, what was Lincoln talking about? Probably, he was evening an old score. Cloaked as a regional slam, his disgust or contempt was aimed at his *family*. Chiefly, without naming his father, Lincoln was excoriating *him*. But Tom was only the grand marshal of a parade. Other participants in the debate over Lincoln's schooling recalled and referred to their opposition at the time with surprising openness.

Dennis echoed Tom's attitude. He said that Lincoln was "lazy, a very lazy man. He was always reading, scribbling, writing, ciphering, writing poetry and et cetera, et cetera." Though he wrote this in his sixties, the old argument remained fresh.[8]

Sally was furniture. As Dennis said simply, "Sarah was cooking for us, she being about 14 years of age." Moreover, Sally was depressed. Dennis described how she would "git so lonesome, missin' her mother, she'd set by the fire an' cry." The distraught young woman either never asked to resume school or, if she asked, she did not persist. Or—her disinterest may reflect a touching and intentional sacrifice on her part to strengthen her beloved brother's chances for more schooling.[9]

Lincoln's nearly complete reticence to mention Sally suggests disappointment. She likely retreated to the shadows. She had once led the way to school for him but did no more. In the early 1820s, one must forgive and pity Sally, "the smart one" and her mother's hope who, after her devastating loss, took up chores and forsook school altogether.[10]

Lincoln's new, mouthy stepbrother, John D. Johnston, two years younger, a hunting, slouchy boy, quickly became Tom's pet and would certainly have adopted Tom's mindset. John would never have stood mute or amenable when Lincoln asked for relief from his share of the farm chores.

Likewise, stepsister Tildy Johnston, by then a giddy 14-year-old, fell opposite Lincoln. One imagines the pout after she said, "Abe was not energetic except in one thing, he was active and persistent in learning." Even in her adulthood, she hit the negative before stating the single positive trait in a comment that could have replicated her whining complaint during the debate.[11]

These spiteful, surly remarks, flung at a supposedly lazy, wayward boy *after* he died, having been President, must have hurt when they were hot. Even alone, Lincoln pushed back. At that time and place, Tom's denial sufficed to end his education. No way existed around Tom's veto. Not only was his word law but, because his earnings belonged to his father, Crawford's fees were beyond Lincoln's reach.

A miracle happened. Enter the fray stepmother Sarah. There was no one else. Sarah's granddaughter, Harriet A. Chapman, recalled Sarah as "a very tall woman, straight as an Indian, fair complexion, very handsome, sprightly-talkative and proud," who back then wore her hair curled. She liked to dress well, and Herndon said that she was buxom.

Sarah must have joined the lone boy, seeing the problem and, to her eternal credit, acting.[12]

Sarah described to Herndon the harmonious relationship that she enjoyed with young Lincoln. "His mind and mine—what little I had— seemed to run together," she said. Endowed with neither mental acuity nor articulate advocacy, Sarah was apparently feisty. Somehow she tilted the balance of power in the cabin. Tom relented, debate ended, and Lincoln resumed school each winter.[13]

Although a great man's youthful exploits are sometimes retroactively exaggerated, Lincoln's educational efforts can scarcely be exaggerated. The record substantiates a continuous and nearly-superhuman struggle from his boyhood up.[14]

His Mother's Example—Maybe

Again, what was his motivation? No wonder Herndon never lectured about Lincoln's education. That Tom and Nancy's son educated himself at all suggests some uncommon factor—but what? We might infer that his intellectual mother was Lincoln's living example, that she had learned, and so could her son, but this, in effect, only kicks the can a generation back: what drove a poor girl in the backwoods of Kentucky to study?

Working on the mystery within a mystery, Nancy read while Tom and many neighbors could not. Specifically, she read aloud or recalled history, the Bible and family biographies. As the weaving shed story strongly suggests, she seems to have applied critical thinking to books including the Bible, a habit that her son picked up. In one word, she was an intellectual.[15]

Lincoln's mother was a rich source of diverse knowledge. She engaged her children in stimulating and relatively deep explorations of the world outside of their isolated farm. A habit of serious conversation took root in him. Lifelong afterward, Lincoln was notable for no capacity at all for small talk, and no patience for fatuous generalities or glib remarks.[16]

Lincoln's Surprisingly Fastidious Curriculum

But what did Lincoln need to succeed? Lincoln never believed in learning for learning's sake. He valued education insofar as it was necessary to accomplish specific tasks. One learned in order to do something. Vocational training and experience mattered as much to Lincoln as book or classroom learning. Functionality ruled. When he gave his Temperance Address, partly in celebration of George Washington, in 1842, he spoke about the equivalent of substance abuse counselors, noting, "Even though unlearned in letters, for this task, none others are so well educated. To fit them for this work, they have been taught in the true school."[17]

And so, again: why did Lincoln seek so much education?

The remarks just quoted are cogent if Lincoln was fitting himself consciously for a public life, particularly, public office. First, to do so, he had to learn to write. Obsession seems to be the right word for his insane effort, by himself, to learn to write. John Scripps, who collaborated with Lincoln on a campaign biography in 1860, made this pathetic practice sound positively jolly. After stating Lincoln's age as having started school in Kentucky "in his seventh year," Scripps wrote, "It was his custom to form letters, to write words and sentences wherever he found suitable material. He scrawled them with charcoal, he scored them in the dust, in the sand, in the snow—anywhere and everywhere that lines could be drawn, there he improved his capacity for writing." But for years was Lincoln writing anything anybody else could read?[18]

Shortly after his stepmother, Sarah Bush Lincoln, arrived in December 1819, Lincoln turned eleven. He was a novice at writing, but he did write his name. Contrasting writing samples as she spoke with Herndon in 1866, Sarah showed them to him. "Here is our old Bible dated 1819: it has Abe's name in it," Herndon transcribed. "Here is Barclay's dictionary: it has Abe's name in it, though in a better handwriting—both are boyish scrawls." In Indiana, without further schooling for some five years, Lincoln practiced but his marks were crude. Dennis Hanks said that Lincoln wrote legibly when he was 12 years old.[19]

Lincoln the Author

By about his late teens, Lincoln became a published author and his now-lost letter to the editor was read and praised outside of the Lincoln family. One of the first settlers in the area, "Uncle William" Wood, then in his early forties, who befriended and mentored Lincoln, witnessed the breakthrough when Lincoln was about 18.

11. The Great Educational Debate

Although Wood took a New York paper, *The Telescope*, for current events and political news, it was Wood's temperance newspapers that caught Lincoln's eye. Wood forgot their names. One potential draw was that these periodicals were politically unaligned (contrary to most newspapers of the day). Wood said of one temperance paper in particular, "Abe used to borrow it—take it home and read it, and talk it over with me. He was an intelligent boy." The subject of temperance inspired Lincoln, who tended toward asceticism.[20]

"One day Abe wrote a piece on temperance and brought it to my house," Wood told Herndon in 1865. Wood said, "I read it carefully over and over."[21]

Ironically, Lincoln's essay had some political slant. (Wood called it a "political article.") Perhaps Lincoln suggested united action to support new legislation but, whatever he wrote, Wood thought that it "excelled for sound sense anything that my paper contained." Wood soon passed the article on to Aaron Farmer, a Baptist preacher, who in turn somehow got one of the newspapers in Ohio to run it.

"I saw the printed piece," Wood recalled, noting that he "read it with pleasure over and over again."[22]

Lincoln could not have had a bigger fan. Wood insisted that Colonel Pitcher, the county's most prominent lawyer, scan it. Pitcher was that evening a captive audience, having stopped to spend a night at Wood's house while he was riding circuit. Wood watched him "read it carefully," after which Pitcher asked Wood about its author.[23]

"I told him one of my neighbor boys wrote it," Wood said. "He couldn't believe it until I told him that Abe did it."

Pitcher knew Lincoln. Pronouncing the article unbeatable, Pitcher got it reprinted in yet another paper. The copy that Lincoln retained clearly meant a lot to him, as he had it in his possession in New Salem, some fifteen years later. One wonders if it provided an outline for his speech at the largest temperance event held in Springfield, in 1842.

Perhaps spoiled by Wood and his vocal chorus of friends, Lincoln's hopes were high enough that he got the local editor, an older friend, Simeon Francis, to publish his temperance speech in full. Lincoln's expectations were totally unmet. Bothered, if not painfully stung, Lincoln finally clipped and sent it to his best friend, Joshua Speed, and asked Speed, then on his *honeymoon*, to read every line aloud. Speed's reply is unfortunately lost.[24]

Book Learning

Lincoln read *Sinbad the Sailor* a dozen times and could recite many of the stories by heart. Before Dennis married and went off on his own, he witnessed the dynamics: Tom objecting, followed by Sarah intervening. As Dennis reported, "Abe'd lay on his stummick by the fire, an' read out loud to me 'n' Aunt Sairy, an' we'd laugh when he did, though I reckon it went in at one ear and out at the other with her, as it did with me. Tom'd come in an' say: 'See here, Abe, your mammy cain't work with you a botherin' her like that'; but Aunt Sairy always said it didn't bother her none, and she'd tell Abe to go on. I reckon that encouraged Abe a heap."[25]

John Hanks, a cousin mentioned earlier, lived with the Lincolns for about four years, beginning in 1823. He seems to have arrived from Kentucky to fill the worker's slot just as Dennis departed. John observed Lincoln closely, having reasons to count the days off granted to his co-worker. "He went to school but little while I was there," John said, "say, one or two months."[26]

Days off during John's residence, he also recalled Lincoln reading at home. John said, "He read *The Life of Washington*, histories, some poetry, all he could get, and learned the most of it by heart, quickly and well, and always remembering it."[27]

But Lincoln was a slow reader and, as he read, his lips moved. (Even in adulthood, Lincoln never flipped rapidly through pages—annoying Herndon, who heard each word.) Seeing and hearing his son read slowly, the teen's barely literate father was irritated to a point of rage. Tom would sometimes "slash him for neglecting his work by reading."[28]

About the time that Lincoln's schooling ceased, the Lincolns decided that its talented student required a book. Possibly after a debate or perhaps initiated by Lincoln himself, but Lincoln was allowed to purchase an anthology, *The Columbian Orator*, its cost taken out of money he earned, funds that technically and legally belonged to his father.[29]

Lincoln persisted in his studies, being as conscious as ever that his mind was the Virginia planter's mind, the mind that his grandmother had "stolen," and his mother had inherited and passed on to him. All minds, he mystically felt, were moved by some power over which they had no control. By this so-called "Doctrine of Necessity," Lincoln might be seen as a virtual instrument of the founders, programed to implement their unfinished work. His blueprint—to be applied to all races—was Jefferson's Declaration of Independence.[30]

By ceaseless night and day activity, before neighbors' hearths, in the corner of an old barn, outdoors and under trees, Lincoln turned himself into his mother. His mother was called "an intellectual" by almost everyone who knew her. He finally read a history of the United States no earlier than 1821 because the book he read was first published in 1821. It was Grimshaw's *History of the United States from The First Settlement as Colonies to the Cession of Florida in Eighteen Hundred and Twenty-One*, a bestseller, at least among Whigs.

Grimshaw, an anglophile born in Ireland who admired the judicial abolition of slavery in the British Isles, followed by the Parliamentary abolition of the international trade in enslaved, immigrated to the United States shortly before the abolition of slavery throughout the British Empire. Buoyed up when he wrote his history text, Grimshaw took slavery to be globally doomed.

Grimshaw filled his pages with the most dramatic events of American history but, more than any other contribution he made to American history, he made Lincoln aware that he was not alone in thinking that slavery was wrong, and that it was destined to extinction. Among other critical comments, Grimshaw wrote, "Since the middle of the last century, expanded minds have been, with slow gradations, promoting the decrease of slavery in North America."[31]

Self-Study on a Shoestring Without the Shoestring

Among the first to observe Lincoln as a student outside of his home was Elizabeth Crawford. When about 20 years old, Elizabeth became the wife of Josiah Crawford. Josiah decided to fix up the cabin for her and paid Tom for his son to daub chinks in their new log cabin with clay. (Daubing in those days was a time-consuming project that began with digging and hauling heavy buckets of clay through unmarked paths of thick woods from banks along the river. Because the green logs of the Crawford cabin were unhewn and unbarked, daubing, always tedious, was especially troublesome.) In the course of digging for clay, Lincoln ran into a vein of creel (red ochre), a treasure to the poor boy of 16 or 17, who gathered some for his educational use.[32]

Elizabeth witnessed Lincoln studying because, when he was

working for the Crawfords more than a mile from home, he stayed overnight with them.

"We had a broad wooden shovel," Elizabeth said, likely referring to a broad, light granary shovel. Lincoln sat and used it as his writing surface, making creel marks instead of pencil. She recalled that he would work out sums and then "wipe off and repeat till it got too black for more."[33]

He would then take the shovel outside of the Crawfords' small cabin and use their carpenter's plane, stripping thin shavings off the surface of the shovel. Likely, he also smoothed it with a file. (She said that he smoothed it but did not describe how.) Next, with some water in a bucket or basin, and a sponge or a cloth, he scrubbed it clean. Elizabeth said that "he would scrape and wash off, and repeat again and again." Elizabeth saw that if he ran out of creel, he wrote out his figures with sharp pieces of soft coal.[34]

"I have seen this over and over again," Elizabeth told Herndon, in a tone of wonder. She said that Lincoln read all of their books and noticed that, when her intermittent boarder was not "studying his books," he was "thinking and reflecting." He was reading and thinking for a purpose. The dot of "education" can be connected to that purpose. At this time, Lincoln spoke openly to one voter about his plans—a practice he stopped altogether when he was only slightly older.[35]

"He said that he would be President of the United States, told my husband so often," Elizabeth said. "Said it jokingly, yet with a smack of deep earnestness in his eye and tone."[36]

The Crawfords knew Lincoln for three or four years, long enough for her to judge that a fire was ablaze inside of him. To get from the Crawfords' cabin to the White House, he knew what he had to do.

"He evidently had an idea, a feeling, in 1828 that he was bound to be a great man," she said to Herndon. For humble Elizabeth, however, ambition was close to a sin, bordering on deadly pride. She reported in that light, "Abe was ambitious, sought to outstrip and override others. This I confess."[37]

He allowed nothing to stop him. Another neighbor observed Lincoln make do while working on his calculations where, for want of a shovel, he used old boards, and found a substitute for lack of creel or coal. Inside an old barn, claiming its quiet space for his mathematical studies, he scavenged. "Having no slate, pens or pencils handy," wrote J.W. Wartman, "he figured all over the smooth parts of some clapboards in an old barn he used to use, with a pencil made of *clay*."[38]

Education by "Necessity"

Shortly after his nomination for President, Lincoln pondered how to tell about his education when the *Chester County (Pa.) Times* wanted biographical information. Pennsylvania was a key state and Lincoln responded with a subtle and intriguing note.[39]

Lincoln wrote, "When I came of age I did not know much. Still somehow, I could read, write, and cipher to the rule of three, but that was all. I have not been to school since. The little advance I now have upon this store of education, I have picked up from time to time under the pressure of necessity."[40]

The phrase "the pressure of necessity" makes absolutely no sense. What necessity? How did a boy, a docile farmer's son "raised to farm work" until he was 22, feel any "pressure" to learn? But Lincoln was truthful. His phrase is a Russian doll that needs unpacking. He was compelled by pressures that felt urgent and real to him—and to anyone else who expected to be President.

That pressure of necessity upon Lincoln was to become all that he ever hoped to be, to satisfy the agenda that he got from his mother, the promise in the Declaration of Independence for which the Virginia planter had fought. As ludicrous as it may seem, "said jokingly but with a smack of deep earnestness in his eye and tone," this American prince in the guise of an ordinary farm boy had to be ready *to be President* and, during his term, he pressed himself to be intellectually able to manage and to complete the unfinished business of the American Revolution.[41]

The readers of the *Chester County Times* got these clues. Lincoln alluded to pressures in a serious but much too succinct explanation of why he learned what he learned. This was perfectly in keeping with Lincoln's reputation and habit of seeming to say everything when he actually revealed nothing.

The Problem Parent and the Problem Period, 1829–30

Lincoln's educational efforts seem to have trailed off just as Tom's hold on his son strengthened. For Lincoln, the end of 1829 and the entire year of 1830 was a wash, as he lingered with his father. Lincoln once excused his father's ignorance of family history "being left an orphan at the age of six years, in poverty, [who] in a new country became a wholly uneducated man," but any understanding of one another varied by the day, dipping down to bare tolerance at times. (In truth, Lincoln's strained list does *not* explain why Tom knew so little of his family history. After all, Nancy was a waif adrift from cabin to cabin, poor and in Kentucky, the "new country" or frontier, her extent of education unknown, yet she told her children about her family, singling out their ancestors, thus, greatly expanding her son's world.)[42]

Overall, Tom had been more of a hindrance than a help to his son. William Wood talked him out of running away from home in 1829. Lincoln stayed with Tom, although the old man was characteristically so stubbornly wedded to bad plans that his son quoted only one saying of his father's: "When you make a bad bargain, hug it the tighter." Somehow, despite everything, Tom Lincoln reigned supreme over Lincoln for over a year. It was as if Lincoln's ambition and ancestors fell away from him for this, one of the most mysterious periods of his life, and Lincoln stuck profitlessly by his old, slow, erring father.[43]

During the winter of 1829–30, Tom planned to sell his Indiana farm and head west. Lincoln, 21 in February 1830, free then to stay in Indiana or to go anywhere he wished, cryptically chose to go with his uneducated and even boastfully ignorant father to clear yet another farm. This was Lincoln's surprising first major decision as an emancipated adult. In March 1830, he followed through and drove one of the wagons in a caravan with his parents and extended family (including Dennis Hanks and his family) moving west, a total of fifteen men, women and children.

In Illinois, Lincoln secondly decided to put his back into clearing, building, fencing, plowing and sowing. For a time, his interest in the larger world was nil. When two of the men in the family were placed in outside farms, Lincoln did not step forward to vacate but stayed with the core group. The nestlings who remained all sickened, coming down in rotation with a "bone-break fever" borne by mosquitoes but then simply associated with moist soil. Lincoln, approaching 22, for his third adult decision, committed with all others to leave the county together.[44]

Given the goals Lincoln entertained from boyhood, his corresponding studies, and the contrasting inertia of the Lincoln family, how can this fallow period be explained? One may guess that melancholy-prone Lincoln was discouraged or depressed, or for a while the Virginia planter's talismanic influence faded and he lost confidence in his high ambitions. But then destiny beckoned (as in Lincoln's philosophy), and just at this point the snow began and the winds howled as the worst winter in many years struck the Illinois prairie, including these discouraged new settlers on their hastily built small farm.

12

The Winter
of the Deep Snow

Now is the winter of our discontent....
—William Shakespeare, *Richard III*

Note: In no other chapter am I conscious of such a high degree of speculation. However, a combat veteran I knew, as honest a man as exists, once told me that it is true that in battle severely injured men say, "Mama." Apparently, trauma triggers a felt need for the primal helper and the perfect rescuer we knew in our infancy. Extending this line of reasoning, at the beginning of 1831, Lincoln literally fell into a terrifying situation that may have reminded him of his infancy and childhood, and of his need for his mother.

While disabled and helpless, Lincoln was tended by a matronly woman who did as Nancy Hanks Lincoln once did, speaking cheerfully to encourage him, urging him on while he enjoyed a respite from a frozen hell.

During this terrible winter, Lincoln suffered from painful injuries of which he never spoke. While he was tended by neighbors whom he did not acknowledge in his autobiographical sketch, he concealed any problem along with his recovery. However, he not only recovered but found within himself just at this time a belated readiness to separate from his father and—to farm *no more*.

How much of this sea change derived from recovery time spent reflecting on what his mother taught him? At the neighbor's home, nothing external appears to explain his transformation. Lincoln's mind never ceased to operate, though. We must pursue slight clues, including whether, forced by trauma, he may have thought this winter about his mother and his fabulous grandfather.[1]

A Winter Like No Other

If fever, poverty, depression, a manifest failure of confidence, a likely fear of the next step or of the unknown, were not enough suffering for Lincoln, he now had to endure a terrible, freezing time. He clung to the Lincoln family for dear life. Clinging to something unsatisfactory had become habitual for him, doing familiar tasks with and for familiar people. So long as he could reason himself to stay with his father, he excused himself from proceeding with education, or in any other way advancing himself and moving on.

That winter, Lincoln reclaimed an earlier, more hopeful self, the good cheer of a youngster full of the devil who told jokes and listened to and memorized vivid stories about Washington suffering in crossing the river at Trenton. These were stories he heard after his family crossed the freezing Ohio.[2]

How did it happen? Even after reading what we know about that winter, anyone is free to say, "All right, I know what the facts are. And I believe that something changed Lincoln. But I still do not know how that happened." We shall come as close as we can to solving the means of change, the mysterious and happy end of an overall mysterious and dark period. The facts are too few to support strong inferences.

An Impoverished Family in a Bad Way

First, the family context of Lincoln's accident, injury and recovery is quickly set. In Macon County, Illinois, the Lincolns had never been so large a group, three generations crowded into a newly built rough bark cabin on land newly cleared and hastily fenced. Dennis Hanks and Squire Hall having been sent off to board elsewhere, moves that left Tom and his second wife, Sarah Bush Johnston Lincoln, with her son, John D. Johnston, 19, Matilda "Tildy" Johnston Hall and her infant boy, Sarah Elizabeth Johnston Hanks and her four children up to eight years old, and Abraham Lincoln, 21.[3]

Moreover, these extended Lincolns had run into bad luck, hindered that fall by a contagious "bone-break fever" that swept through the family. Each case required a week or two for recovery and close care by those still standing upright. Downtime of the victims and time needed to care for and nurse those afflicted through their fevers rippled through routine schedules, left chores undone and spawned dysfunctional chaos. In his memoir, Lincoln said that the "ague" was like nothing they were "used to" and that they grew "greatly discouraged."

111

The climax of his account may be the saddest words Lincoln ever wrote: "They determined on leaving the county." The Lincolns were refugees whose plan was flight.

The next thing that Lincoln added was, "They remained, however, through the succeeding winter, which was the winter of the very celebrated 'deep snow' of Illinois." Here is the winter of Lincoln's discontent, also a major turning point. The transformation of Lincoln is indisputable. The man who refused to leave his father's side, the man who had come of age but continued to balk leaving, the man who lived narrowly within his family, was by winter's end an independent man, a man capable of taking care of himself and of others, his senses fully alert, awake to a new day.[4]

But first, the storm. After a deceptively warm December before Christmas, a sudden blizzard that lasted three days deposited several feet of snow. Howling winds shaped the snow into huge dunes which, when coated by freezing rain, solidified into a lunar landscape, obstacles to the movements of men and beasts. The wind thereafter seemed never to stop, day and night, until March. All that while, the Lincolns were in the center of the storm, in the center of the prairie, slammed daily by the worst and most unremitting winter in a hundred years.[5]

Presumably after talking with Lincoln, although omitting Lincoln's accident and the Warnicks, Scripps crafted a short paragraph printed in Lincoln's campaign biography as follows:

> The winter of 1830–31 is memorable to this day among the early settlers of Illinois, by reason of the deep snow which fell about the last of December, and which continued upon the ground for more than two months. It was a season of unusual severity, both upon the settlers and their stock. Many of the latter perished from exposure to the cold and from hunger, while the former, especially the more recently arrived of their number, were often put to great straits to obtain provisions. Of these hardships the Lincolns and their immediate neighbors had their full share, and but for Abraham, whose vigor of constitution and remarkable power of endurance fitted him for long and wearisome journeys in search of provisions, their suffering would have been often greater.[6]

Scripps shaped things accurately. Duty called and duty answered had been to then the story of the young man's life. Lincoln had been an obedient child and, while growing up, hardly deviated from the model son of a farmer. On March 1, 1830, in Indiana, he had every right (having just turned 21) to set his own course—but he did not. His father was moving west to Illinois, and Lincoln compliantly drove the team of oxen that hauled the family's largest wagon, taking on the most difficult role for a 200-mile trek through poor roads, swamp and rushing rivers. Once in Illinois, he put his back into cutting and fitting logs into a cabin, barn and outbuildings, clearing land, plowing and sowing, fencing in about ten acres as the new Lincoln farm. The experiment had failed. Everything had been in vain. But when the family decided to flee the region that they believed to be infected, Lincoln had joined in planning to exit the county along with them.[7]

One counter to the possibility that Lincoln was begging is the possibility that he was bartering. He was an able woodsman. Chopping or "rail-splitting" was virtually his trademark skill, and a service needed by landowners like Sheriff Warnick. The reported fact that Lincoln "that winter" split a thousand or more rails for Warnick requires analysis. When did he perform this service? If winter may be taken to mean the onset of snow and cold, the earliest would be about Christmas. If it was January, then he did not fall through the ice until late January or even early February. But he had to have done his work before March 1, 1831, when he and others rowed their canoe to Springfield, and, thus, December before his accident or February after his accident makes sense. (It could even be that he was going to the Warnicks' to work, as it were, on the day of the accident.)

But again, and in any case, Lincoln was no hero on the cold January morning that he crept out of the cabin door. No attempt to be daring led him to trek through the frozen woods. Sheer desperation and not recklessness led Lincoln to risk attack by roving packs of wolves that thrived that winter, moving fast on the crusted icy surface of the deep snow, in which cattle, deer and men floundered. During hard times, neighbors helped neighbors. His family's needs alone motivated him. The Lincolns were unfeigned "charity cases." Their best-off neighbor, Sheriff William Warnick, was his destination. After weeks of bitter cold, high winds and snow, Lincoln was saving his father, then in his fifties, as well as the women of the cabin, and John D. Johnston, his laggard stepbrother, two years younger, from exposure to the cold.

To the Warnicks

Maybe Lincoln wanted to travel alone for speed or weight. He walked—he may have had skis to distribute his weight better and accelerate his movement—on the Sangamon River. It offered a natural roadway. In any case, he had to cross it. To understand the importance of speed, one must imagine a wilderness under conditions that made reducing minutes of exposure to the howling cold winds matter greatly. As he slogged along, the ill-fed, ill-clothed, shivering 21-year-old, despite a woolen scarf, would have seen the vapor of every breath. He had no time or energy to spare to toss a heavy rock in front of him to make sure the ice could bear his weight.

Lincoln would have left the cabin to outward appearances a pitiable, ragged beggar ducking down low to avoid high and howling winds. Headed, in effect, to the only functioning welfare agency in the cursed county, Lincoln may have carried a knife for protection or even an ax. Dangers were real. Men froze to death when lost. Lincoln and Scripps both omitted the report of a wagonload of pioneers headed west, caught in a blizzard, who had died snowbound, their remains lying undiscovered until spring.[8]

On his way, Lincoln fell through ice on the river.

In a shocking instant Lincoln was transported there, alienated from everybody, even his past warm self. Soaked upon immersion, if not nearly drowning in icy waters, upon surfacing Lincoln had to scramble in order to climb up over wet, impossibly slippery, cracking ice to the banks. His clothes then began to freeze to his body and soon he was walking as if a corpse in a stiff shroud of ice.[9]

His numbing legs in motion, he had to think quickly and execute immediately. Possibly, of course, he was nearer to the Warnicks than he was to the Lincoln cabin but, about two miles apart, neither his family's cabin nor Warnick's farm would have been very nearby. To the Warnick farm Lincoln proceeded, step by painful step, covering as much as a mile for perhaps an hour. The better-stocked Warnick cabin beckoned as more practical than a return home, even if farther away. Under horrific circumstances, Lincoln willed himself to stay awake.

He was now scrambling in trackless, possibly unfamiliar woods. The snow was a foot or two high, with crust, when he was not scaling drifts that rose up over his head. As his body temperature sank, though his life depended on speed, he would have been hampered by waves of torpid delirium. As his feet were numbed by frostbite, he would have often lost his footing. He would have arrived at the Warnicks' door crippled and in an unmistakably desperate condition, his heart close to its end run.

Mrs. Warnick

By third party accounts, Mrs. Nancy Warnick met him. According to the *History Book of Macon County*, Mrs. Warnick, the former Nancy Griffin, about 47 in 1831, was the mother of ten in a house big enough to serve as a tavern. Her husband, who had been born in North Carolina and came west to make his fortune, was serving his first two-year term as sheriff at a time that county officials practically equaled governmental power. No man cast a bigger shadow in Macon County than Warnick, not only the sheriff but also the largest landowner in Macon County, a mover and shaker, a powerful politician and, in effect, the last resort of the poor in his county. (It was supposed, without cited source, that Lincoln had regularly visited the Warnicks "to court Polly Warnick," the third eldest Warnick child, about Lincoln's age and then unmarried.)[10]

No doubt terrified into a frenzied series of acts, Mrs. Warnick had him strip his icy clothes—doubtless, had to assist in this torture for the man whose clothing had frozen to his skin—and to soak in cold water, especially his horrifyingly blackened feet, before she had him lie back on a bed, a table or a bench and applied goose grease, skunk oil and rabbit fat to his feet and bandaged him up with a dressing of cotton strips.[11]

Of course, she would have fed her bedbound patient warm liquids, soup and such other food as she had on hand, and he could tolerate. Between regular, gentle rubbings of his tender, now burning feet and toes with the folk remedy, Lincoln would have been forbidden to walk. Compelled to rest, he was transported from the frozen, slow thinker whose every thought and act had been directed for months to work and to unsuccessful efforts to warm himself. He had fallen into a livelier, more luxurious, successful and leisurely household than any he had known, in which meals were both certain and ample, logs for the fire were handy, and people conversed without shivering and coughing.

The cosmic answer to the question of why Lincoln crossed the river was not for food but to discover what he was made of. At the Warnicks' home, Lincoln found comfort and relief. But "comfort and relief" are not normally life changing and, after those weeks with the Warnicks, Lincoln's senses were manifestly alive as never before. His memoir shows it.

Simultaneously, his feet and toes were saved, although Mrs. Warnick may have had to cut and remove (with scissors or knives?) some of the dead skin. Punctuated by spikes of pain, gradually, over dreadful and largely sleepless weeks, the hero's scarred and granular "proud flesh" covered his frostbitten wounds.

Finally, probably on horseback with Sheriff Warnick, and probably with a sack of food needed for his family's bare survival, Lincoln returned to the cabin a different man. After weeks with well-fed, well-clothed, warm, educated and stimulating company, joining the Lincolns lost all savor. Moreover, his near-death experience, submerged in the Sangamon River and then dragging through the frozen woods near it, opened his eyes. As if reborn, Lincoln pondered what to do with the rest of his life.

The Hiring, the Turning Point

The winter of the deep snow formed a turning point in Abraham Lincoln's life. Before the winter ended ("about the 1st of March, 1831" by his memoir), Lincoln decisively pulled away from his family in a canoe headed south. This dark winter, Lincoln's earliest crucible of change, nonetheless rigidly resists close exploration. It is a swirl of partial and contradictory memories.[12]

Within the fog, historical justice fairly obliges us to try to gauge at least how large a role Sheriff Warnick and his wife, Nancy, had in Lincoln's transformation—a stunning one—from passive hanger-on of the poor Lincoln family into an active, ambitious and independent man. We know that Lincoln interacted that winter outside the family farm with few people, the Warnicks among them. And we know from Lincoln's own words that he contracted to go to New Orleans, probably on a handshake, with a complete stranger, one Denton Offutt, an eccentric entrepreneur who dreamed of building a commercial empire.[13]

Lincoln wrote, "(d)uring that winter, A., together with his stepmother's son, John D. Johnston, and John Hanks, yet residing in Macon county, hired themselves to one Denton Offutt" to take a flatboat from Beardstown, Illinois, to New Orleans. No place of hiring was given. Yet, using probabilities, where would a traveler be directed who, in the middle of that terrible winter, was seeking to hire workers or simply needed a bed for the night and feed for his horse? In that benighted county, would it not be Sheriff Warnick's farm, soon officially turned into a tavern and designed for guests from its original construction?[14]

Lincoln did not mention this, but he also did not mention anything else about that winter or about his fall through the ice. But it would be aesthetically balanced and fitting if the reliable last resort of help to residents of the county, and the hostess who was so kind, facilitated the hiring that led to the next year's wonders and, indeed, to the rest of Lincoln's life.

It was probably not so much that Offutt was persuasive as that Lincoln, notwithstanding the warning scar over his left eye that still throbbed in cold from a terrifying fracas three years before, was ready to be persuaded. Offutt, a prairie P.T. Barnum who spouted big, wild plans, a "harum-scarum," overwhelmed Lincoln's normal caution and high inertia. Lincoln signed on with the stranger for a hazardous journey to New Orleans. Lincoln ignored all clues that joining Offutt was a bad idea (his less-captivated cousin, John Hanks, soon left Offutt, before their boat left St. Louis).[15]

Incidentally—or perhaps *primarily*—putting a thousand miles between himself and his father and his woeful, impoverished family, he joined a man who suspiciously seemed to favor making deals with entire strangers over those who knew him. Opinions and sentiments that had formerly ruled Lincoln no longer did. Lincoln ebulliently declared his independence.

On the Other Side of the Turning Point

In his outline for Scripps, after describing his trip down to and back from New Orleans in fond and loving detail, one superfluous, self-congratulatory datum Lincoln held up like a jewel. He positively reveled in his independence, writing that he was next "for the first time, as it were, by himself" in New Salem.[16]

Something more than suffering must have occurred in early 1831. In his text, Lincoln covered his life from age seven to age 21, and the deep snow in a sprint of sixty lines. By contrast, beginning with March 1, 1831, without any prelude or explanation, almost one-fourth of his outline, fully 70 lines of his 288-line sketch, covers about one year, running from his canoe ride about March 1, 1831, through to the early summer of 1832.[17]

Similarly exuberant, scarcely a year after Lincoln rose from his bed at Sheriff Warnick's farm and walked on his own two feet, he was seeking public office. He addressed his fellow citizens of Sangamon County in a handbill dated March 9, 1832, also run in the newspaper. Announcing his candidacy for state legislator, Lincoln confided no greater ambition than of "being truly esteemed of my fellow men, by rendering myself worthy of their esteem."[18]

If the Warnicks did not themselves stand as his exemplars of his ambition in 1832, then the spooky but related answer may be that his ambition, after over a year of distraction, depression or discontent, arose from recently revived memories of his blessed, cool and heroic "angel mother."[19]

Grammar

The question of why, in January or February 1831, Lincoln changed his mind and finally separated from his family might be inferred from a later ripple. The same man who later said that keeping resolutions was the chief gem of his character, instead of keeping his "vote" to leave the Macon County with everyone else, went to New Orleans as a hired hand on a flatboat and then settled by himself in New Salem. Was he fleeing from or moving to something? Apparently, both.

That is, once unfettered, Lincoln resumed studying. He freed himself from an educational obstacle. He slipped a zinger at his father into his autobiographical sketch, "After he was 23 *and separated from his father*, he studied English grammar."[20]

Lincoln, quickly a war veteran after he had journeyed safely down to and back from New Orleans, soon operating a small store with a partner, consciously shook off his father's dark shadow over his education. He expressly associated his grammar studies with *separation from his father*. The point is intriguing, as if speaking and writing correctly required *distance* from his ungrammatical father's presence—as if his father had somehow stultified him.

We can follow the episode unfolding in real time one morning over breakfast in New Salem, as recalled by a resident. Lincoln stated his interest between bites, presumably at the Rutledge tavern, possibly as a neighbor's guest. He said to the local teacher, Mentor Graham, "I had a notion of studying grammar."

Graham caught on right away that this young man had lost interest in farming. But, even so, Graham, who made part of his living teaching grammar and literacy, offered no free instruction.

"If you ever expect to go before the public in any capacity, I think it is the best thing you can do," Graham replied, without committing himself.

"If I had a grammar, I would commence now," Lincoln said, with a likely long glance at the teacher. Although Graham offered no grammar, he said, "I know of a grammar."

12. The Winter of the Deep Snow

The Berry-Lincoln store, New Salem, where Lincoln studied and mastered grammar and the art of surveying, teaching himself with books. He did the same with law, reading books borrowed from John Stuart, a Springfield lawyer and volunteer officer whom he met during the Black Hawk War, and who later became his first law partner (Sture Olson, from the Lincoln Financial Foundation Collection, courtesy of the Indiana State Museum).

Apparently being quizzed and disclosing that the book was in Vance's farmhouse, six miles away, Graham witnessed next how Lincoln "got up and went on foot to Vance's and got the book. He soon came back and told me he had it."

Nothing held Lincoln back from mastering grammar now. He was going to scratch its rules on his steel plate or, as Graham put it about the experienced autodidact, the young man "then turned his immediate and almost undivided attention to English grammar."[21]

13

A Meditation on Lucy Hanks, Her Impact on Her Daughter, and on Lincoln

> Some people are your relatives but others are your
> ancestors, and you choose the ones you want to have as
> ancestors. You create yourself out of those values.
> —Ralph Ellison

Like Grandmother, Unlike Grandson

Lincoln, who knew Lucy's name and may have met her once or twice, told Herndon no very coherent or complete story about her. We owe scholars, not Lincoln, for the facts noted here:

1. Lucy Hanks was born in Richmond County, Virginia, to Joseph and Nancy or "Nanny" Hanks in about 1765. She was their first child, followed finally by eight siblings, four brothers and four sisters.

2. In about April or May 1783 (though perhaps earlier), when she was about 17, she became pregnant with a child born in February 1784, a girl she named Nancy Hanks.

3. The father of this child may have been a rich, landed planter with a good mind.

4. She apparently left the baby in care of her parents, and departed from their home but still (in another couple of years, around 1786) joined them in settling near Elizabethtown, Kentucky.

5. Lucy bore another illegitimate child, a second daughter she named Sarah Hanks.

6. As noted, a grand jury indicted Lucy for fornication but prosecution lapsed when she married Henry Sparrow. Henry was

an impecunious Revolutionary War veteran and former Virginian who farmed for a living. She may have looked younger than her 22 years; she signed an affidavit, still extant, that she was of age to marry. How she met Henry and how they came to marry—whether he was her unindicted co-partner in crime, for example—is as obviously important to know as it is irrecoverably lost.

7. Without recorded dates of birth, she thereafter bore two or three children. This number enlarged after Joseph Hanks died in 1794, when she took Nancy under wing for a period of up to a year or so, before Nancy went to live next with Elizabeth Hanks Sparrow (Lucy's younger sister), who had married Thomas Sparrow, Henry's younger brother, and lived nearby.

8. Lucy eventually had eight children while married to Henry Sparrow, two of whom became ministers, denomination unknown. Lucy continued to reside in Elizabethtown until she died in 1835. (It is, thus, possible that when the Lincolns made their way from Hodgenville to the Ohio River to cross over into Indiana, they stopped to visit or stayed a night or two with her. Lincoln, at age seven, may have thus known Lucy, who would then have become the only one of his grandparents that he ever saw and talked with.)[1]

The sole surviving document partly in her hand is a paper filed in applying for a license to marry. She was then 22 but must have looked younger: the document, signed "Lucey Hanks," on its face confirms her literacy to that extent and in its content affirms that she was of age to marry, daintily without stating her age. The life she led before she became a bride had resulted in two illegitimate children and a grand jury's indictment of her for fornication. The grand jury named no male co-defendant; presumably, *she* was seen at sole fault criminally. Albeit unfairly, the implication was that *she* irresistibly tempted one of Adam's kin to sin.[2]

What was his possibly riotous grandmother to Lincoln, and Lincoln to his grandmother?

Although Lincoln dubbed Lucy Hanks "poor and credulous," she certainly sounds more poor than credulous. Without ever escaping poverty, however bare her cupboard, an element of romance infused Lucy's time on earth, to her family's and her neighbors' consternation. Perhaps she was never credulous. Perhaps her grandson, by definition no witness of her youth, granted her that adjective by sheer courtesy.

Lucy was clever enough for her purposes as she hunted for a

husband. Disappointments may have hindered her but never entirely stopped Lucy. Her quest for freedom had costs. Her relationship with her family suffered. She departed the Hanks home early. Her father left her out of his will, and she inherited nothing. When her daughter, Nancy, finally came to live with her, it was not a good fit. Within a year or two, Nancy moved on to be raised by Lucy's younger sister, Elizabeth.

Storytellers and readers normally treasure the ups and downs of lovers. "Love's Labor's Lost" survived while "Love's Labor's Won" withered away unpublished. Of Lucy Hanks's failed courtships and impassioned liaisons, however, only the tale of her disastrous first coupling with the Virginia planter truly survived. Of her long marriage, the one that followed her signed affidavit, neither Lincoln not anybody else said anything. How Lucy Hanks won Henry Sparrow, or how he won her, we do not know. Manifestly, they shared some grounds for contentment: although poor, they stayed together for decades, and their marriage was fruitful. She bore many children, ostensibly by Henry, a Revolutionary War veteran and subsistence farmer. No story in this. Of this happier and duller narrative Lincoln breathed not one word.

The Myriad Mysteries of Lucy Hanks

In reckoning Lucy's importance in Nancy's life and in her grandson's, one asks simple questions. For example, what was the Bible to her? And slavery? The same questions may be asked of her husband, Henry Sparrow. Although these questions seemingly seek esoteric trivia about two obscure people who died long before the Civil War, it is not so. Their justification is collateral: how did *Nancy Hanks* react to these people?

Two of Lucy's sons gravitated toward the ministry. From this, a natural implication arises of a household in which the Bible was read. A notch beyond that reasonable implication, more speculative but realistic enough, is that Lucy at some point, possibly dramatically, "got religion." On the way to or in marriage, perhaps she reformed.

Or was Henry Sparrow the religious one? Which of them, if either, initiated a family habit of humanizing figures in the Bible? Did Lucy tell her sons histrionically about Daniel in the lion's den and Christ on the cross? Not least, did she originate a little playlet enacting Zebedee the bad father? Did that playlet, as well as Lincoln's documented boyhood performances as a "little minister," reciting sermons and imitating his own minister, in any way derive from his Grandmother Lucy?

Henry Sparrow's application for a pension as a Revolutionary War veteran. Henry was married to Nancy Hanks's mother, the mysterious Lucy Hanks. Her marriage to Henry squashed prosecution of Lucy's indictment by a grand jury for fornication (courtesy Jay Garner, Richmond County historian).

Lucy the "poor and credulous" seems a sentimental fiction. She was the interesting one, the thief of hearts and minds, as it were. Lincoln said nothing about his minister uncles, or about Henry Sparrow, the real Revolutionary soldier and his grandmother's husband. Lincoln, by implications of his question story, wanted it known that his grandmother knew how to avoid detection and correction as she evaded the most important of her parents' mandates to ensnare the most prominent nobleman near her, eligible bachelor or not. Lincoln's image may have been his mother's, and his mother's image—may have been Lucy's own coinage.

Lucy, who engaged the attention of a man to marry her with a fornication charge over her head, had inner resources. She was not a woman to tangle with or to cross. What we know about her is consistent with a headstrong, willful girl, finally a formidable and clever female making her way in life.

We wish we knew more because this obscure woman's thoughts may have been of great historical importance. Was it *Lucy* who first found and favored the Rev. Jesse Head and his fiery opposition to slavery? Is it possible that Lucy opposed slavery in part to bring down the Virginia planter who snubbed her in her time of travail? Was her target not so much slavery as the rich planter? Did this woman recruit her daughter to believe in this cause, and did Nancy go on to inculcate her children? Was the Emancipation Proclamation set in motion by Lucy Hanks's grudge against her jilting lover, the Virginia planter?

There are no answers to such questions. The breadth and duration of Lucy's impact on her daughter and on her famous grandson is opaque. That an errant or reformed or vengeful Lucy Hanks was historically significant one may guess but nobody will ever prove.

Nancy and Lucy

Why did Lucy not get along with Nancy? Lucy seems to have been a physical woman without much use for high-flown words or ideals. She may have been cynical; she had some reason to disbelieve the sincerity of others. On the other hand, Nancy's world was mental, and her head was full of ideas and ideals. Neighbors called Nancy an "intellectual" which implied that she did not ramble or grunt, expressed cohesive thoughts, and engaged in monologues embedded with a richer vocabulary than most of her contemporaries used. We know from Dr.

Graham that she held firm opinions about rights, government, slavery and equality, and that she could be outspoken. Were Lucy and Nancy oil and water?

The Virginia planter, Nancy's constant companion, became the parent she told her children about, not her mother. Her Washington stories implied that her father served with General Washington, which was possibly a claim that she never made directly. (How much of her father's history did Nancy actually know?) In teaching her children, or in response to their questions, Nancy eventually seemed to have shared several variants of the story of her parents. Her keen intelligence, in the often-cited phrase of F. Scott Fitzgerald, afforded her "to hold two opposed ideas in mind at the same time and still retain the ability to function."

Nancy's versions (the versions Lincoln shared in 1851) might nonetheless be seen as two sides of the same moral coin. Both versions revolve around unmet duties. Neither the Virginia planter *nor* the woman lived up to societal expectations. The woman's duty to be chaste, the man's duty to protect a young woman, the duty of lover to lover, the parents' duty to children, were imperiously ignored by a shameless "nobleman so-called" and by a young woman (although, cogently, Lincoln *never* called her young, or excused her by reason of minority).

One imagines that Nancy may have first told a simple cautionary tale to the little auditors at her feet, the moral of which was a variant of honesty as the best policy. That would be all until or unless she later delighted them when they grew older by presenting her mother, their grandmother, instead as a charming and clever trickster. As in Lincoln's tellings to Herndon, that more questionable version would have come last.

Lincoln's Refinements of the Original Story

Arthur W. Frank wrote in his classic *Letting Stories Breathe*, "a story that people become caught up in because it holds them in suspense, engages their imagination, and calls for interpretation" is not necessarily "a *good* story, in the sense of encouraging goodness among those who tell and retell it."[3]

What Lincoln told Herndon was a good story but not a *good* one. In essence, Lincoln gave Herndon mismatching stories and inconsistent characters. By his follow-up questions, Lincoln declined to leave intact, no pun intended, the "poor and credulous &etc." woman bedded down and then tragically abandoned. Instead, with two quick rhetorical questions, each pregnant with an affirmative answer, Lincoln depicted a wanton woman whom he nonetheless admired. The series featured a happy ending. The stories' redeeming social value was unambiguous: a lively, bright natural child was born, thrived, and in turn bore a baby who was Lincoln, with high hopes—i.e., all's well that ends well.

The narrative story Lincoln first told Herndon, one that may have comforted his mother and boosted her self-esteem, Lincoln *modified* to do the same for him and to explain his own origins, and still-flowing hope, a story which he ended with a hearty "God bless my mother."[4]

"What Ifs" Reviewed

What if Lucy told Nancy? If so, how was the Virginia planter, her former lover, the erring knight, described? Could Lucy have resisted crowing over how clever she had been? Or did Lucy by then have a religious bent, generating the moral of the story, that Nancy must be on her guard in dealing with men?

On the other hand, what if Lucy's husband, Henry Sparrow, a poor man with many children whose origin he may have doubted, offered a vulgar version of his consort's "theft" of male seed?

What ifs abound, whether living with her mother and stepfather, or her Aunt Nancy Sparrow and her new husband, or in any Hanks cabins where she may have heard several variants of the old yarn of her conception.

Lastly, what if imaginative Nancy served as her own source? Lincoln's first story is of a princess with an absent parent, faraway, rich and royal, from whom the child was separated at birth to grow up with different, less gifted, poorer parents—a classic fantasy. It sounds too good to be true, a consoling restorative for a daughter who longs for an ever-absent father. Compensating for dysfunction, filling a void in her life, Nancy had cause to come up with a wonderful origins story, a highway out of the chaos that was swallowing her up.

Narratologist Arthur W. Franks is again helpful on point. Professor Franks wrote, "Stories inform in the sense of providing information, but more significantly, stories give form—temporal and spatial orientation, coherence, meaning, intention, and especially boundaries—to lives that inherently lack form."[5]

Whatever Nancy heard, along with what she made up, she finally cherished as her origins story. Any possible passionate love affair burned off without a trace. The terrors and travails of abandonment vanished. What may have begun as a lust-driven scandal and a factual basis for opprobrious gossip and blame evolved into something else, mild and richly meaningful. Worn down like sea glass, what her son shared with Herndon was a traumatic event that had lost its sharp edges long before.

The Virginia Planter's Enduring Shadow (Maybe) and the Three Damsels

Questions arise because all witnesses agree that Lincoln governed his appetites severely. Herndon said that "Lincoln had terribly strong passions for woman—could scarcely keep his hands off them" but that "honor and strong will" put out these fires. Herndon claimed up close personal observations, saying that had "seen pretty women make advance to L which were rejected." Judge David Davis, a friend who was often with Lincoln on circuit, said, "Lincoln was a man of strong passions for women. His conscience kept him from seduction. This saved many, many a woman."[6]

Did Lucy become a sympathetic character for her grandson, and the Virginia planter a cautionary figure? Did the planter's bad example drive Lincoln to chastity? When Lincoln himself presented his core identity, which he called "the chief gem of his character," it was *keeping his resolves*, and wanting "in all cases to do right, and most particularly so, in all cases with women."[7]

Did that Quixote-like mission reflect revulsion at the Virginia planter's misbehavior in the 1780s? In a cluster fifty years later in New Salem, a village of fewer than 200 people, Lincoln quickly identified no fewer than three damsels in distress.

Many readers will readily recall Ann Rutledge as Lincoln's first love, who died of a fever when young. Not so many will remember Nancy Burner, a fortuitous name for a lass of smoldering passion. And then there was Mary Owens, to whom Lincoln proposed by letter. Lincoln seems to have been drawn compulsively to any woman in distress who ought to be married. Nancy Burner, Ann Rutledge, Mary Owens, and, later, Mary Todd and Sarah Rickard all reflected either abandonment, rejected proposals or broken engagements.

Nancy Burner seems to have been first. The least interesting aspect of Lincoln and Nancy Burner is whether they slept together. It was reported that Lincoln had his way with Nancy, but this is impossible to verify and needless to debate. What is clear (and significant) is Lincoln's concern over the welfare of a young, never-married girl. Nancy seems to have been socially backward, if not intellectually limited. After Nancy was publicly shamed by one "Slicky Bill" Green, Lincoln's co-worker at the mill, Lincoln fanned the flame between Burner and an eligible suitor, a physician. The result Lincoln engineered was the marriage of a girl as "poor and credulous" as Lincoln's grandmother.[8]

The connection between Lincoln and Ann Rutledge likewise involves abandonment and shame. She was in a hellish state, neither married nor free to marry, the victim of apparent abandonment (if not of seduction). She had pledged herself to a man who disappeared. Although he showed up again in New Salem after she died, in the interim, just as for Nancy Burner, Lincoln labored to redeem another man's debt. Jolted into action by a woman jilted, Lincoln himself courted Ann Rutledge, but she took sick and died.[9]

Thirdly, Lincoln's first preserved love letter was his signed, written marriage proposal to Mary Owens. The first time Lincoln wrote the word "woman" or "women" was twice when he was 28, both in the same letter to Mary Owens. Although he was reluctant to follow through, he felt too invested not to propose.[10]

Again, does poor and credulous Lucy, or the sinful Virginia planter stand behind these three attempted rescues?[11]

Or was it Lucy's daughter, Nancy?

The Family Marriage Conundrum, Mary Owens and Others

Lincoln's mother embodied difficult, missed, or broken paths to the altar. Her initial legal and social status was determined by its *absence*: she was born outside of marriage. Likewise, Lincoln probably knew that, before Nancy, Tom proposed to Sally, who declined. Then, when Nancy and Tom wed, the bride may have been pregnant. One must guess what else Lincoln heard and retained to write in his twenties about having "a point of honor and conscience in all things, to stick to my word, especially if others had been induced to act on it."[12]

Lincoln described straining to make an honor-bound offer of marriage to Mary Owens. "At once I determined to consider her my wife; and this done, all my powers of discovery were put to the rack, in search of perfections in her, which might be fairly set-off against her defects."[13]

Lincoln at last conceived that his envisioned "wife's" *mind* might answer. However, the young man found it hard to convince himself. He protested too much "that the mind was much more to be valued than the person." He hoped to comfort himself with that idea, he emphasized, because "in this, she was not inferior, as I could discover, to any with whom I had been acquainted."[14]

Was Lincoln's mother also a smart but plain woman? Was Lincoln regressing to an old feeling of attraction for his mother's mind and wit and an aversion to her "person"? No matter how exaggerated his ludicrous letter may have been, was its core correct—was his mother ugly in her son's eyes? It was a struggle few sons would acknowledge or even admit to themselves—but he did assert categorically that this intelligent woman in whom he could see no allure reminded him of his mother.

Her saving feature was finally some type of facial regularity: "I tried to imagine she was handsome, which, but for her unfortunate corpulency, was actually true. Exclusive of this, no woman that I have seen, has a finer face."[15]

Curiously, when Lincoln wrote to Mary Owens proposing marriage, he compared himself against richer men. *Wealth* had been the Virginia planter's key characteristic. Lincoln asked Mary whether she could accept living in a town with "a great deal of flourishing about in carriages" where she would be "poor without the means" of hiding her poverty. Without using the H-word of heroism, he asked if she could bear that "patiently."[16]

After New Salem, besides Mary Todd, Lincoln courted one truly poor woman, a much younger girl of his acquaintance. He was 32 and she was 17. They had known one another for several years. Lincoln was 28 or 29 upon first meeting Sarah Rickard, then 13 or 14. He had indulged her young whims and taken the adolescent on innocent outings. At 17, Sarah, without her parents near, was a poor relation living (along with her younger brother) in her married older sister's boarding house. Lincoln made a fatally poor choice of witty words. When he said to Sarah that "Abraham ought to have his Sarah," she took it to be one of his pleasant jests and laughed. Stymied, Lincoln did not propose again but instead resumed his courtship of his abandoned and unhappy Mary Todd.[17]

At least subconsciously, if not consciously, Lincoln kept replicating 17-year-old Lucy Hanks's situation as her vicarious rescuer after the fact, with twists each time, nudging women toward marriage. He helped to see Nancy Burner, age 17, married. He consoled (if he did not propose to) Ann Rutledge, age 17. He definitely proposed to 20-year-old Mary Owens, overcoming his reluctance but not hers. He got engaged but broke off courting 22-year-old Mary Todd, to resume it later. He proposed to Sarah Rickard, age 17.

Can we agree that this was *in toto* odd serial behavior by a shy man? In New Salem, Greene said, in his small one-room store, that Lincoln would not wait on women customers. And remember Judge Davis, who likewise declared that Lincoln, by shying away, had saved many a woman's honor.[18]

Lucy's fall *may* have cast a long shadow, as Lincoln practiced on improving on the family response to young women.

14

What Lincoln Told
Neither Herndon Nor
the Special Correspondent

> Lincoln is the great unknown—the silent—the reticent—
> the incommunicable....—William "Billy" Herndon (1887)

Missing Elements

From his two stories, the narrative and the interrogatory one, Lincoln withheld several elements common to stories and typical in other stories that Lincoln told. An analysis is called for, an attempt to determine what Lincoln was aiming at by so shaping his stories to Herndon. The facts are that to Herndon, Lincoln did not:

- name his grandfather, the Virginia planter;
- *expressly* state that the planter was an enslaver;
- fully specify the planter's offenses;
- offer the lovers' respective ages;
- embrace any emotions;
- describe the historical context;
- explain the necessity for lifetime secrecy;
- blame anybody;

When Lincoln stopped talking, these many elements, elements that we are fully entitled to expect, were missing from his stories. A ninth omission surfaces when Lincoln's personally bizarre goal of an immortal name is factored in.

Let us go through these with a goal of appreciating why Lincoln edited and withheld so much. Because the inclusion of these elements would have changed his abstract sketches into more conventional stories,

131

what we hope to nail down are the stories that Lincoln held back and chose not to tell, in a sense, the complete story behind the partial stories he told.

The Name of His Grandfather, the Virginia Planter

In his most explicable omission, Lincoln left out the name of the Virginia planter. Little time need be spent on this. Either Lincoln stopped short of naming a name or he did not know it in the first place. The most reasonable possibility is that he did not know it.

Really, only if Caroline Dall's bizarre notes are sorted out to imply that, in Washington as a Congressman, Lincoln somehow traced and found his grandfather from undisclosed clues, presumably from his mother—he definitely spoke with Herndon soon after his term expired and he returned to Springfield—then he knew but withheld this information. In that case, Lincoln chose to reveal a stripped-down story and deny both Herndon and posterity access to his actual lineage.

Likely, though, the Dall note is rubbish. Likely, if Nancy ever knew her father's name, she preferred not to tell her children. She wanted them to be encouraged to learn, not to undertake a visit that could prove unpleasant both to them and to a surprised old fellow in Virginia.

(One must also accept the possibility that Nancy made up the "Virginia planter." Children fantasize and she was a once deprived if not a neglected child, a human being who might benefit from fantasy's comforts. Idealizing and fantasizing absent parents is a common psychological balms. If the rich, well-born, aristocratic, prominent "Virginia planter" was Nancy's fantasy, it would be simply prudent for her not to give her father any name.)

At bottom, the omission of this element may be taken to reveal nothing about Lincoln's editing or storytelling design and creative skill. The contrary is true of other omissions, especially the next, the planter's status as an enslaver.

The Planter's Status as an Enslaver

In reality, although the "planter" was presented baldly *sans* plantation, his status as an enslaver was strongly implied. For example,

132

Herndon referred to him as a "nabob" and an "aristocrat," and quoted Lincoln directly for the adjective that the man was a rich planter. In the region of Richmond County, Virginia, the operation of a plantation with free labor was impractical. Economics of that time and place clearly required a rich planter either to own enslaved workers or hire enslaved labor from other planters.

Due to the strength, close to certainty, of this implication, Lincoln's omission was only of a plain statement that the planter was an enslaver. The decision to omit this bears analysis: the emperor has no clothes. Essentially, once having declared his grandfather's occupation as planter, and his situation as wealthy, the only way that Lincoln could protect his ancestor from the imputation that he was an enslaver would have been by explicit denial. "Although a rich planter, he was unique in having no participation in slavery. He employed strictly free labor on his farm," Lincoln would have been telling Herndon in that case, implausibly.

By a devious and distracting ploy, Lincoln made no comment. He did not weigh in one way or the other on his grandfather's participation in the common lot of Virginia planters, slavery. This omission simultaneously left open (as undiscussed) the possibility of an "enlightened enslaver," that oxymoronic spectrum of enslavers who acted in some way via manumission of enslaved workers after they died, or who were open to enslaved freeing themselves by purchase, or who at least thought of and spoke of slavery as evil, and destined to fade away.

This last seems to have been Lincoln's working proposition, that it was his hope (or belief without evidence beyond his own mother's anti-slavery utterances) that this rich planter abhorred slavery. After all, the woman who was this planter's daughter evidenced abhorrence of slavery.

Herndon, whom Lincoln was addressing, was an abolitionist. Herndon was forever hounding Lincoln to strengthen his opposition to slavery. Lincoln would have liked to say that his grandfather abhorred slavery but lacking proof, his integrity precluded that. Hence, he did not address slavery at all.

The main desire Lincoln had as storyteller was not to tag this rich planter expressly with being an enslaver. He did not place in Herndon's hands anything about slavery to publish after his death. In Lincoln's mind, given his idealized image of a slavery-hating grandfather, Lincoln had not resisted the pull of an ancestral acceptance of slavery, or consciously taken a path contrary to his grandfather's imagined or projected philosophy. To say nothing was best, keeping his grandfather where the founders stood, founders about which Lincoln so often and so publicly spoke.

The Planter's Offenses

Next after slavery, the most outstanding and morally horrifying editing Lincoln did was in understating the planter's offenses. Lincoln left it ambiguous whether the planter was an adulterer. That he clearly abandoned his lover, seemingly *after* her pregnancy, was apparent, although Lincoln never made this explicit. It was a charge he did not make against the accused, *nolle prosequi.*

Whether the planter made false promises to obtain Lucy's favors is unclear but suggested when Lincoln said that his grandmother had been "poor and credulous."

On the other hand, Lincoln crafted ambiguity by his follow up interrogatory story, when he held his grandmother up in wry admiration as Prometheus with a swollen belly. By this premise, Lucy fell that her baby might rise: his trickster grandmother *stole* the best brains and bloodline within her reach. She could have done no better for any child of hers. To match his meaning, his question may have ended with a smile or even a hearty and triumphant laugh.

This premise loops back or ties up to undermine the planter's supposed taking shameless advantage of a poor and credulous girl, because that narrative is displaced and replaced by the scenario of a foolish gentleman who thought that he was taking advantage of a wily woman but was, in reverse, being manipulated into making her pregnant. Lincoln reduced the guilt burden on the planter to that degree.

Lincoln ought to have reported whether the planter was an adulterer, a conscienceless seducer, and, possibly the denouement being his worst act, an abandoner of a pregnant woman. Having enjoyed her surrender, he left Lucy to community scorn, to paternal wrath, to economic and emotional hurt for the rest of her life and their baby's. But Lincoln spent no words or time on these offenses. All too clearly, he intended to frame the rogue in an abstract light, holding no brief as prosecutor but instead as his after-the-fact enabler and eraser of faults.

Both of Lincoln's main characters all but vanish into outline. Lincoln never clarified their respective motives and personalities. He is simply a wealthy planter of Virginia and she is poor and credulous. The couple's affair, whether romantic, lustful, hopeful, passionate, etc., goes flatly uncharacterized and insipid.

Although he smoothed the edges of the culpable cavalier, Lincoln offset his editing by adopting a rigid moral code in his own life. As noted in the prior chapter about Lucy, Lincoln aimed to assist woman, especially young women, in distress or marginally mistreated, either by offering marriage or by arranging for their marriages. He seems to have proposed to three women before Mary Todd accepted his offer, fourth, each time because he always wanted to do right by women. It was such a core part of his being that he made up for omitting to describe in 1851 any ancestral deviation from classic, chivalric acts.

Ultimately, to use a pun, Lincoln told an inoffensive story. Grandparental flaws faded, any unsavory relationship was blurred. Lincoln's tandem stories to Herndon leaped to the outcome, the baby, the lively bastard. Lucy gave birth off-stage and then Nancy, too, until Lincoln himself fills the screen, concluding in a quavering voiceover, "God bless her!" That is, God bless mother for having me, shaping me as I am and setting me in pursuit of my yet-hoped-for high and noble goals. To that story the planter's offenses were obstacles to omit, and he did.

The Lovers' Respective Ages

The lovers barely breathe in Lincoln's narrow, inoffensive story world. The man's weakness was implicitly his appetite. He indulged himself. That it was at cost of the virginity of a 17-year-old girl, an overseer's eldest daughter, possibly his own overseer's daughter, is unstated. (We know her age roughly and her father's station in life from other informants and documents.) An older man took advantage of an underage girl. By omitting to state her age—he did not even call her "young"—Lincoln afforded his female Prometheus myth to bloom, *and* avoided amplifying his grandfather's offense list.

Emotions

Lincoln's stories scanted emotion. Lincoln passed Herndon a small glass of distilled family tree without bubbles. He told nothing for effect except his *cri de coeur* blessing of his mother at the end. Otherwise, feelings about his grandfather, his grandmother, and (behind the scenes) his great-grandparents and their community are abstract or omitted entirely.

Any feelings about love, pregnancy, loss, and empathy with the feelings of others, her parents and siblings, are completely missing. Under scrutiny, this may be more about Lincoln than about storytelling strategies. Long prior to 1851, Lincoln had girded himself up to contend against feelings or emotions, which he called "passion."

Lincoln's exaltation of unemotional reason began with his first public address. Lincoln presented himself as a survivor standing among surviving kin of the Revolutionary generation. He came close to saying that his passionate planter grandfather was a veteran. At the lyceum in Springfield in 1838, he pursued passion as his topic—and his target. Rejecting extended passion, he advised all present, "Passion has helped us; but can do so no more. It will in future be our enemy. Reason, cold, calculating, unimpassioned reason, must furnish all the materials for our future support and defense."

He loved the theme of reason with—dare one say—a passion. In 1842 he again raised his origins story, again drained of emotion. The head must rule the heart, thought must trump feeling, Lincoln argued. "All hail Reason!" he told his audience. The happy day would come when no drunkards or enslaved persons inhabited the earth. Off-stage, we sense that passion brought the planter to his knees but, by reason, he could rise above, control appetite and eliminate the injustice of slavery. (Although Herndon was actually in the audience in 1842, he did not carry over Lincoln's paean to reason as a gloss to adorn the passionless story Lincoln shared with him in 1851.)

In sum, his mother possessed a mind that she would not trade for legitimacy. All hail, Reason! All hail a story without heroes—unless Nancy, the resultant lively, smart bastard was the hero, and Lincoln did call her "heroic."

The Historical Context

Dennis Hanks told Herndon that Nancy was the daughter of Henry Sparrow and Lucy Hanks Sparrow. Henry Sparrow *had* served as a soldier during the Revolution. Lincoln, as if caught between Henry Sparrow as his putative grandfather and the Virginia planter, tread lightly around his ancestor's military service in 1851, as before the Springfield

Lyceum in 1838. Rather than fall between two stools, Lincoln seated himself squarely on neither but passed by the chance.

Contrary to Lincoln's custom and the custom of storytellers in general, the story is without historical context. As Lincoln left matters, the planter did not take sides, serve in the military, voice opinions on the issues of the day, including slavery (notably in the Northwest Ordinance) but instead stood out as an "idiot" in the original sense of that ancient Greek term, applied to any adult male who failed to take part in civic business.

Here it is superficially incredible that Lincoln would omit the historical context, his favorite era, the setting of more speeches than any other time. As a result, he made no allusion to the big event of his grandparents' time, the Revolution, or the planter's role in it. Although the story was a personal one, as some sort of romance, thus framed it had no connections to Virginia, to nation building, to politics or to slavery.

Outside of this day with Herndon in the buggy, Lincoln had blended or merged his grandfather with the founders, the Revolution, 1776 and the Declaration of Independence, as well as opposition to slavery. Here, stage-center and singularly was the tragicomic episode of a "nabob's" seduction of a credulous maid.

Is any explanation possible?

Yes … because Lincoln incorporated *himself* into *this* story. *Lincoln* proposed that his hopes were connected to the 1780s. From these people of Virginia of the Revolutionary period, Lincoln asserted that he drew both his contemporary identity and *what he hoped to be.* His future hopes were the proverbial "moral of the story." After he blessed his mother with advance gratitude, he ended his origins story. Unfortunately, to Herndon, he only hinted at this content. To this day, that point remains to be eked out or it is missed.

The Necessity for Lifetime Secrecy

Lincoln never explained his grounds for lifetime secrecy. Perhaps he could not explain without giving up the protection that secrecy was intended to insure. Maybe his grounds are obvious: no one airs their family's dirty laundry in public. Another possible motive was that Lincoln never wanted *the public* to think of him as an aristocrat. Besides Herndon, Lincoln let nobody know that he was descended from the First Families of Virginia. According to Anita E. Kelly, a psychologist who has made a study of secrets, defining secrecy involves answering the question: Secret *from whom*? Here, the better answer might be that Lincoln was intent upon keeping his ancestry secret from *potential voters*.[1]

Certainly, he was not waiting in 1851 for a still-warm 1780s family scandal to cool down, or for his mother to pass. Nancy Hanks Lincoln had been in the ground over thirty years. Nobody living could be hurt by his revelation but him, and he could not be hurt—except at the polls, where men might not vote for a Virginia planter's grandson. Lincoln wished not to offend. Southern agitators might stir up ridicule and scorn for him as a hypocrite or traitor to his family. (Stephen Douglas did so during the 1858 debates, as we shall see.)

About slavery, Lincoln governed his tongue closely. He did not feel alone in this. He bit his tongue and believed that "the great body of the Northern people do crucify their feelings, in order to maintain their loyalty to the constitution and the Union."[2]

He imposed secrecy on himself as well and, because our drifting minds tend to visit our secrets, Lincoln must have thought often of his mother *and* of the Virginia planter. But he could celebrate neither publicly. Rather than lie or obfuscate, he said nothing of his mother, whom he loved and privately blessed and in secret praised as the source of all he was or would ever be. In order not to alienate his constituency, which in 1851 was a purely hypothetical and future national constituency, he said nothing. That was probably the secret behind his secret.

Blame

One does not know whether either or both of the lovers are to be blamed for their fruitful dalliance. This baffling result reflects Lincoln's philosophy, which Herndon detailed with a specificity unavailable from any other contemporary. Because Herndon was in a perfect position for about twenty years to hear and observe Lincoln, he is an ideal informant about Lincoln on blame. His discussion of Lincoln's philosophy amounts to an explanation of why we find nobody to blame even after hearing these short ancestral stories.

Herndon said that Lincoln as a general rule, "never praised or blamed a man—never eulogized a man nor condemned him—I never heard him compliment mortal man nor did I ever hear him condemn mortal man. In praise or blame he was equally chary—equally passive—equally negative: it was neither good lord nor good devil."[3]

They were not cautionary tales for anybody else; only Lincoln, privately and inward, managed his behavior to an extreme degree to avoid the planter's bad example.

Memory

When one knows more about Lincoln's attention to the dead, an absorption close to obsession, one looks in vain for references for a deliberate reference to the *memory* of the deceased.

In Lincoln's philosophy, resurrection was by remembrance. Did Lincoln's disclosures to Herndon mean anything else? This is the hardest nut to crack. He explicitly linked his mother and his Virginia planter grandfather to his highest hopes. But tacitly, was Lincoln not honoring the dead? We need to explore this phenomenon further. Examples abound, such as the Gettysburg Address, an oration to dedicate a cemetery.

For Lincoln, the afterlife was not celestial but conscious. Humans survived—if they survived—not in heaven but in heads. Accordingly, so long as people thought about, talked about, wrote about the Virginia planter, just so long—and no longer—would he live.

Although Lincoln in 1851 said nothing aloud about immortality or honoring the dead to Herndon, his favorite and much-recited poem provides entry into Lincoln's mindset. The poem, John Knox's "Mortality," begins:

> Oh! why should the spirit of mortal be proud?
> Like a swift-fleeting meteor, a fast-flying cloud
> A flash of the lightning, a break of the wave
> He passeth from life to his rest in the grave.

Dr. Jason Duncan in New Salem introduced Lincoln to "Mortality." Not for nothing, the poem was also known as "Immortality." Motivated by concern over both, Lincoln memorized the poem. Some who heard his impassioned recitations thought that Lincoln must have written it. When Lincoln said no, he sometimes injected that he "would give all I am worth, and go in debt, to be able to write so fine a piece as I think that is." Lawrence Weldon was impressed to note specifically, "Tasteful composition, either of prose or poetry, which faithfully contrasted the realities of eternity with the unstable and fickle fortunes of time, made a strong impression on his mind."[4]

Part Two—Reflections

Back in the Lincoln cabin in Indiana, Lincoln in his teens wrote his *own* mortality poem:

> Time, what an empty vapor
> 'tis and days, how swift they are,
> Swift as an Indian arrow,
> fly on like a shooting star.
> The present moment just is here,
> then slides away in haste,
> that we can never say they're ours
> but only say they're past.[5]

Scholars who infer a morbid Lincoln obsessed by death are half right, but only half. Mortality certainly moved him. But—so did immortality. In another poem in the 1840s, Lincoln wrote about "living in the tombs," although the word "living" ought to be stressed as emphatically as "tombs." He waxed poetic over the dead who lived in memory, defining memory as falling exactly

> between Earth and Paradise:
> O memory! thou mid-way world
> 'Twixt Earth and Paradise,
> Where things decayed, and loved ones lost
> In dreamy shadows rise.[6]

If we are to understand Lincoln, a *sine qua non* is that Lincoln believed in an immortality of consciousness. Remembered, you never die. When in 1851 in his buggy with Herndon Lincoln pared off one individual, unnamed by him, for discussion from out of all of the Revolutionary generation, he was probably dead. Few soldiers and sailors of the Revolution were left. The last signer of the Declaration of Independence, Charles Carroll of Carrollton, a Maryland enslaver who saw slavery as a great evil and opposed it in policy, had died in 1832. The last Virginia planter signer, Thomas Jefferson, had died on the same day as John Adams, July 4, 1826.

When Lincoln conversed with Herndon, by bringing up his mother and grandfather, he was granting them added life. From the obscure dead, he was saving his mother and grandfather from being forgotten. As he phrased it in his own poem, Lincoln was raising "loved ones lost" as "dreamy shadows." The stakes were cosmically high. The Virginia planter's immortality depended upon his grandson's recalling him. Herndon's posthumous disclosure of what Lincoln told him would do more. The boon for the Virginia planter (and for Lincoln's mother) was possible immortal life. This book is now a part of that.

140

Herndon never fully understood that he was being given a sacred duty. His partner's raw words required a rigorous analysis that Herndon never gave them. Because Lincoln withheld too much and chose to be sketchy and ambiguous, Herndon may be forgiven. It is left for us, the living, to gather the clues and perform the belated honoring of Lincoln, Nancy Hanks Lincoln, and her father, each of us now between Earth and Paradise in our own memory and consciousness.

Discussion

Professor Frank made a conclusion quite apt to review here: that stories are told to salvage lives from calamities. From an extended study of stories around the world, he realized that, in general, characters make good from their mistakes, and stories end with hope.

For this last to be true in Lincoln's telling, for his stories to work, he himself has to be seen as the hope. Perhaps to optimize this recognition, to etch hope most sharply and memorably Lincoln's hopes as the point of his stories, the absence of a setting and the suppression of complex characters was mandatory. In essence, the storyteller, three-dimensionally, stepped out of the simplified stories on that day in 1851.

Professor Frank suggests four criteria for "less dangerous" stories (the best kind of stories). They are:

1. openness to other stories,
2. characters acknowledge mistakes and work to set things right,
3. cooperative characters praised, and
4. antagonists with names, faces and purposes that cannot be immediately dismissed.[7]

Here, the first criterion is certainly satisfied. The gaps in the ambiguous storyline Lincoln spun were as fine as the linen threads with which his mother won prizes as a girl. He left everything open to the point of being airy. Second and third, however, Lincoln left out—if he ever knew it—Lucy's (questionable) sacrifice in leaving the baby with better parents than she could then be. The heroism of cooperative characters is missing in the telling, although likely present in old Virginia. Fourth, the *ostensible* villain, the Virginia planter, despite ample means and power, lust and appetite, shows no redeeming cooperation, does not acknowledge any mistake or work to right his wrong. Yet, by a sort of jiu-jitsu, Lincoln upends his indifferent villain *outside* of the story proper. From years of promoting patriotic proxies, he had idealized his ancestor in a Revolutionary prequel, first unveiled in hints at the Lyceum in 1838, until this man's legacy of qualities and Revolutionary goals could not be dismissed. If anything, his qualities and Revolutionary goals cannot be exaggerated in terms of impact on Lincoln. He did not state this to Herndon, but we understand the Virginian's *omitted rich complexity.*

Altogether, Lincoln—had he sworn to tell the truth, the whole truth and nothing but the truth—would have been obliged to tell a story that omitted none of these elements, and (after revealing his grandfather's name, if he knew it), without shading things, then to say something like:

> My grandparents conceived a child outside wedlock as the Revolution ended in which my grandfather took part, supporting the Declaration of Independence in 1776. As Washington began to furlough home to the volunteers from Virginia, this Virginia planter, an enslaver, a brilliant and rich man, ambitious and prominent, returned home with an eye to sow his wild oats despite either being married or having marriage plans to a member of the First Families of Virginia.
>
> A young girl of about 17, my grandmother, managed in turn to set her cap for him, and became pregnant by him, to which he reacted by shamefully abandoning her and their baby. She was left with no option but to return in shame to her father's home and give up the child to their care. Moreover, the planter's misbehavior set Lucy on the primrose path, and she was thereafter used by several men for their pleasure without regard to her needs or dignity.
>
> Their baby, Nancy, heroically overcame the miseries and difficulties that she, thus, inherited along with her brilliant mind as the planter's abandoned daughter. Independently, or through a local minister's preaching, she saw the light of Jefferson's declaration and promise of equality, and applied it to oppose slavery, which doctrine she taught her children. I cannot recall a time when I did not think and feel that slavery was wrong. The sight of the enslaved crucifies my feelings. All that I am or ever hope to be I got from my mother, God bless her.

Much of this remained untold. Lincoln carefully and consciously cut and pasted the much shorter story of his origins into the less palpable and more abstract one that he wanted people to remember him by after he was gone.

15

The Farmers
and the Enslaved

Every blade of grass is a study.—Abraham Lincoln

The Undocumented Lincoln

Lincoln, a farmer's son among a people who lived and worked mostly on farms, said accurately that he had been "raised to farm work." He never said that his liberation from farming may have been a close call, but it possibly was. Up to and after age 21, farming was his occupation. For how long was Lincoln mesmerized to farm for a living? He went with his family to settle in Illinois, where he cleared land and planted crops, seemingly without resentment or fretting, drawing up no plans to escape the usual labors of a farmer.

Only by unplanned chance with a total stranger, the vigorous personality of Denton Offutt, did he decide to take a flatboat for his second trip to New Orleans. His separation from farming thereafter became permanent. After that trip, Lincoln ran Offutt's store in New Salem and, from that point, never seems to have thought seriously about farming again.[1]

Fussing Over Farming or Planting

Despite his Virginia planter grandfather, no Southern plantation was ever Lincoln's model farm. In fact, he avoided the words, only rarely speaking or writing "plantation" or "planter." He revealed his distaste more expressly when he was in his early thirties. His Kentucky friend, Joshua Speed, had urged Lincoln to join him in "farming." For Speed, a "farm" was a plantation, and in suggesting farming, Speed meant not guiding a plow but farming with enslaved labor, the enterprise in which he himself was contentedly engaged. (Speed did not free those enslaved at his Farmington plantation until Federal law positively and finally required this of the border states.)

Lincoln not only declined Speed's invitation—which probably included incentives, such as possibly co-signing a mortgage (Speed's original letter is unfortunately lost)—Lincoln rejected the offer emphatically. He wrote, "As to your farm matter, I have no sympathy with you. I have no farm, nor ever expect to have; and, consequently, have not studied the subject enough to be much interested with it. I can only say that I am glad you are satisfied and pleased with it."[2]

By rights, Speed's suggestion (especially if, as likely, he had proposed incentives) ought to have been harder to reject. Speed, his best friend, born in Kentucky like Lincoln, was not only a planter but a planter with whom Lincoln had stayed enjoyably for a month in August 1841. As an element of the invitation, living near one another was a great lure. At the time of Speed's offer in early 1842, Lincoln was a bachelor, a trial lawyer for three years, going on four, who had just lost one partner, John Todd Stuart, and was undertaking to practice under a new one, Stephen Logan, a sour man with whom his relations were cold from the start. Lincoln had never been diffident about relocating, moving from Kentucky to Indiana to Illinois, and he had in the past unhesitatingly traveled up and down the Mississippi.

Thus, Lincoln's decision to dismiss the thought—to insist that he had not studied it—to state that he had no interest in it—at first challenges *credibility*. His wording of no "sympathy" with his closest friend on the "farm matter," is insistently shrill. But then it becomes obvious: that his curt rejection reflects a lifelong rejection of plantation farming. Before Speed's offer, long before, the planter's grandson who had almost nothing but agricultural savvy and experience in farming, had given thought to the occupation of the Virginia planter, and was revolted by it.

Lincoln's remark was, thus, truthful and his cold tone was intentional. Although Lincoln's opposition to slavery can only be documented back to the 1830s, he said once that he could not remember a time that he did not oppose slavery. He plausibly cheered on the total eradication of slavery irrelevantly at the tail end of a speech he delivered on temperance in the early 1840s. His bristling reply to Speed suggests that he always had such feelings but kept them private for decades but before he spoke out.[3]

By standards of his time, it would have been politically savvy for

Lincoln to have accepted Speed's invitation and to have become a planter in 1842. To the political aspect Lincoln was far from indifferent. In this respect, Lincoln's moral values alone distinctly stood between himself and undertaking his ancestral occupation.

His prejudice later led him to ridicule farmers who became President. Lincoln said nothing of it to Speed but later, in a moth-to-flame way, Lincoln publicly and playfully toyed with the concept of farming—with a plantation, and enslaved labor—as a qualification for the Presidency. Of course, since George Washington, candidates for President had often been planters. The absence of a plantation in Lincoln's resume came with inherently adverse political consequences. Ingeniously, in 1852, Lincoln targeted this specific presidential criterion for ridicule.

The nominee of Lincoln's party in 1852 was Winfield Scott, a West Point graduate and career military man who had never farmed. Lincoln came to his rescue. Lincoln—not a farmer in his adulthood either—invited himself to defend the nominee's Achilles heel against Stephen Douglas's derogation of Scott for never having been a farmer or planter.

Creating a *reductio ad absurdum*, Lincoln began by saying that he could not fathom how being a farmer *or a physician* qualified a man for public office. The example of a physician he injected as a political insider's joke: it was funny because, as party members well knew, no physician had ever been President.

"Whatever of sound views of government is acquired by the physician and farmer, is acquired not in their regular occupations, but by reading and reflection in the hours of relaxation from their regular occupations. It is probable that the leisure time for such reading and reflection would, in time of peace, be quite as abundant with an officer of the army, as with a physician or farmer," Lincoln said, comically handling each of the occupations with ostentatiously equal seriousness.[4]

Lincoln, who had never been a general, did not beat Washington's drum or otherwise tout Scott's military service. He invented a "physician" qualification when "farmer" was his real and sole target. By hindsight, we see that he was defending his *own* path as a non-farmer to a future hopeful nomination.

A Brief History of Lincoln and "Plant"

Lincoln insisted that farming came with moral questions. In 1854, "plant," a word that Lincoln did not speak or write, he began to utter.

The first time that the Virginia planter's grandson is known to have said "plant" was at Bloomington, Illinois, when he told a crowd, "If we admit that a negro is not a man, then it is right for the Government to own him and trade in the race, and it is right to allow the South to take their peculiar institution with them and plant it upon the virgin soil of Kansas and Nebraska." He was responding to the great issue of 1854, whether slavery could be expanded into the Territories.[5]

Next, in Peoria, he used "plant" again when he spoke in scorn of the casualness by which a farmer might decide whether to go into cattle or to "plant" tobacco. He criticized Judge Douglas's *laissez faire* view that "whether a new country shall be slave or free, is a matter of as utter indifference, as it is whether his neighbor shall plant his farm with tobacco, or stock it with horned cattle. Now, whether this view is right or wrong, it is very certain that the great mass of mankind takes a totally different view. They consider slavery a great moral wrong; and their feelings against it, is not evanescent."[6]

In Chicago, for the third time on record Lincoln used the word "plant," as he whipped up his rhetoric. He threw back his head and asked, "How is it, then, that Judge Douglas infers, because I hope to see slavery put where the public mind shall rest in the belief that it is in the course of ultimate extinction, that I am in favor of Illinois going over and interfering with the cranberry laws of Indiana?" He repeated his charge that Douglas was indifferent to "the question of whether a man shall pasture his land with cattle, or plant it with tobacco—so little and so small a thing, that he concludes, if I could desire that anything should be done to bring about the ultimate extinction of that little thing, I must be in favor of bringing about an amalgamation of all the other little things in the Union."[7]

As we weigh what Lincoln said in 1854, we might consider that, before he declined Speed's invitation to farm in 1842, the same moral grounds were available to him back then, even though unexpressed.

The Wisconsin Wonderland

The funny thing was that farming actually appealed to him. When Lincoln addressed those attending the Wisconsin State Fair in 1859, he spoke of farming in terms of cultivation of the human mind. He revealed his "reflection, that no other human occupation opens so wide a field for the profitable and agreeable combination of labor with cultivated thought, as agriculture."[8]

He took flight as a poet in virtual botanical ecstasy, saying, "Every blade of grass is a study; and to produce two, where there was but one, is both a profit and a pleasure. And not grass alone; but soils, seeds, and seasons—hedges, ditches, and fences, draining, droughts, and irrigation—plowing, hoeing, and harrowing—reaping, mowing, and threshing—saving crops, pests of crops, diseases of crops, and what will prevent or cure them—implements, utensils, and machines, their relative merits, and how to improve them—hogs, horses, and cattle—sheep, goats, and poultry trees, shrubs, fruits, plants, and flowers—the thousand things of which these are specimens—each a world of study within itself."[9]

Lincoln avoided the minefield of crops like cotton, tobacco, hemp, sugar cane, or rice. He avoided the moral dimension of farming that had separated him dramatically from Stephen Douglas and which stood behind his curt dismissal of a farm offer in 1842. The words "plant" or "planter" were not mentioned. Altogether, he said nothing to which a Virginia planter might take offense; he touched briefly upon slavery, neutrally as a minor aspect of a debate over the so-called "mud-sill" economic theory.[10]

On the other hand, the late Tom Lincoln may possibly have made an uncredited cameo appearance late in his celebration of the ideal cultivated farmer. The casual lifestyle of a certain subsistence farmer whom Lincoln had once known might have stimulated the tail end of this sentence: "The thought recurs that education—cultivated thought—can best be combined with agricultural labor, or any labor, on the principle of thorough work—that careless, half performed, slovenly work, makes no place for such combination."[11]

Searching for the Virginia Planter

Virginians did come to settle in Kentucky and in Indiana. For how many years in his boyhood did Lincoln hope in vain to meet the Virginia planter? Even as an adult in Illinois, he was poignantly on the alert to spot any Virginia planters in particular. In such run-ins, though, he was also on guard. He had first to determine if they were pro-slavery, testing them immediately on this point before making closer acquaintance. One who passed his test was Ward Hill Lamon.

Lamon, later one of Lincoln's first biographers, moved from Berkeley County, Virginia, to Danville, Illinois, in the late 1840s, where his attire led him to stand out. Upon meeting him, Lincoln expressed his certainty about Lamon.

"I should know at a glance you were a Virginian," Lincoln said. Lamon wore a swallow-tail coat, white neck cloth and ruffled shirt, which Lamon himself admitted was "an astonishing outfit for a young limb of the law in that settlement."[12]

Lincoln told him, "You Virginians shed barrels of perspiration while standing off in a distance and superintending the work your slaves do for you. It is different with us. Here it is every fellow for himself, or he doesn't get there."[13]

To the charge Lamon pled not guilty, responding instead that he detested slavery. Upon that exchange, they were, Lamon said, "from that hour, friends for life."[14]

Lincoln's test was for friendship only. Politically and professionally, he had no hesitation about associating with planters. He looked for their "better angels," aspects of recognition that slavery was evil. One he idealized was Henry Clay, his "beau ideal of a statesman," a living paradox who owned a plantation worked by some 200 enslaved persons but who also served as the president of the emancipation-sponsoring American Colonial Society. Lincoln literally eulogized Clay as a co-author of the Missouri Compromise that "drew a line" to limit slavery in 1820. Similarly, without concern over crossing boundaries, Lincoln married Mary Todd Lincoln, the daughter of a prominent Kentucky enslaver's family. Her virtues, however, included a deep and consistent hatred of slavery.

16

Lincoln and His Ancestors

It is for us the living, rather, to be dedicated
here to the unfinished work which they who
fought here have thus far so nobly advanced.
—Abraham Lincoln, Gettysburg Address (1863)

Back Endlessly to the Revolutionary Ancestors

Richard Brookhiser, an expert in the Revolution, in his compre-
hensive book, *Founder's Son,* analyzed Lincoln's speeches and writings. Brookhiser demonstrated that the chief historical resource Lincoln
drew on in defense of the Union *and* opposing slavery were the deeds
and writings of the generation that fought the Revolution and drafted
and ratified the Constitution and the Northwest Ordinance.[1]

As noted earlier, Lincoln's first extended speech, his 1838 "Lyceum
Address," suggests that his mother's stories stirred him still and that
he believed in and deeply cherished his Revolutionary roots. In this
address, Lincoln mingled "memory," the Bible, stories of the Revolution,
and the pervasive influence of "passions" in support of the "noblest" of
causes.

As a reader of history, and of the writings of Thomas Paine, Nancy
seems to have directed her boy to her intellectual colleagues of Revolutionary times. They became his allies. His grandfather became something more. Dennis Hanks recalled Nancy telling her son that his blood
was a good as Washington's. Lincoln's ancestors became his strengths in
times of stress.

Some years were harder than others. Charles Strozier wrote, "For
some reason a special dread descended on Lincoln in that spring of
1848." Strozier then quoted from Lincoln's April 16, 1848, letter to Mary:
"In this troublesome world, we are never quite satisfied. When you were
here, I thought you hindered me some in attending to business; but now,

having nothing but business—no variety—it has grown exceedingly tasteless to me. I hate to sit down and direct documents, and I hate to stay in this old room by myself." Yet it was at this low point that Lincoln thought of his paternal grandfather and sent out several inquiries for information.[2]

In October 1854, people gathered in Peoria to hear Lincoln speak alongside Douglas. They got to hear something more significant: Lincoln's first dedicated anti-slavery speech, widely considered his first transcendent oratory. He approached matters from his hybrid Northern-Southern identity. "Before proceeding, let me say I think I have no prejudice against the Southern people," Lincoln told his audience in what was, if anything, an understatement. Lincoln felt as one with Southern planters.[3]

He had warm feelings toward men like Henry Clay, whom he eulogized, and Zachary Taylor, an enslaver in Louisiana, whom he also eulogized. Taylor, as President, loudly opposed and officially condemned the introduction of slavery into territory newly acquired from the Mexican War, to acquire which he himself had fought.

It was no unprecedented fantasy for Lincoln to picture his grandfather as a Virginia planter with a conscience and a deep desire that slavery would end. Logic suggests something that Lincoln never said directly and clearly—because Lincoln always knew that slavery was evil and he had inherited his grandfather's mind and ambition, their thoughts ran together. Lincoln would not demonize the South.

Lincoln said immediately of Southerners,

> They are just what we would be in their situation. If slavery did not now exist amongst them, they would not introduce it. If it did now exist amongst us, we should not instantly give it up. This I believe of the masses north and south. Doubtless there are individuals, on both sides, who would not hold slaves under any circumstances; and others who would gladly introduce slavery anew, if it were out of existence. We know that some southern men do free their slaves, go north, and become tip-top abolitionists; while some northern ones go south, and become most cruel slave-masters.[4]

He expressed sympathy:

> When southern people tell us they are no more responsible for the origin of slavery, than we; I acknowledge the fact. When it is said that the institution exists; and that it is very difficult to get rid of it, in any satisfactory way, I can understand and appreciate the saying. I surely will not blame them for not doing what I should not know how to do myself. If all earthly power were given me, I should not know what to do, as to the existing institution.[5]

He said in practical terms, "When they remind us of their constitutional rights, I acknowledge them, not grudgingly, but fully, and fairly; and I would give them any legislation for the reclaiming of their fugitives, which should not, in its stringency, be more likely to carry a free man into slavery, than our ordinary criminal laws are to hang an innocent one."[6]

The sole position upon which Lincoln stood consciously contrary to *current* Southern leaders concerned the expansion of slavery. He argued that was nowhere constitutionally protected. Indeed, the Constitution had forbidden the importation of enslaved captives into the country from abroad after 1810. This Lincoln emphasized, saying, "But all this; to my judgment, furnishes no more excuse for permitting slavery to go into our own free territory, than it would for reviving the African slave trade by law. The law which forbids the bringing of slaves *from* Africa; and that which has so long forbid the taking them *to* Nebraska, can hardly be distinguished on any moral principle; and the repeal of the former could find quite as plausible excuses as that of the latter."[7]

Douglas got miserably personal, targeting not only Lincoln but his *parents*. Encouraged by crowd noises as he spoke, warming up an attack on Lincoln's Southern roots, Douglas said, "I do not know that a native of Kentucky is more excusable because raised among slaves, his father and mother having owned slaves, he comes to Illinois, turns Abolitionist, and slanders the graves of his father and mother, and breathes curses upon the institutions under which he was born, and his father and mother bred."[8]

Transparently, these remarks scalded Lincoln. Technically, Lincoln, born and raised in Kentucky, was "born and raised among slaveholders"—but as "a native of Kentucky" only. Douglas's statement that "his father and mother having owned slaves" was untrue, but Douglas, by one generation, nearly hit home. Nobody ever came closer, by accident, to the truth.

With that wound, Lincoln became dangerous. Herndon vouched for the fact that Lincoln's wrath against Stephen Douglas was distinctive. "I never heard Mr. Lincoln praise but two men—Jefferson & Clay, & I never heard him censure but one—Douglas."[9]

In his final debate with Douglas, Lincoln and Douglas sparred over a quotation in which Henry Clay alluded to the noble men of '76. The turf played into Lincoln's hands. It was his grandfather writ large. Lincoln reviewed the phrase ("the noblest band of patriots that ever assembled in council") and its context, the Declaration of Independence and the premise that slavery was evil.[10]

Douglas Demonized

Douglas had made matters personal and familial. In the universe of all possible insults, this one inflamed Lincoln who, in his heart, knew he had been descended from a rich Virginia planter, and that in his veins flowed a mix of the First Families of Virginia. Of this Douglas knew nothing while he played with fire.[11]

Lincoln advanced on Douglas personally, attacking his integrity. In August 1858, before friendly audiences, he aimed both barrels, one at slavery and the other at Douglas, whom he charged with lying about his own and Henry Clay's position on slavery.[12]

In a newspaper report of his speech (the speech itself being lost), Lincoln disavowed any claim for Whig support, "unless he could show from Mr. Clay's printed speeches that he stood upon the very ground occupied by that statesman, and that Douglas's position was as opposite to it as Beelzebub to an Angel of Light. In proving this point—reading extract after extract from the speeches and letters of Henry Clay, contending nobly and greatly for the 'ultimate emancipation of the slave'—Mr. Lincoln remarked that he believed Douglas was the only statesman of any note or prominence in the country who had never said to friend or enemy whether he believed human slavery in the abstract to be right or wrong."[13]

Lincoln finished up with a thunder that brought hands to clapping intermittently, "These communities, by their representatives in old Independence Hall, said to the whole world of men: 'We hold these truths to be self-evident: that all men are created equal; that they are endowed by their Creator with certain unalienable rights; that among these are life, liberty and the pursuit of happiness.'...In their enlightened belief, nothing stamped with the Divine image and likeness was sent into the world to be trodden on, and degraded, and imbruted by its fellows."[14]

At this point, after cheers, Lincoln said, "If you have been inclined to believe that all men are not created equal in those inalienable rights enumerated by our chart of liberty, let me entreat you to come back. Return to the fountain whose waters spring close by the blood of the Revolution."[15]

Poised at that instant upon his grandfather's shining moment, he went for the jugular: Think nothing of me—take no thought for the political fate of any man whomsoever—but come back to the truths that are in the Declaration of Independence. You may do anything with me you choose, if you will but heed these sacred principles. You may not only defeat me for the Senate, but you may take me and put me to death. While pretending no indifference to earthly honors, I do claim to be actuated in this contest by something higher than an anxiety for office. I charge you to drop every paltry and insignificant thought for any man's success. It is nothing; I am nothing; Judge Douglas is nothing. But do not destroy that immortal emblem of Humanity—the Declaration of American Independence.[16]

Clearly, what motivated Lincoln transcended his desire for office. He expressed willingness to shed blood for the principle of equality as embodied in the Declaration. Although no one dies to become a Senator, he could have thought that somebody might kill him for what he was saying. His anxiety was apparently unfeigned; he had signed off a short note a few days before this speech, "If life and health continue..."—but he continued to ride about Illinois with boldness and daring, preaching the equality of all men against all risks.

A year later, an essay by Douglas appeared in the widely distributed *Harper's Weekly* newspaper, offering Lincoln a specific target. Lincoln summarized for his rebuttal the point on which he felt that Douglas was most vulnerable, "where he endeavored to link the men of the revolution to popular sovereignty."[17]

The Cooper Union Speech and Gettysburg

Lincoln then sought to destroy Douglas. He shaped his Cooper Union speech to separate "the men of the revolution" forever from Douglas. With this tactic, he might bring down the man he hated—*by means of* the idealized family he loved, whom Douglas had defamed. This drama played out in Cooper Union on the night of February 27, 1860, when Lincoln, who had once ridiculed Zebedee sitting in his boat guarding his servants, employed the founders to demonstrate that the enslavers abhorred slavery and dedicated their public lives to arresting slavery in place and to speeding its demise. Because these founders were the public proxies of his own idealized grandfather, the Virginia planter, his victory was especially and personally satisfying.[18]

Aiming at Douglas, that arch defamer of the planter's memory and his line of descendants, Lincoln said, "The Supreme Court, in the Dred

Scott case, plant themselves upon the fifth amendment, which provides that no person shall be deprived of 'life, liberty or property without due process of law'; while Senator Douglas and his peculiar adherents plant themselves upon the tenth amendment...."[19]

He did not stop with accusations. Senator Douglas and justices of the Court were now planting slavery where slavery had never been planted before, in the Constitution itself and within its Bill of Rights— but Revolutionary allies were lined up alongside *him*, opposed to slavery's expansion or permanence. Although historians have since picked away at his proofs and underlying numbers, that night, before a packed, awed house, when Lincoln concluded that the majority of the founders stood against the expansion, and for the extinction of slavery, he seemed to those assembled to speak with near-divine authority.

We hear in his Cooper Union speech how his origins dazzled him. Lincoln and the founders were one. He took on their agenda as his to implement. The sense of continuity possessed him. After the election, after Lincoln defeated Douglas, and after Douglas had died, we hear Lincoln again looking back in the careful choice and order of his words at Gettysburg.

Muffled in grammatical subtlety, word order was key. Richard Brookhiser sagely noted that, had Lincoln at Gettysburg meant a "birth of new freedom" he would have said so. Instead, standing among the dead, honoring them, Lincoln looped back to the Founders and spoke of re-birth. After the recent and climactic battle, Lincoln did not foresee but *saw* in that violent clash of arms the resumed throes of the original Revolution in a "new birth of freedom."[20]

PART THREE

Recapitulation

17

Lincoln's Hope
of an Immortal Name

In this temple, as in the hearts of the people
for whom he saved the Union, the memory
of Abraham Lincoln is enshrined forever.
—Lincoln Memorial, Washington, D.C.

What the Boy Thought

One luxury of our times is the celebrity interview, during which famous and/or important people answer questions. We hear everything about their parents, stories of their childhoods, and view photographs, movies or video recordings that show scenes that humanize these people. We lack the Barbara Walters questions from which we might know what Lincoln thought of his mother, his childhood fears, the most influential book he read in his boyhood and why, that time he fell through the ice.

We have Lincoln's address to the New Jersey legislature as President-Elect on February 21, 1861. Lincoln shared his boyhood thoughts—the *only* time he ever did—with these men during the stressful week before he was inaugurated. Lincoln's reverie before the New Jersey legislature is noteworthy as an account of the processes of his *boyhood mind*. Lincoln essentially described himself as an imaginative boy who was stirred by stories of the Revolution. He told legislators in New Jersey what he thought (as a boy in Indiana) had motivated the first enlistees of Washington's volunteer army.

"Away back in my childhood, the earliest days of my being able to read," Lincoln began, revealing that he read Parson Weems's biography of Washington. Much as at the Lyceum Address in 1838, except in first person, Lincoln said,

17. Lincoln's Hope of an Immortal Name

I remember all the accounts there given of the battle fields and struggles for the liberties of the country, and none fixed themselves upon my imagination so deeply as the struggle here at Trenton, New-Jersey. The crossing of the river; the contest with the Hessians; the great hardships endured at that time, all fixed themselves on my memory more than any single revolutionary event; and you all know, for you have all been boys, how these early impressions last longer than any others.[1]

This is when he shared his boyhood thoughts: "I recollect thinking then, boy even though I was, that there must have been something more than common that those men struggled for."[2]

The assembled legislators were likely disappointed. Caught up in the events of their day, anxious over news of secession, eager to hear Lincoln's response, legislators hoped for an update and Lincoln instead seemed determined to lull and distract them with this old account of a long-ago march of the rebels at Trenton. Instead of a revelation, his speech seemed a rebuff.

But that was because his message was over their heads.

He was answering the question, "Mr. Lincoln, what events particularly of your boyhood are important for the country to know about you as hostilities are starting to seem imminent?"

When Lincoln invoked the generation of Washington and alluded to boyhood memories, early impressions, vivid and lasting, how could his *grandfather* not be on his mind, of whom he had first heard as a boy? Lincoln chose the very reflections that had led him to "make himself of account," to study, to stand for office, and all the while to draw a line around slavery. With heroic blood coursing in his veins, he identified with men struggling for a great cause, and being *remembered* for that. He was going to be firm.

Did no legislator wonder why no account of the Revolution "fixed" itself in the boy's imagination so deeply as the struggle in Trenton? Or why Lincoln as a boy pored over an account of relentless sufferings in the field during the winter campaign? Did any of them connect it especially to personal experience in "crossing of the river" by Lincoln's family, hazarding the broad Ohio in December 1816, before a cold winter in a lean-to in the hills of Spencer County, "partly on account of slavery"?

Moreover, there was his recollected episode. Lincoln "fixed" on the first year of the Revolution—*before* the French alliance, *before* success at Trenton, *before* confidence was high—a period much like early 1861. Before the legislators, he revived his boyhood concentration on what was inside these suffering mortals. Not success or even hope but the importance of their *cause* drove his youthful thinking, which led to his conclusion that "something more than common" was the wind in these men's sails.[3]

Such thinking was demonstrably filed for instant recall, and drawn upon in stressful times. This type of analysis was not singular but representative of Lincoln's thinking. He pondered why people were willing to suffer. In his family's case, the great event of his childhood, the move to Indiana, he combed for cause. He discerned a dispute over title, yes, but from some other evidence their sacrifices were undertaken "partly on account of slavery." He knew what motivated him. He had inherited ambition. Unspoken in New Jersey in 1861 but clear from what Lincoln told Joshua Speed in 1841, public recognition remained his reason for living. He had even stated it in his naïve but candid handbill when first running for elective office in 1832. "Why are you running, Mr. Lincoln?" He had pondered long enough to answer without hesitation, telling the people that he desired to be "truly esteemed of my fellow men, by rendering myself worthy of their esteem."[4]

A Terrible End Feared

On no rational basis and for decades, Lincoln feared meeting a "terrible end." Then, on April 14, 1865, he was bloodily struck down like his grandfather, Abraham Lincoln, albeit indoors in a theater rather than outdoors in a cornfield. For the nation's future reverence, the government official who emptied the President's pockets preserved all that he carried. The collection resides at the Library of Congress and may be seen to this day.[5]

One of the half-dozen objects on Lincoln's person that night was a linen handkerchief. Linen was the same fabric which his mother had been so adept at making and in teaching her cousin to weave. It was also the material of the shirts she had hand-sewn for her boy in his youth. Closer inspection shows it to have been embroidered "A. Lincoln." President Lincoln was carrying around with him *his name in red letters*. One recalls Dennis Hanks telling Eleanor Atkinson about Lincoln as a boy writing his name and inviting attention to it. "Look at that, will you?" he would ask Dennis more than once in the cabin in Indiana, noting proudly, "That stands for me." His cousin remembered the youth standing and studying it "for a spell" before concluding that his name "appeared to mean a heap to Abe."[6]

Lincoln had two grandfathers, one whose name he carried and used whenever he signed anything, the other of whom was, to him, nameless, the mysterious and idealized Virginia planter. Ironically, of the planter Lincoln knew much more, including qualities he felt that he replicated. Through his mother, and her father's "blood," Lincoln knew who he was and all that he hoped to be—and, in this incarnation, he was determined that his name would outlive him. He would defeat his painful *athazagoraphobia.* For Lincoln, who longed to be remembered, to be celebrated along with his link to a noble cause, the embroidered handkerchief was but a memento of that goal, carried about everywhere, even when he relaxed, off duty, on a night out with his wife at the theater to see a comedy.

Thus passed Lincoln, who seriously and frequently confronted the challenge of death. No other topic of literature so dominated his mind. Lincoln's taste for morbid and lugubrious poetry exceeded Poe's. No other American President ever wrote about "living in the tombs." Haunted by the dead, ancestral specters beside him, Lincoln elevated the *remembered* over the *forgotten.* He did not foresee Heaven or Hell. He foresaw immortality or obscurity. What Lincoln thought rewarded a good life was an eternal memory. To be forgotten was Hell. This schematic drove his decisions and shaped his life. He aimed to deserve being remembered.

Lincoln's Unremembered Relatives

Apparently, name immortality had to be earned, in Lincoln's book. When Lincoln was three or four, his mother delivered a sickly child, his brother, whom the parents named after his father, Thomas Lincoln, Jr. The tiny infant died in three days. Curiously, Lincoln, in his 1860 autobiographical sketch, had nonetheless left the child nameless. Lincoln simply said that he had a "younger brother, who died in infancy." One might conclude that the baby died unnamed—except for confirmation of his name unexpectedly over a century later, in 1933, when a Works Public Administration crew discovered a small apparent tombstone on which the letters "T L" had been carved. Closely examined, the letters looked like the initials Tom Lincoln carved into furniture that he made and occasionally sold.[7]

Lincoln's mother died, possibly after months of deteriorating health, possibly within a week or two of contracting "the milk sick" in

August 1818, when Lincoln was nine. Then his sister died (along with her baby, who would have been Lincoln's nephew) on January 20, 1828. These losses of a brother who struggled for breath for days after birth, of his mother as she failed in an agony of several days and, most suddenly and unexpectedly, of the brilliant sister to whom he was close, along with her baby, all before Lincoln was 19, may have scarred him emotionally but naming these relatives whom he clearly had loved was rare for him. Given his normal compassion, and his own emphatic pursuit of an immortal name, and fear of being forgotten, why did he not write their names often, along with stories or anecdotes in the cases of his mother and his sister? Why did no engraved stone with her name top his mother's grave?

Except for eulogizing Henry Clay, William Henry Harrison, Zachary Taylor, and Bowling Green (a failed or aborted attempt), something held him back from performing the exact service that he deeply desired for himself. He did not always name the names of the dead. It was as if a superstitious reluctance, not to remember the names of those who had not *earned* immortality in human consciousness.

Notably, when Lincoln rose to speak in eulogy it was not for a friend or his family, it was for a man linked to a cause. Perhaps the element of advancing a cause was a prerequisite for an immortal name. Consistent with his statement to Joshua Speed in 1841, and his letter of thanks to the Manchester workingmen and their families in 1863, naming names was cheating unless the deceased had won immortality by taking steps and making sacrifices to advance the cause of humanity.

There are counterindications. Lincoln could (and did) inscribe names in the family Bible, including his father's. Beside his name, Lincoln calculated and wrote exactly how long the old man had lived, to the day, possibly to predict how many more years, months, weeks and days he might have himself. Beside other relatives' names, he wrote nothing.

Lincoln's Background Surfaces—Almost

Lincoln expressed his agenda in Trenton days before assuming the Presidency, when he struggled—by a sort of induced trance of boyhood proxy memories—to attain the same vision that the Virginia planter had believed in and suffered for. Without using the word slavery or its antonym, equality, he next reviewed how Washington and Jefferson—read them as proxies for his Virginia planter grandfather—influenced his decisions and mandated his moves. He who had ears in Trenton that day was invited to hear: The President-Elect's goal went back prior to the compromises of the Constitution, before the United States was independent, to the time when the Declaration was the exclusive operative document, to the cause as sheer ideals for which men suffered, fought and died. He avowed, as if he had raised his hand before the legislators and swore an oath, to bear the mindset of Trenton in 1776, to redeem the promises that Jefferson wrote.

Lincoln could not tell the legislators the secret that his mother was emphatic about his blood being as good as Washington's. He could not directly admit his lineage. He danced around the great hope espoused in the Declaration of Independence, while he could not acknowledge the familial nature of the cause. However, he could and did approach equality by indirection, saluting Thomas Jefferson.

Lincoln told them,

> I am exceedingly anxious that that thing which they struggled for; that something even more than National Independence; that something that held out a great promise to all the people of the world to all time to come; I am exceedingly anxious that this Union, the Constitution, and the liberties of the people shall be perpetuated in accordance with the original idea for which that struggle was made, and I shall be most happy indeed if I shall be an humble instrument in the hands of the Almighty, and of this, his almost chosen people, for perpetuating the object of that great struggle.[8]

In accordance with "the original idea," Lincoln visualized leading this "almost chosen people." Gifted by hindsight, none of us can read those words without seeing between its lines something close to the surface of Lincoln's *inherited* agenda. He was not only to defend the Union, the Constitution and the liberties of the people but something *more* than national independence—the clarion call of 1776, *Jefferson's promise*, and the object of the Revolutionaries from the first year, present when Washington crossed the river but not yet finished. He would speak more clearly later about a new birth of freedom, one that might bring on equality and end slavery for all time on this continent.

Logically and naturally, we recall from about ten years earlier what Lincoln told Herndon confidentially:

> My mother inherited (her father's) qualities and I hers. All that I am or hope ever to be I get from my mother—God bless her.[9]

Afterword

This book was written to enable readers

1. to recover what it was like for Lincoln to be Lincoln; and,
2. to experience awe and wonder upon realizing just how narrow and past-bounded the path was that Lincoln followed to learn, to lead, and, finally, to limit slavery's time in his country.

I have documented the shadowy but constant and influential figures of his mind on that journey, largely from his own words. One of his key ancestors was a complicated gentleman, as Lincoln's label for him ("nobleman so-called") indicated, a man whom he likely never met, while the other, this Revolutionary Virginia man's intellectual daughter, was present from the beginning of Lincoln's consciousness until he was nine and lost her. This book displays what can be known about Lincoln's origins, so long secret and, once published, so long discounted. The case made here is that, just as he told Herndon, one man and the one woman above all others shaped who Lincoln was and all that he ever hoped to be.[1]

Corroboration exists. During his last interview, Dennis Hanks, Lincoln's first cousin, once removed, told a cordial woman reporter from Chicago about the day the baton was passed. He overheard Nancy, then in her mid-thirties, tell her eight- or nine-year-old son that his blood *was just as good as Washington's*. Then, apparently afraid that he had said too much, Dennis backed off, saying that Nancy may have exaggerated.[2]

It was the Lincoln family's open secret. Nancy's words offer a solution to the mystery behind the otherwise miraculous rise of Nancy's slow-learning son, whom everything seemed to puzzle and who was a nuisance with his questions. Tom Lincoln thought that there was no sense in sending him to school, that what the kid needed was a back of the hand. After his mother died, Lincoln did quiet down. Another of Lincoln's cousins, John Hanks, recalled no questioner but a "bashful," "not a brilliant boy" who was "somewhat dull."[3]

But his mother had already told Lincoln that he had a good mind and leadership skills by *inheritance*—specifically from her Virginia planter father. The boy was driven to be what he was and all that he ever hoped to be by a Virginia planter. Lincoln authorized Herndon to speak after Lincoln died, to tell about the blood kin to whom he owed everything.[4]

With near unanimity, Lincoln biographers have resisted the idea. In the 1890s, Ida Tarbell published a Lincoln quote in *The Early Life of Lincoln*, "I don't know who my grandfather was, and I am much more concerned to know what his grandson would be." Although Tarbell seemed to be her own source of the made-up quote, her point nonetheless thrives to this day. The great David Donald began his classic biography of Lincoln stating flatly, "Abraham Lincoln was not interested in his ancestry."[5]

Further ironically, Lincoln himself preceded these family-scanting biographers in sanitizing his origins. By Lincoln's autobiographical outlines, Nancy Hanks Lincoln was born in Virginia, lived to marry and bear children, then died and was buried in Indiana. He wrote nothing of his Virginia planter grandfather. On the stump, Lincoln did not boast about his family. When he talked to troops, it was as his *father's* son.

On the other hand, when Lincoln could invite audiences' attention to the founders (whom he sometimes called the "fathers"), among whom Virginia planters figured so prominently, he did. Lincoln followed his mother, as she had been heard orating in backwoods debate by Christopher Columbus Graham. Lincoln praised the Declaration of Independence and its author, Thomas Jefferson, to whom he once offered "all honor," and he uniquely cheered the immortal name of Washington "in its naked deathless splendor."[6]

Lincoln never doubted his lineage, and lineage impelled Lincoln to learn much more than a farm boy would ever need, to seek a seat in the state legislature when he was first able to vote, to persist in politics, and, not least, by an inherited script to complete the Revolution's unfinished business, i.e., slavery's eradication.

Thus, Nancy's encouragement and stirring stories contributed to saving the Union. In a Churchillian paraphrase, never have so many owed so much to so few scraps of facts, if facts at all. We cannot be sure that Nancy's solace was not her own invention. But, in this book, we are concerned with Lincoln's belief. Because Lincoln was brought up from his youngest days as the descendant of a "broad-minded" planter, the dream of liberation beat within his heart. To him, his grandfather, alongside other Virginia planters, stood not only for independence in 1776 but for human equality. For public praise of the planter, the founders were proxies.[7]

Throughout his life, Lincoln circled back again and again to the Revolution, his grandfather's generation's finest hour, and most often and most publicly drew strength from the Declaration of Independence. What Lincoln told Herndon—"My mother inherited his qualities and I hers. All that I am *or hope ever to be* I get from my mother—God bless her"—is best understood in that context.[8]

It was this Lincoln who was elected President. After he swore the oath and sat where Washington and Jefferson once sat, he had time to savor the thought that he was to them what his mother taught him he was: blood kin through her father, his brilliant grandfather, the broad-minded Revolutionary, the Virginia planter. However, President Lincoln, who cited census figures in debating Stephen Douglas, had to have pondered the dark possibility also that enslaved cousins of his were stooping and tending fields not far away, in plantations along the Rappahannock River.[9]

I conclude by offering the final stanza of "To Helen," Edgar Allan Poe's 1848 reverie about the guiding eyes ("two sweetly scintillant Venuses") that lead him, after an enchanted, noble world has otherwise vanished:

> But now, at length, dear Dian sank from sight,
> Into a western couch of thunder-cloud;
> And thou, a ghost, amid the entombing trees
> Didst glide away. Only thine eyes remained;
> They would not go—they never yet have gone;
> Lighting my lonely pathway home that night,
> They have not left me (as my hopes have) since;
> They follow me—they lead me through the years.
> They are my ministers—yet I their slave.
> Their office is to illumine and enkindle-
> My duty, to be saved by their bright light,
> And purified in their electric fire,
> And sanctified in their elysian fire.
> They fill my soul with Beauty (which is Hope),
> And are far up in Heaven—the stars I kneel to
> In the sad, silent watches of my night;
> While even in the meridian glare of day
> I see them still—two sweetly scintillant
> Venuses, unextinguished by the sun!

Appendix A:
Lincoln: Uncertainty, Probabilities and the Census of 1850: A Speculative Essay

The number side of Lincoln came out when he first took the public stage, when he bridged uncertainties by using *probabilities*. The earliest uncertainty he publicly confronted was whether his grandfather had served in the Revolution. What he wanted he got through probabilities. Service in arms was the touchstone of gallant manhood for a Virginia planter whose blood—as his mother told him—was "as good as Washington's." To claim it for his unnamed and misty ancestor, and personally bask in a descendant's corollary pride, he executed a mathematical coup.

Before an audience in January, 1838, during his "Lyceum Speech," Lincoln labeled all present—including himself, grammatically—"legal inheritors." He crept up on claiming an ancestor who served during the Revolutionary War by his statistically justified premise that "nearly every adult male had been a participator in some of" the battles of the Revolution. Lincoln told those assembled to hear him that "a husband, a father, a son or a brother, a *living history was* to be found in every family." In short, as a new resident of Illinois's new capital, Lincoln introduced himself to people as a survivor of fighting kin of the Revolution standing among other surviving kin on the basis of—sheer probability.[1]

Twenty years later, when debating Stephen Douglas in Chicago in 1858, he used numbers to make another point. He had numbers to work with because in the 1850 U.S. Census, census takers counted persons who had "three-eighths to five-eighths black blood" as "mulattoes." Instructions to census takers in 1850 included these: "Be particularly careful to distinguish between blacks, mulattoes, quadroons, and octoroons. The word 'black' should be used to describe those persons who have three-fourths or more black blood; 'mulatto,' those persons who have from three-eighths to five-eighths black blood; 'quadroon,' those persons who have one-fourth black blood; and 'octoroon,' those persons who have one-eighth or any trace of black blood."[2]

In reply to Douglas, contrasting New Hampshire and Virginia, Lincoln limited himself to review relevant and chilling census figures. New Hampshire at the prior census (1850) had 184 so-called "mulattoes" while, Lincoln said in a long, teasing question, "In the Old Dominion—in the Democratic and aristocratic State of Virginia—there were a few more mulattoes than the census-takers found in New Hampshire. How many do you suppose there were? Seventy-nine thousand seven hundred and seventy-five—twenty-three thousand more than there were in all the free States!"[3]

Lincoln, a deep and logical thinker, did not share all of his thoughts. One thought in particular—that he may have had enslaved cousins, descendants of the same Virginia planter who was his grandfather, working in the nearby fields of Virginia—seems a likely part of his mental landscape, with consequent historic impact, given his compassion and sensitivity (Pixabay.com).

The enslaved of the 1850s included infants, their parents in their 20s and 30s, the infants' grandparents and a layer of living great grandparents. Accordingly, if a Virginia planter violently or by coercion forced himself upon an enslaved woman in the 1780s or thereafter, and these liaisons led to live births, when those babies grew up to reproduce, an increasingly larger group of enslaved so-called "mulatto" inhabitants of Virginia existed to be counted in 1850. It is not without irony that Lincoln, the grandson of a Virginia planter, paid particular attention to the 1850 census.

As if numbers were his best friends, his wizardry had come out early. Proof exists as a homemade arithmetic book. Sheets of then-rare, precious paper sewn together, preserved, and partly reprinted in *Collected Works*, demonstrate his early adolescent interest. He was figuring out numerical mysteries just as he began to read books and write intelligibly. He ciphered at least as often as he wrote as a young man. Lincoln studied in New Salem in his early twenties to be a surveyor—his first profession—and never ceased thereafter to be active in the pursuit of mathematics. After he married, Lincoln took on Euclid and worked his way through all twelve books of geometry, carrying them in a saddlebag when he rode circuit. In his forties, in his law office, to Herndon's consternation, Lincoln tried to "square the circle" for several intense days. That Lincoln likewise brought statistics into speeches as a strength he enjoyed flexing.[4]

In 1858, unlike 1838, he addressed the crowd without a hint of any personal application. Only with our greater scope of awareness from our perspective (after the Herndon revelation) can we discern something that his audience could not hear. Lincoln, a most logical man, teetered on the brink of claiming enslaved relatives. His own probabilities surrounded him. The official data of the census suggested—*without* proving—that his grandfather's blood circulated not only in him, and in his children, but also in persons enslaved in Virginia. What was sound reasoning in 1838 remained sound in 1858, but with this difference: it was not said aloud in 1858.

To his 1838 audience, Lincoln had floated a numerical and grammatical construct to support an implied claim of a Revolutionary soldier in arms in his family tree. That 1838 probability-based suggestion is missing in 1858 although Lincoln was most certainly aware of his grandfather as a rich, potent planter who took advantage of a young *white* woman. (He actually barely knew anything more about the man.) It follows that where consent was legally immaterial,—and children born of liaisons with enslaved women were reckoned by planters as so much additional valuable property—a lusty and potent enslaver was as likely to be tempted, if not more tempted, to take advantage of *Black* women. Lincoln chose no grammatical formula to hint at the most realistic result of these facts in combination: that he had enslaved half-uncles and half-aunts, born in about the 1780s, and descendant enslaved cousins.

Of course, what Lincoln hinted at implicitly in 1858, he doubtless knew long before. Planters and their "aristocratic" friends exercised a grotesque variant of *droit de seigneur*. Abolitionists documented serial rapes, a staple horror in the orations of most opponents of slavery. By entirely logical surmise, immersed in such data, Lincoln was necessarily less sure than most white men of his time that he did not have enslaved cousins whose labor, knowledge and skills were stolen from them.

The 1850 census was not his only moment of contemplating the unjustifiable loss of freedom. He pondered as well the unfairness of lighter people enslaving darker people. In an undated note of the 1850s, he seemed driven to write a cautionary note, as if aghast:

"If A. can prove, however conclusively, that he may, of right, enslave B.—why may not B. snatch the same argument, and prove equally, that he may enslave A?—You say A. is white, and B. is black. It is color, then; the lighter, having the right to enslave the darker? Take care. By this rule, you are to be slave to the first man you meet, with a fairer skin than your own. You do not mean color exactly?—You mean the whites are intellectually the superiors of the blacks, and, therefore have the right to enslave them? Take care again. By this rule, you are to be slave to the first man you meet, with an intellect superior to your own."[5]

Lincoln left his note unfinished. Was it, finally, too personal to finish? On its face, these expressions had no personal application. No direct claim was made. We know from it, however, that Lincoln mulled over the arbitrariness of slavery and of intellect not at different times but in the same sitting, his pen in hand—and that both factors carry a familial relevance. *Ergo*, if the planter whose blood and brain Lincoln himself inherited in his time had brilliant children of many hues, how unfair and arbitrary was life for these *relatives*. But Lincoln braved thinking through these facts only up to a point, with no personal or familial application.

This Appendix neither establishes that Lincoln *had* enslaved relatives nor that he did *not*, but only that he *may* well have thought that he *did*. Publicly, he limited himself to the census and made no allusions to his own grandfather in Virginia. The degree of probability that Lincoln had enslaved relatives is uncertain. He only knew with certainty and inferred from official statistics the general truth that with slavery came so-called "mulatto" children.

Lincoln, the unacknowledged grandson of a rich planter, could not escape the long shadow of these facts any easier than could acknowledged members of the first families of Virginia. The vision of kin who might be working the fields anywhere in the South may have tormented him, but Lincoln spoke of his torment only in general in a letter to a Kentucky planter who was his closest friend, Joshua Speed. To Speed Lincoln confided what the sight of enslaved people made him feel, and that "the great body of the Northern people do crucify their feelings" out of loyalty to the Constitution and Union. He said nothing to his best friend about a horror peculiar to him and his conscience personally.[6]

By limiting himself to the census and making no allusions to his grandfather, Lincoln nonetheless did not avoid Southern demagogues' attacks. They branded Lincoln as a friend of the enslaved and even caricatured him as Black. Lincoln never confided to paper or to any witness his feelings about this intended calumny, a surreal caricature that reflected a possible familial *truth.*

What Lincoln did publicly was to rise often to speak in opposition to the expansion of slavery, and to categorize slavery as an evil that had to be eradicated. Uncertain of all branches of his family tree, Lincoln found refuge in the certainty of the promise of the Declaration of Independence. He became familiar with and certain of the record of the founders on slavery, and certain of their consensus that slavery was on a course of extinction, which they welcomed. Upon this certain knowledge, Lincoln spoke about slavery publicly. That the existence of his promiscuous and potent Virginia planter grandfather suggested the strong possibility that he was himself part of a family half-free and half-slave is an idea that, if he thought, he kept solely to himself. If the thought had the power to make him miserable, he bit his lip and kept quiet.[7]

And yet, not only the 1850 census may have brought home that possibility, and not only in Lincoln's adulthood but back in his boyhood, when his mother was alive. Perhaps Lincoln had joked about the topic with his mother. One might relevantly compare and contrast Lincoln's reply to Douglas in 1858 against a young boy laughing with his mother in about 1818, playing with and mocking a patriarch he dubbed "Zebedee," by asking, "Who was the father of Zebedee's children?" with the implied answer, "Not Zebedee."

Is it possible that Lincoln's outwardly merry notes disguised a tragic *family* tune?

Is it possible that what mother and son shared in the weaving shed that day was actually *one layer deeper* than Dennis Hanks could have grasped?

When his mother called him a "nasty little pup," was it because Lincoln was teasing her about something that she had disclosed to him? Did he and she handle that day, albeit only remotely in the form of Biblical or literary parody, intellectual and intellectual-in-training, a painful and deeply sensitive family theme?

If so, Lincoln thus came up with a few words embodying the greatest of her father's offenses, the greatest of any father's offenses: at the weaving shed some forty years before his 1858 debate with Douglas and his remarks about Virginia census figures, he asked, in essence, when is a father no father?

Lincoln would grow up to take up on the debating stage such paternity as a serious and tragic aspect of slavery. He would speak again in different words in many future speeches to many audiences—that a father is no father when he fathers an enslaved child.

Of his own personal sense of a blood relationship with toilers in the fields who were treated by law as chattel, of a constant vicarious suffering under the whip of the master, of a vision founded firmly on numbers, logic and probability that his family lived on both ends of the spectrum that he spoke about when he hailed freedom and hectored slavery, he left the public (and us) without more clues than stated here.

Appendix B:
Lincoln's Schooling
(An Approximation)

AGE 5 (?)	October–December, 1814	Zachariah Riney
AGE 6 (?)	October–December, 1814, 1815	Caleb Hazel

NOTE: The first two teachers, in 1814 and 1815, were small "blab schools" or ABC reciting elementary classes conducted in Kentucky by part-time teachers who farmed for a living. Short terms were held each winter after the crops were harvested. Lincoln's first teacher was one of his best. Riney, a native of Maryland, and a Catholic who knew some Latin, was also one of the few schoolmasters who persisted in the profession for decades.

A LONG INTERRUPTION (WHEN RESETTLED IN INDIANA), FOLLOWED BY:

AGE 12–13	12 weeks (?)	October–December, 1814, 1821–22(?)	Andrew Crawford
AGE 13–15	12 weeks (?)	October–December, 1814, 1822–24(?)	Azel W. Dorsey
AGE 15–17	4 weeks (?)	October–December, 1814, 1824–26(?)	James Swaney

NOTE: HI 128, (John Oskins, September 16, 1865), (Oskins placed Lincoln's and his time with Swaney in 1826, when Lincoln would have been 17); HI, 121, (David Turnham, September 15, 1865), (Turnham's list of their Indiana teachers starts with Dorsey, then Crawford, both before 1826 [Sally Lincoln's wedding], and, last, Swaney); HI 28, (Dennis Hanks, June 8, 1865), ("Abraham went to school with his Sister Sally on Knobb Cr in Hardin Co Ky some 3 or 4 weeks when he was 6 or 7 years old—to

171

a man by the name of Hazel and he got about Six months Schooling while he lived in Indiana the teachers name not now recollected."); 4 C.W. 62, (Lincoln to John L. Scripps, *c.* 1860), Lincoln listed Crawford, "Sweeney" and Dorsey "successively" as his Indiana schoolmasters.

Dorsey, an entrepreneur and land speculator, left teaching for more lucrative pursuits and installed his apprentice-clerk, James Swaney, to teach after him. Swaney (whose first and last name Lincoln did not correctly recall), the youngest teacher he ever had, perhaps five years older than Lincoln, was probably the least trained or capable. Lincoln probably spent little time with Swaney. I believe that Lincoln correctly recalled Crawford as his first Indiana teacher, and that, interpolating Oskins and Turnham, as well as Lincoln's sputtering memory of Swaney, Dorsey's apprentice clerk, Swaney was his last.

A total of some thirty to forty weeks in classroom studies in the two states seems about right. Lincoln estimated "in aggregate less than a year." 4 C.W. 62 (Lincoln to John Scripps, *c.* June 1860).

(Besides this formal schooling, in time with monumental effort Lincoln taught himself grammar, surveying, Shakespeare's plays and the poetry of Robert Burns, memorized poetry, worked his way through the twelve books of geometry by Euclid, and read scientific treatises on various subjects, including lightning and electricity.)

Appendix C:
Lincoln's Early Encounters
with Enslaved Persons
and Statements About Slavery

Approximate Date	Event
1809–16	Living in Kentucky, site of many unrecorded but likely sightings of enslaved people
December(?), 1816	Move to Indiana "partly on account of slavery"
July(?), 1826	First trip to New Orleans; attack by seven enslaved men, permanent facial scar
Summer(?), 1827	Work on locks and canal in Louisville, a huge project including enslaved workers
March 1831	Second trip to New Orleans; possibly witnessed hanging of a runaway from enslavement
March 1837	Legislative protest in favor of Congressional power to restrict slavery
August 1841	Visit to Speed's plantation, Lincoln a sympathetic witness of enslaved persons on steamboat
February 1842	Temperance Address includes Lincoln's first public vision of a slavery-free world
January 1849	Lincoln authors bill to restrict slavery in District of Columbia
September 1854	Speech in Peoria against expansion of slavery, followed by many other addresses and official acts

Appendix D:
Lincoln's Campaigns
for Public Office

1832	Run for state legislature (loss)
1834	Run for state legislature (win)
1836	Run for state legislature (win)
1838	Run for state legislature (win)
1840	Illinois Elector for Whig ticket (loss)
1844	Campaigner for Whig ticket (win)
1848	Run for Congress (win)
1854	Run for United States Senate (loss)
1858	Run for United States Senate (loss)
1860	Run for President (win)
1864	Run for President (win)

Chapter Notes

Preface

1. Charles B. Strozier, *Lincoln's Quest for Union: Public and Private Meanings* (Chicago: University of Illinois Press, 2nd ed., 1987) (hereafter, "Strozier"). Strozier, a psychotherapist as well as a biographer, introduced the Virginia planter as historically significant almost forty years ago. "It seems that, as a child, Lincoln had worked out a rather elaborate genetic myth that both explained and nourished his separateness from his family and environment," *id.*, 8. Among many other contributions, Strozier raised the importance of Lincoln's mother's illegitimacy and of the long scholarly duel over Nancy's illegitimacy in opening his book, *id.*, 3–7. While not twins, his book and this one are at least distant cousins.

A Note on Method and Sources

1. Douglas L. Wilson and Rodney O. Davis, eds., *Herndon's Informants: Letters, Interviews, and Statements About Abraham Lincoln* (Chicago: University of Illinois Press, 1998) (hereafter "HI"), 256 (E.R. Burba, May 25, 1866). Quotes, including Burba's, are offered in standard English, with correct spelling and modern punctuation, except when a purpose is served by retaining unvarnished original wording or dialect.

2. Quotes drawn from Professor Gordon-Reed's groundbreaking article, "Rebellious History," *New York Review of Books* (October 22, 2020); no endorsement by Professor Gordon-Reed of views in this book ought to be inferred.

Chapter 1

1. Strozier, 3. His first chapter carefully sorted out what was known about Lincoln's mother, what was unknown, and what Lincoln believed. It was especially by developing the last that Professor Strozier so markedly advanced the field of Lincoln studies.

2. HI 5 (John Hanks, May 25, 1865), 37 (Dennis Hanks, June 13, 1865), 454 (John Hanks, c. 1865–66).

3. HI, 113 (Nathaniel Grigsby, September 12, 1865).

4. William E. Barton, *The Paternity of Abraham Lincoln* (Vol. 2), 340, which may be viewed online at http://www.ebooksread.com/authors-eng/william-e-barton-theodore-g-soares-and-sydney-strong/the-paternity-of-abraham-lincoln-volume-2-tra/page-28. Accessed 8/3/2017.

5. CAUTION: My goal is a modest one: to demonstrate and to follow, as closely as the record permits, the links between Lincoln and certain "flesh of his flesh and blood of his blood," namely, his mother and her father, whom Lincoln once personally characterized as keys to who he was and all that he ever hoped to be. What I am attempting to present is a family story. Although many of Lincoln's speeches are quoted and enslaved people are referred to, along with the Constitution and the Civil War, this is not a complete analysis of Lincoln's speeches, a book about slavery, or a treatise on the Constitution, its flaws or the causes of the war. Nor does this book track the centuries-long American dialogue about race, slavery and equality by state, by

district, in Congress, in the churches, by politician, party, group or individual. For one example, the contradictions and limits of Thomas Jefferson's attitudes and positions on these yet burning topics fall beyond the scope of this short book. No reader looking for full coverage of these subjects will find it here. This book is likewise far too limited to follow in any detail Lincoln's complex and circuitous journey to the Emancipation Proclamation. Doctoral theses and of a host of scholarly books already exist on this worthy and inexhaustible subject. I devote a single chapter to the moment Lincoln signed the proclamation, and what a contemporary document suggests may have been in his mind on that occasion, when he gave no address. The beginning and the end of this story is how each of these two ancestors influenced Lincoln to see "the wrong of slavery" and to clarify "the rights of man." No one should draw broader implications. For example, that Lincoln repeatedly evangelized Jefferson's purported promise of equality and his 1776 list of inalienable rights is historical fact proven here, as distinct from any implication that Lincoln's view of Jefferson is historically accurate. (Historically, we know that, during the delegates' sparring over the wording of the Declaration of Independence, Jefferson's attack on chattel slavery was left on the cutting room floor. To grapple with Lincoln's shifting emphases and interpretations of the positions of the founders, I yield the floor to Harold Bloom. *The Anxiety of Influence: A Theory of Poetry* (New York: Oxford University Press, 1973, 2nd ed., 1997), explains how later authors practice so-called "creative misreading" in order to clear "imaginative space" around earlier authors who would otherwise block them from thriving in their time.) Now, on with the story—of Lincoln and two of his ancestors.

6. HI 36–37 (Dennis Hanks, June 13, 1865)("Slavery did not operate on him," i.e., upset Tom; but he "could beat his son telling a story—cracking a joke"), 96 (A.H. Chapman, September 8, 1865)(Tom Lincoln was "very fond of a Joke or story & of telling them"), 145 (Harriet A. Chapman,

December 17, 1865) (Tom "Walked rather Slow never seemed to be in a hurry").

7. Douglas L. Wilson and Rodney O. Davis, eds., *Herndon on Lincoln, Letters* (Chicago: University of Illinois Press, 2016) (hereafter "LL"), 129 (William H. Herndon, November 24, 1882). All but unanimously, reliable informants described Nancy Hanks as thin. Conversely, Sarah seems to have been proportionally fleshed or, in Herndon's phrase, "finely developed and buxom." LL, 203 (William H. Herndon, January 19, 1886); HI 68 (Samuel Haycraft, June 1865) ("Her mother thought she was too proud, simply because the poor girl tried to make herself look decent and keep in the fashion of that early day.")

8. Chapter 8 covers Nancy teaching her cousin, a released Indian captive, in weaving and in English.

9. HI, 613 (Robert L. Wintersmith, March 23, 1887).

10. Roy P. Basler, ed., *Abraham Lincoln: His Speeches and Writings* (New York: The World Publishing Co., 1946), 6.

11. Roy P. Basler, ed., *The Collected Works of Abraham Lincoln* (New Brunswick, NJ: Rutgers University Press, 1953) (hereafter "C.W."), 1 C.W. 6.; Robert Havlik, "Some Influences of Thomas Paine's Age of Reason Upon Abraham Lincoln," *Lincoln Herald*, 104 (Summer, 2002), 61–70; Michael Burlingame, *Abraham Lincoln: A Life*, Vol. 2 (Baltimore: Johns Hopkins University Press, 2008), 83.

12. Thomas Paine, *The Rights of Man* (1791).

13. Thomas Paine, *Common Sense* (1776). HI 171–72 (Abner Y. Ellis, January 23, 1866) ("I think he read some of Tom Paine's works as he frequently spoke of Paine's *Common Sense*."

14. Eric Foner, *Tom Paine and Revolutionary America* (2005) Oxford University Press, 2nd edition, xxxii. Graham fell into the pro–Southern camp of Kentuckians.

15. 4 C.W. 61–62. ("This removal was partly on account of slavery; but chiefly on account of the difficulty in land titles in Ky.")

16. Lincoln in his adulthood had a recurring dream that he viewed as ominous. Upon awakening from it, he always

expected news of a battle or of some other important event. Lincoln described the dream to cabinet members and a reporter for the New York Herald, in which he "seemed to be on some singular, indiscernible vessel ... moving with great rapidity towards an indefinite shore." Ward Hill Lamon, Recollections of Abraham Lincoln, 1847–1865, (Lincoln: University of Nebraska reprint, 1994), 118–19. The family's move to faraway Indiana, into the unknown wilderness, required a trip on a large ferry across the broad Ohio River. Seven-year-old Lincoln's first stomach-tightening voyage— and the reasons for it, partly on account of slavery—may have never left him.

17. 7 C.W. 281 (Lincoln to A.G. Hodges, April 4, 1864) ("I am naturally anti-slavery. If slavery is not wrong, nothing is wrong. I cannot remember when I did not so think, and feel.")

18. HL, 100 (William H. Herndon, March 6, 1870). See Chapter 5.

Chapter 2

1. 3 C.W., 511 (Abraham Lincoln to Jesse W. Fell, December 20, 1859).

2. *Ibid.*; HI, 23 (John Hill, June 6, 1865), HI, 39–40 (Dennis Hanks, June 13, 1865).

3. Strozier, 9; also, Harrison, 18 (Nancy "could read" and she possessed "an excellent memory and could recite long prayers and Bible passages to her children."); the literacy controversy will never be resolved to universal satisfaction, but the gray area of *functional* literacy exists, if Nancy read, but not well. HI 615 (John Hanks, June 12, 1887) (of Tom Lincoln that "he could read little, he could not write"). This may explain why her children were sent to school to learn their letters. Scarce money was paid to learn the alphabet when Sally was eight and her brother was six. Even so, the "slow" boy left Kentucky without reading. At nearly eight years old, he had only "acquired the alphabet." (This was in a text that Lincoln proofread and let stand in 1860. Harrison, 25); HI 37 (Dennis Hanks, June 13, 1865).

4. See chapter 5.

5. See HI 107 (Sally Bush Lincoln, September 8, 1865) ("he never lost that fact or his understanding of it... He would hear sermons preached—come home—take the children out—got on a stump or log and almost repeat it word for word.") HL 162 (William H. Herndon, November 12, 1885) ("he was intensely thoughtful—persistent—fearless and tireless in thinking. When he got a thought—fact—principle—question he ran it down to the fibers of the tap root—dug it out; and held it up before him for an analysis...")

6. Matthew 4:21.

7. Luke 5:4.

8. HI 37 (Dennis Hanks, June 13, 1865). Dennis Hanks, born ten years before Lincoln, was a waif taken in by a married aunt, Elizabeth (Hanks) Sparrow, and her husband, Thomas Sparrow. When the Sparrows both died of the "milk sick" during the same summer that Nancy Hanks Lincoln died, then–19-year-old Dennis moved in with the remaining Lincolns. Richard Lawrence Miller, *Lincoln and His World; The Early Years, Birth to Illinois Legislature* (Mechanicsville, PA: Stackpole Books, 2006) (hereafter "Miller"), 44.

9. The door may have been propped open or the shed may have had a window. The existence of a "weaving shed" in use helps date the joke to 1818, the year Lincoln turned nine. A weaving shed (presumably, the loom inside as well) would have been completed only after the land had been cleared, crops sown, the main cabin built and furnished, a privy dug and set up, and, probably, Tom's own work shed for carpentry, if not a barn as well. This would reasonably have taken most of 1817. Given cold and limited sunlight, Nancy would have been using her weaving shed in the spring or summer of 1818 at the earliest. The two words "weaving shed" likewise imply Tom's care for his wife. For Tom, a slow man on his best day, to build this weaving shed was no small task. But the weaving shed was, as Virginia Woolf visualized, "a room of her own" for Nancy. Besides, the weaving place was a sanctuary. It replicated the cherished space where she had excelled from childhood in fabric work, spinning

and weaving, and where she had once taught her beloved cousin, Sarah Mitchell. Lincoln may have counted on his mother, ahead of anywhere else or any other time, being in a good mood and receptive to his homemade joke at work in her weaving shed.

10. I go by the weaving shed story as originally told by Dennis Hanks, which ended in mutual laughter as follows: "One day when Lincoln's mother was weaving in a little shed, Abe came in and quizzically asked his good mother, 'Who was the father of Zebedee's children?' She saw the drift and laughed saying, 'Get out of here you nasty little pup, you.' He saw he had got his mother and ran off laughing." HI, 37 (Dennis Hanks, June 13, 1865). By comparison, Jesse Weik's summary notes (made around 1886) concluded with Nancy irritated, "Abe ran in room while old lady was weaving at window and asked Mother who was father of Zebidie's children—this fretted old lady." (Dennis Hanks, c. 1886?)

11. Eleanor Atkinson, *The Boyhood of Lincoln* (New York: Doubleday, Page & Co., 1908) (hereafter, "Atkinson"), 35. The use of Atkinson's 1908 book, *Lincoln's Boyhood*, by historians and Lincoln biographers has been stinting because Atkinson became a well-known novelist. However, she originally trained as a schoolteacher and went into journalism in Chicago. The book derives from articles published in the *Chicago Tribune*, January 28, 1889, 1, which reasonably establishes the fact that she did interview Dennis Hanks at length in his home. Her book's format, including dialect, brought out the folksy character of the interviewee much as in a novel. When scrutinized, though, her factual content is consistent with the vast majority of other sources and informants on points covered. Her book is only slightly more expansive than her articles and what is new was peripheral. For example, neither his mother's stories of Washington nor her statement about his blood were sensational or ground-breaking from Atkinson's perspective).

12. 1 C.W. 265 (Abraham Lincoln to Joshua F. Speed, January (3?), 1842).

13. Professor Strozier in his book demonstrated that Lincoln spent his life to create in the Union the complete family which he had never had. A related nuance may be raised: was it *his mother's* dream of a family uniting or rescue by her father that spawned her son's desire for close group connection? Fragmentary evidence remains only that she employed her father, idealized, to inspire her son's ambitions and his pursuit of learning.

Chapter 3

1. David Herbert Donald, *Lincoln* (New York: Simon & Schuster, 1995), 19; Michael Birmingham, *Abraham Lincoln: A Life* (Baltimore: Johns Hopkins University Press, 2009); Bunn to Henry S. Pritchett, n.p., January 12, 1905, SC210 (copy), Ihi.

2. HI 57 (John W. Scripps letter to Herndon, June 24, 1865); Herndon's *Life of Lincoln, The True Story of a Great American Life* (Chicago: Belton, Clark & Co., 1889) (hereafter "HL"), 15.

3. HL 16. See also Chapter 5.

4. See this chapter below, an 1858 speech especially.

5. Atkinson, 8.

6. E.g., Miller, 4; HI 95 (A.H. Chapman, *ante* September 8, 1865).

7. Lincoln wrote to cousin Jesse Lincoln that "the story of [Abraham Lincoln's] death by the Indians, and of Uncle Mordecai, then fourteen years old, killing one of the Indians, is the legend more strongly than [most prominent of] all others imprinted upon my mind and memory." 2 C.W. 217 (Abraham Lincoln to Jesse Lincoln, April 1, 1854).

8. LL 173 (WHH to editor of Religio-Philosophical Journal, December 4, 1885) ("He has said to me more than once, 'Billy, I feel as if I shall meet with some terrible end.'"); Strozier, 28–29, posited nights of fear and "emotionally laden" moments that Lincoln long carried in memory, possibly aggravated by incomplete or interrupted mourning after his mother's death.

9. Besides a will Lincoln drafted for a client, he used the word "grandson" in exactly three writings of his own, only

once identifying himself as the grandson of Abraham Lincoln in an 1854 letter to Jesse Lincoln, and in two letters before and after his Gettysburg Address. He delivered the Address on November 19, 1863. He referred to a grandson status in requests for favors to two young men. The last occasion was a letter for a West Point applicant on November 20, 1863. A slightly earlier letter simultaneously *notes the grandson's ancestor as a memorialized name*: "Executive Mansion, Washington, Hon. Secretary of Treasury: October 26, 1863. My Dear Sir: The writer of the accompanying letter is one of Mrs. L[incoln]'s numerous cousins. He is a grandson of Millikin's Bend, near Vicksburg—that is, a grandson of the man who gave name to Millikin's Bend. His father was a brother to Mrs. L's mother. I know not a thing about his loyalty beyond what he says. Supposing he is loyal, can any of his requests be granted? and, if any, which of them? Yours truly, A. LINCOLN."

10. Atkinson, 18–19.

11. 1 C.W. 1 (copybook verses, c. 1824–26).

12. 4 C.W. 61 (Lincoln to John L. Scripps, c. June, 1860).

13. HI 197 (Joshua Speed, February 7, 1866).

14. *Ibid.*

15. *Ibid.* This powerful fear remained even after he regained control of himself. In 1863, Lincoln referred to their conversation when Speed visited him at the White House. Also, Lincoln wondered aloud gloomily once to Herndon in a similar vein, saying, "How hard, oh, how hard it is to die and leave one's country no better than if one had never lived for it. The world is dead to hope, deaf to its own death struggles, made known by a universal cry. What is to be done? Is anything to be done? Who can do anything and how can it be done? *Did you ever think of these things?*" (emphasis supplied) (WHH to Ward Hill Lamon, March 6, 1870).

16. HI 48 (John B. Helm, June 20, 1865).

17. 3 C.W. 499 (Lincoln speech in Chicago, July 10, 1858).

18. *Ibid.*

19. "We hold this annual celebration to remind ourselves of all the good done in this process of time of how it was done and who did it, and how we are historically connected with it; and we go from these meetings in better humor with ourselves—we feel more attached the one to the other, and more firmly bound to the country we inhabit. In every way we are better men in the age, and race, and country in which we live for these celebrations." *Ibid.*

20. *Ibid.*

21. *Ibid.*, 500.

22. All but one of the Presidential candidates Lincoln supported were sons of Virginia planters. See footnote 268.

23. See chapter 11, section 6.

24. *New York Tribune*, July 26, 1885, 3; quoted in Burlingame, *The Inner World of Lincoln* (Chicago: University of Illinois Press, 1997), 237.

Chapter 4

1. 1 C.W. 455 (Lincoln to Solomon Lincoln, March 6, 1848), 1 C.W. 459 (Lincoln to David Lincoln, March 24, 1848), 1 C.W. 459 (Lincoln to Solomon Lincoln, March 24, 1848), and 1 C.W. 461 (Lincoln to David Lincoln, April 2, 1848). He also replied at 2 C.W. 217 to Jesse Lincoln (Lincoln to Jesse Lincoln, April 1, 1854), and at 4 C.W. 37, Lincoln to Richard Lincoln, April 6, 1860) and at 4 C.W. 117 (Lincoln to John Chrisman, September 21, 1860). Besides this family tree correspondence, Lincoln unavoidably used "grandfather" in two business letters and in the outlines of his life for campaign biography. (To explain that he had been named for his "paternal grandfather.") The sole casual use of the word occurred at 4 C.W. 131 (Lincoln to David Turham, October 23, 1860) ("I suppose you are a grandfather.")

2. 4 C.W. 60–67 (Lincoln to John L. Scripps, c. June 1860).

3. 1 C.W. 9 (Lincoln to the people of Sangamon County, March 9, 1832).

4. LL 43–44 (WHH to Caroline Healy Dall, November 30, 1866), *n*1 and text.

5. Douglas Wilson, "Keeping Lincoln's Secrets," article in *The Atlantic* (May 2000).

6. At the author's request, Richmond County native and local historian Jay Garner kindly summarized the situation that would have greeted Lincoln, had he visited in 1848. No legend or local lore suggests that Lincoln did so. (As noted, many of this book's illustrations are courtesy of Mr. Garner.)

7. Griffin Murdock Fauntleroy and Elisha Lingan Hall, as well as planter Richard Beale, have been suggested by Paul Verduin, the dean of experts on Lincoln's antecedents. Michael Burlingame, in his *Lincoln: A Life*, vol. 1, Chapter One, noted, "Paul H. Verduin, 'New Evidence Suggests Lincoln's Mother Born in Richmond County, Virginia, Giving Credibility to the Planter-Grandfather Legend,' *Northern Neck of Virginia Historical Magazine* 38 (1988): 4354–89, and 'Plantation Overseers, Patriots, Pioneers: New Light on Lincoln and His Hanks Forbears,' unpublished paper delivered at the Lincoln Home, Springfield, 12 February 1992." An interesting omnibus article gathering and comparing several conflicting theories is Christopher Challender Child's "The Maternal Ancestry of Abraham Lincoln; The Origins of Nancy (Hanks) Lincoln; A Study in Appalachian Genealogy," *New England Ancestors*, Vol. 4, No. 1 (Winter, 2003), 25–29, 55. Various family tree charts (of which there are five) feature Joseph Hanks, Abraham Hanks, Griffin Murdock Fauntleroy, Elisha Lingan Hall, Thomas Hanks, and James Hanks as possible "Virginia planters."

8. 3 C.W. 116 (Stephen Douglas in Jonesboro, September 15, 1858).

9. *Ibid.*, 117 (Lincoln in Jonesboro, September 15, 1858).

10. *Ibid.*

11. HL 15.

Chapter 5

1. See LL 195 (WHH to Jesse W. Weik, January 10, 1886). Dennis Hanks said that Lincoln "took his disposition and mental qualities from his mother." HI 598 (Dennis Hanks, c. 1886?)

2. Herndon wrote, in different letters, concerning the year, without being certain. See LL 100, 118, 246, 283; also, Lincoln and Mary lost their youngest son, their treasured, bright four-year-old Eddy, in early 1850. In early 1851, Tom Lincoln, his father, died at 73. Soon afterward, Mary's grandmother died, with whom Mary had been close after her own mother died young and her stepmother proved difficult. Around the time of their ride to the Menard County courthouse, Herndon described Lincoln as "sad, gloomy, hopeless," and "soured." HL 100. In addition, political progressives like Lincoln had no future. Herndon summarized that Lincoln's "hope and fame were at their lowest ebb. The compromise measures of 1850 had apparently sealed the fate of the slave forever, and there seemed to him no hope of doing good to his fellow-man." LL 118.

3. 3 C.W. 511 (Lincoln autobiography for J.W. Fell, December 20, 1859) ("absolutely nothing to excite the ambition for education").

4. HI 497 (Robert B. Rutledge, December 4, 1866) (on Lincoln's habit of writing whole pages of books to fix what he read in his mind); HI 499 (Joshua Speed, December 6, 1866) (on his mind as a "piece of steel.")

5. LL 155 (WHH to Isaac N. Arnold, October 24, 1883); *Id.*, 246 (WHH to Truman Bartlett, June 24, 1887); letter from William H. Herndon to Wendell Phillips, May 12, 1857, Wendell Phillips Papers, Houghton Library Harvard University, cited in HL, xix; F.B. Carpenter, *Six Months in the White House* (New York: Current Literature Publishing Co., 1907), 283–84.

6. These fragments derive from an 1866 pen portrait quoted in David Donald's *Lincoln's Herndon* (New York: Alfred A. Knopf, 1948), 234.

7. Douglas Wilson, "Keeping Lincoln's Secrets," *Atlantic Monthly* (May 2000), 78; LL 158 (WHH to Jesse W. Weik, October 21, 1885).

8. HL 100, 294.

9. HL 100.

10. *Ibid.*

11. William H. Herndon and Jesse Weik, eds., Douglas L. Wilson and Rodney O.

Notes—Chapter 6

Davis, *Herndon's Lincoln: The True Story of a Great Life* (Chicago: University of Illinois Press, 2006), xxviii, 130.

12. One of Herndon's most thorough discussions of Lincoln's fatalist beliefs is contained in LL 208–210 (WHH to Joseph Fowler, February 18, 1886).

13. LL 100 (WHH to Ward Hill Lamon, March 6, 1870); published in the first edition of Herndon's biography, with Jesse Weik, HL 16.

14. LL 117 (WHH to Caroline Healy Dall, March 3, 1874) ("Mr. Lincoln told me himself that his mother was an illegitmate (*sic*), but was very, very intellectual."); HL 16 ("broad-minded, unknown Virginian"). Broad-mindedness was an element of Nancy's make-up, too. LL 264 (WHH to Truman Bartlett, October 1887) (Nancy Hanks Lincoln was "a broad minded—liberal—generous-hearted—quickly sympathetic woman ... Lincoln himself told me much of this description of his mother.")

15. LL 68 (WHH to Charles H. Hart, March 2, 1867) (*emphasis in the original*).

16. Lincoln's Presidential ambitions were in play so long before 1851 that allusion to them would not be anachronistic but 1851, a year of political sidelines, was a surprising year to vest any hope in them. What Lincoln only implied, that he took "increased devotion" to an imperishable cause from honored dead, would climactically flower in the Gettysburg Address. One may even here it encapsulated in a pun—that the living be "dedicated" (dead-i-cated). Lincoln, if anybody, was deadicated; one of his few preserved poems included the line "I'm living in the tombs." 1 C.W. 368 (Lincoln to Andrew Johnston, February 25(?), 1846).

17. LL 100 (WHH to Ward Hill Lamon, March 6, 1870).

18. HL 310. ("I have heard him say it a dozen or more times.") (WHH to Jesse W. Weik, January 23, 1890).

19. LL 294 (WHH to Jesse W. Weik, January 4, 1889).

20. HL 16.

21. LL 283 (WHH to Joseph Fowler, October 30, 1888).

22. LL 37 (WHH to Isaac N. Arnold, November 20, 1866); *Id.*, 47 (WHH to David L. Cronyn, December 3, 1866).

23. HL, xxxiv, Editors' Introduction.

24. HL 16. That day, as soon as another traveler rode up beside them, Lincoln, reanimated, told stories and enjoyed entertaining reminiscences in turn. *Id.*, 17.

Chapter 6

1. Clippings of articles from *New York Herald* (August 13, 1860), and an edited, shorter form of the same in the *Chicago Press & Tribune* (August 15, 1860). (Enlarged microfiche copies of each courtesy of National Archives).

2. Michael Burlingame, ed., *Lincoln's Journalist, John Hay's Anonymous Writings for the Press, 1860–1864* (Carbondale: Southern Illinois University Press, 1998).

3. Clipping of article from *New York Herald* (August 13, 1860), and an edited, shorter form of the same in the *Chicago Press & Tribune* (August 15, 1860).

4. *Ibid.*

5. Jay Garner, a local historian of Richmond County during the Revolutionary period, provided the author with a tantalizing account of a potential link between anti-slavery Baptists and the Hanks family while living in that county, through and just after the birth of Nancy Hanks: "In the case of Joseph Hanks, he was a plantation overseer for William Peachey in Sharps for many years starting in 1761. He also was later an overseer for the widow Mrs. Frances Webb (who lived near the Hanks family residence) in the 1770s, and then finally for Fauntleroy and Beale in 1782. Hanks had trouble getting paid by Webb in 1773 so he filed a suit against her, and in 1782, Fauntleroy and Beale both failed to pay him and again he was forced to take court actions for payment. "In the 1770s, several religious meetings were held by the Baptist in lower Richmond County. These groups held meetings in secret in various believer's homes. The early Baptists preached the autonomous doctrine of the faith and used it to argue against slavery. By 1782, an anti-slavery movement within the state had gained enough traction that the Virginia General

Notes—Chapter 6

Assembly passed the 'Act to Authorize the Manumission of Slaves.' This law allowed freedom to the enslaved without having to ask for government approval. Additionally, the local Baptists found a major supporter in the form of Hannah Lee Corbin (Hall) when she moved to Woodberry, a manor house near the confluence of the Rappahannock River and Farnham Creek. Hannah openly encouraged 'free thinkers' to hear the Baptist message at her house and several large meetings were held there. The meetings at Hannah's started to bring in other prominent local colonial leaders, such as Robert Carter III of Nomini Hall in neighboring Westmoreland County. Carter had served for two decades on the Virginia Governor's Council—the upper house of the Virginia colonial government that consisted of 12 men appointed by the King of England to advise the governor—and had considerable land holdings. Carter attended several of the Baptist meetings at Woodberry (as it is documented in his diary on record at Duke University) and in 1791, he undertook one of the largest manumission efforts by a single individual in pre–Civil War Virginia. Carter eventually freed all of his 500 enslaved persons by his act. It is widely believed that the Hanks family converted to the Baptist faith around 1780 and heard many of the same sermons that Carter heard against the institution of slavery. Therefore, with Joseph Hanks being frustrated by plantation owners not paying him for his services, coupled with his new-found Baptist religion that promoted free thinking, personal accountability to God, and anti-slavery, it would seem the seed for slavery abolition within the Hanks family may have started in our small remote area of the Northern Neck of Virginia."

6. Harold Holzer, Craig L. Symonds and Frank J. Williams, eds., *Exploring Lincoln: Great Historians Reappraise Our Greatest President* (New York: Fordham University Press, 2015), 10 ("Lincoln's Role in the 1860 Presidential Campaign" by William C. Harris.) On that relaxed evening in his home, Lincoln cited neither published documents nor firsthand knowledge. Although his engagement with Southerners and Southern leaders was spotty, it was not non-existent. Born and raised until age seven in Kentucky, and as a young man twice a visitor on business to New Orleans, where he seems to have attended an auction of enslaved persons (if not also the hanging of two fugitives from slavery), he visited Joshua Speed's hemp plantation outside Louisville, Kentucky, in 1841. He also spent two years in Washington, D.C., which included an auction block where enslaved persons were bought and sold, where the seizure of a fugitive from slavery once occurred at Mrs. Spriggs's boarding house while he lived there, and where he heard and met Southern leaders like Alexander Stephens, who embodied the cultured Southern gentleman and once moved Lincoln to tears. ("I just take up my pen to say, that Mr. Stephens of Georgia, a little slim, pale-faced, consumptive man, with a voice like Logan's has just concluded the very best speech, of an hour's length, I ever heard. My old, withered, dry eyes, are full of tears yet," Lincoln wrote to Herndon on February 2, 1848, 1 C.W. 448.) Stephens, Clay, Calhoun and other Southern men co-existed with him under the large American sky. For Lincoln, it was as if he drew a tempered approach from his sense of being the grandson he was of a Virginia planter. Only in this *family*-centered interview did Lincoln allege a broadly shared secret "abhorrence" of slavery in "many" Southerners. (Parenthetically, Lincoln's admiration for conflicted Henry Clay, who owned over a hundred enslaved and was the founding president of the American Colonization Society, tends in this direction. But Lincoln's best friend, an enslaver, Joshua Speed, felt no abhorrence and vigorously defended slavery.)

7. Conflicted enslavers existed. One of the best documented among the founders was George Wythe, a Virginia judge for whom Lincoln's "beau ideal" of a statesman, Henry Clay, clerked at age fifteen. Wythe, an early mentor of Thomas Jefferson and a signer of the Declaration of Independence, hired back as workers some of the enslaved whom he freed. See Joyce Blackburn, *George Wythe of Williamsburg*

(New York: Harper & Row, 1975), 114, 123–27. Wythe also held in one case that Virginia's Declaration of Rights included Blacks among "all men" being born free and equal, although his ruling did not survive appeal. *Biography of George Wythe,* Colonial Williamsburg website, Colonial Williamsburg Foundation, http://www.history.org/almanack/people/bios/biowythe.cfm, accessed 4/13/2018.

8. Lincoln did condemn so-called "breeders" or traders whom he saw as irredeemably evil, but this was a demonization licensed by Southerners themselves, whom (he felt and said) despised the class, too. See 2 C.W. 322 (Lincoln to Joshua Speed, August 24, 1855).

Chapter 7

1. 1 C.W. 279 (Lincoln's "Temperance Address," February 22, 1842).

2. 5 C.W. 319. (Abraham Lincoln to Border State Representatives, July 12, 1862).

3. 6 C.W. 65 (*Note,* quoting from resolution of Manchester citizens, January 1, 1863).

4. 6 C.W. 63 (Lincoln to the Workingmen of Manchester, England, January 19, 1863).

Chapter 8

1. HL 22. Interestingly, one gush of exposition of his mother was triggered by his *father's* death. LL 309 (WHH to James Wilson, October 15, 1889) ("Mr. Lincoln himself said to me in 1851, on receiving the news of his father's death, that whatever might be said of his parents, and however unpromising the early surroundings of his mother may have been, she was highly intellectual by nature, had a strong memory, acute judgment, and was cool and heroic.")

2. *Ibid.,* 84 (WHH to Ward Hill Lamon, February 25, 1870).

3. Besides Graham's report, weaving and teaching weaving, see

4. HI 63 (John T. Stuart interview, late June 1865); 7 C.W. 512 (Lincoln to Indiana volunteers, August 22, 1864).

5. 7 C.W. 512 (Lincoln to Indiana volunteers, August 22, 1864).

6. HL 16. ("He said, among other things, that she was the illegitimate daughter of Lucy Hanks and a well-bred Virginia farmer or planter ... broadminded, unknown Virginian."); (NOTE: HL 416, *n*66, "'The content and interpretation in the Herndon-Weik biography was Herndon's; the composition was largely Weiks' (Donald, Lincoln's Herndon, 318). As noted above and elsewhere, the editors of the present edition, while in basic agreement, would qualify somewhat both parts of Donald's conclusion.")

7. For the 1860 interview, see Chapter Six.

8. A.M. Jukic, D.D. Baird, C.R. Weinberg, Dr. McConnaughey, A.J. Wilcox, "Length of human pregnancy and contributors to its natural variation," *Human Reproduction,* Vol. 28, Issue 10, 2848–55 (October 2013). https://doi.org/10.1093/humrep/det297.

9. Nancy's birthdate enjoys a consensus, but it is not completely unchallenged. It matters because if Nancy was actually born a year or two earlier, the furlough theory collapses, and some weak circumstantial evidence does indicate that Nancy was born in 1782 or 1783. That is, in 1782, Lucy's serious and responsible father, a farmer and the overseer of two adjacent plantations alternately, scouted for land in the west. That year he found a new place suitable for his family, a hundred miles west of Richmond County. Some scholars infer that Joseph Hanks needed distance in 1782 in order to protect his family from stinging gossip about his wayward young daughter and harsh criticism of himself as a supposedly irresponsible father.

Scholars who infer that the Hanks family's move was economically driven hold stronger cards. They conclude from official records that Joseph Hanks's services were much in demand, but enslavers were not speedy payers. Richmond County court records show that Hanks sometimes had to sue for his salary. These scholars conclude that the patriarch of a large family wanted to move in order to work for his more reliable self. In context, a lot of people of that time did move west for their own betterment. There is, moreover, no evidence that there *was* any scandalous talk about the Hanks family in Richmond County.

By 1784, everything was ready for a move to the land Joseph Hanks had claimed in 1782 in what is today Mineral County, West Virginia. Joseph soon moved his family even farther west, to Kentucky. For no documented reason, the idea of Kentucky appealed to Joseph Hanks more than whatever he found in Mineral Springs. See also Paul H. Verduin, "New Evidence Suggests Lincoln's Mother Born in Richmond County, Virginia, Giving Credence to Planter-Grandfather Legend," *Northern Neck of Virginia Historical Magazine* (December, 1988), Vol. 38, No. 1, 4354–89.

10. HI 779, Appendix, "Brief Outline of the Joseph Hanks Family," by Paul H. Verduin is the best-researched and most detailed chronology of Nancy Hanks and her relatives. Every scholar owes Mr. Verduin for this solid foundation.

11. Lincoln's disclosures to Herndon would stand as his own invention or fantasies if they did not relate back to Nancy. She is posited as the first spinner of Lucy's incarnation as the trickster thief.

12. See Miller, 10, for a concise and realistic narrative of Nancy's situation.

13. Louis Austin Warren, *Lincoln's Parentage and Childhood, A History of the Kentucky Lincolns Supported by Documentary Evidence* (New York: The Century Co., 1926), 65. Mrs. Vawter was said to be a granddaughter of Sarah Mitchell. *Id.*, 66. See this chapter, section 7.

14. LL 280 (WHH to Jesse W. Weik, October 8, 1888).

15. LL 307 (WHH to James H. Wilson, October 1, 1889).

16. LL 100 (WHH to Ward Hill Lamon, March 6, 1870); Atkinson, 17–18.

17. Miller, 11, summarized, "Nancy's physical appearance is lost; tall or short, fat or thin, color of hair or eyes—all are forgotten." The sole issue I take with Miller is based upon near unanimity and emphatic statements that she was thin or slender. See note 111.

18. HI 403 (David Turnham, November 19, 1866); 4 C.W. 209 (Lincoln to

crowd in Pittsburgh, Pennsylvania, February 14, 1861).

19. HI 5 (John Hanks, May 25, 1865) ("spare delicate frame"); *Id.*, 37 (Dennis Hanks, c. June, 1865) ("spare made"); *Id.*, 94 (Nathaniel Grigsby, September 4, 1865) ("medium size"); *Id.*, 403 (David Turnham, November 19, 1866) ("more spare made than otherwise").

20. Miller, 11; HI 635 (Henry C. Whitney, August 29, 1887).

21. See an essential document, the fruit of countless hours of often tedious research, the Appendix of *Herndon's Informants*, at HI 779, "Brief Outline of the Joseph Hanks Family," by Paul H. Verduin. With a few minutes' study, much becomes clear about Nancy Hanks's chaotic world and moves among households (Joseph Hanks, Henry Sparrow, Thomas Sparrow, probably others) until her incorporation into the stable home of Richard Berry in about her mid-teens.

22. HI 82 (WHH to Ward Hill Lamon, February 24, [1870]) ("Mr. Lincoln told me himself that his mother was a bastard—a child of a Virginia nabob."); HL 83 (WHH to Ward Hill Lamon, February 25, 1870) ("In the first place Lincoln himself told me that his mother was a bastard.")

23. Warren, 64–70.

24. HI 585 (Mrs. C.S.H. Vawter, February 20, 1874).

25. *Ibid.*, 584–86 (Mrs. C.S.H. Vawter, February 20, 1874).

26. Nancy Stark Jorgensen, an artist and accomplished weaver familiar with all stages of the processes described helped me (with limitless patience on her part) get this technology right. Thanks, Nancy!

27. 1 C.W. 456 (Lincoln to Solomon Lincoln, March 6, 1848) ("Owing to my father being left an orphan at the age of six years, in poverty, and in a new country, he became a wholly uneducated man; which I suppose is the reason why I know so little of our family history.")

Chapter 9

1. Nancy certainly enjoyed weaving and handling fabrics; by her late teens, she may have served the Berrys (or even

"hired out") as a seamstress. On Nancy's learning to read the Bible and to fit and sew dresses at the Berrys' home, and for other Presidential parent explorations, see Doug Wead, *The Raising of a President: The Mothers and Fathers of Our Nation's Leaders* (New York: Simon and Schuster, 2005), 111.

2. Tom retained interest in Sally and kept tabs on her whereabouts and her status. After Nancy died, Tom, in his forties, not only journeyed to propose for a second time to Sally, then an impecunious and indebted widow with three children, *but also* spent money to square debts for her freedom to take him as her husband. Adhesion to bad ideas was so typical of Tom that his son quoted only one saying of his father's: "If you make a bad bargain, *hug* it the tighter." 1 C.W. 280 (Lincoln to Joshua Speed, February 25, 1842).

3. HI 96 (A.H. Chapman, *ante* September 8, 1865); HI 613 (Robert L. Wintersmith, March 23, 1887).

4. LL, 281 (WHH to Jesse W. Weik, October 10, 1888).

5. HL 100 (WHH to Ward Hill Lamon, March 6, 1870) (Lincoln ended by asking, "Is it because it is stolen?" That remark is separately analyzed in the following text.)

6. Tom was not likely very verbal or lyrical. The form of his proposal to his second wife, Sarah Bush Johnston, was "You need a husband and I need a wife." June 14, 1806 transactions noted by Harrison, 21, cited from Louis A. Warren, "Mr. and Mrs. Thomas Lincoln at Home," *Lincoln Lore* 1105 (June 12, 1950): 1.

7. 1 C.W. 456 (Lincoln to Solomon Lincoln, March 6, 1848); HI 107 (Sarah Bush Lincoln, September 8, 1865); HI 454 (John Hanks, c. 1865–6); HI 499 (Joshua Speed, December 6, 1866) ("I am slow to learn and slow to forget that which I have learned—My mind is like a piece of steel, very hard to scratch anything on it and almost impossible after you get it there to rub it out.")

8. Did Sally exhibit prodigious brainpower in childhood, only to fall back as she reached puberty? *Rapid* early child development scared Lincoln. When his and Mary's first-born, Robert Todd Lincoln, betrayed signs of being on the fast track, Lincoln worried. He reached out to his closest friend, Joshua Speed, to whom he looked for advice on the most intimate matters. Lincoln wrote Speed that Robert "talks very plainly—almost as plainly as anybody. He is quite smart enough. I sometimes fear he is one of the little rare-ripe sort that are smarter at about five than ever after." 1 C.W. 391 (Lincoln to Joshua Speed, October 22, 1846). Speed's reply, if any was made, was not saved by Lincoln. Speed, although married, was childless. Any advice he could offer would have been chiefly accrued through growing up near the middle of fifteen children on the plantation of Judge John Speed and his wife, Elizabeth.

9. Atkinson, 17. ("He could read 'n write. Me'n Nancy l'arnt him that much, an' he'd gone to school a spell; but it was nine miles thar an' back, an' a pore make-out fur a school, anyhow," a claim Dennis also made to Herndon, HI 37 (Dennis Hanks, June 13, 1865); Robert Bray, *Reading with Lincoln* (Carbondale: Southern Illinois University Press, 2010); Bray studied the data as closely as anyone, estimated Lincoln's literacy to date from about 1822, when he was thirteen; a homemade practice copybook survives from about 1822–24, when Lincoln was thirteen to fifteen, copies of twenty pages of which were published at the beginning of the first volume of the *Collected Works*.

10. HI 135 (Augustus H. Chapman, October 8, 1865), n. 2 (Lincoln's lines "are from the first two stanzas of a hymn by Isaac Watts, "The Shortness of Life and the Goodness of God.") See Isaac Watts, *Hymns and Spiritual Songs*, 1707–1748, ed. Selma L. Bishop (London, 1962).

11. HI 97 (A.H. Chapman, *ante* September 8, 1865) (Tom "took the world easy"); HI, 113 (Nathaniel Grigsby, September 12, 1865) (Tom was "a piddler—always doing but doing nothing great"); Tom seems to have learned to read and to have "read his bible" only as an older man, appearing to his grandson "to border on the serious—reflective." The "stories" he told seem to have been only the one about the day that Indians killed his father. HI, 533 (Thomas L. D. Johnston, c. 1866).

12. Atkinson, 17–18.

13. HI 37 (Dennis Hanks, June 13, 1865).

14. HI 245 (Elizabeth Crawford, April 19, 1866); LL, 280 (WHH to Jesse W. Weik, October 10, 1888).

15. LL 101 (WHH to Ward Hill Lamon, March 6, 1870).

16. 1 C.W. 117–19 (Lincoln to Mrs. Elizabeth Browning, April 1, 1838); some scholars conclude that Lincoln's letter is to be read literally as an accurate description of Nancy Hanks Lincoln's late-stage appearance. However, the letter is on its face a comical and exaggerated account of Lincoln's failed romance. Its incidental and unflattering description of a toothless old woman, supposedly his mother, might equally be rejected as a caricature or figure of fun. His mother actually died in her mid-thirties, about age 34 or 35.

17. 3 C.W. 511 (Lincoln to Jesse W. Fell, December 20, 1859).

18. 1 C.W. 114 (Lincoln's "Lyceum Address," January 27, 1838).

19. *Ibid.*

20. *Ibid.*, 115.

21. *Ibid.*

22. *Ibid.*

Chapter 10

1. 1 C.W. 378 (Lincoln to Andrew Johnston, April 18, 1846); 1 C.W. 61 (Lincoln to John W. Scripps, c. June, 1860).

2. Evidence now lost revealed that Lincoln associated his sister with his mother. Herndon copied entries in Lincoln's handwriting in the Lincoln family Bible, including "Nancy Lincoln was born February 10th, 1807." HI 110 (WHH notes, September 9, 1865). This Freudian slip substituted "Nancy" for "Sarah." The top of the first page was torn and is now lost; when John D. Johnston made a copy before it was lost, he silently corrected Lincoln's entry as "Sarah Lincoln." See 2 C.W. 94–95 (1851[?] family record).

3. HI 62 (Lincoln autobiography to John L. Scripps, c. June 1860).

4. HI 113 (Nathaniel Grigsby, September 12, 1865).

5. HI 104 (Dennis Hanks, September 8, 1865).

6. HI 99 (A.H. Chapman, September 8, 1865) ("no beds or bedding or scarcely any ... no dishes except a few pewter and tin ones ... the children were suffering greatly for clothes..."); *Id.*, 106 (Sarah Bush Lincoln, September 8, 1865) ("Abe was then young—so was his Sister. I dressed Abe & his sister up—looked more human.")

7. Tildy seemed smitten, following behind and horsing around heedlessly with her new "big brother." HI 110 (Matilda Johnston Moore, September 8, 1865) ("One day he was going to the field to work, I ran—jumped on his back—cut my foot on the axe.")

8. Miller, 75.

Chapter 11

1. HL 41 (Dennis Hanks, June 13, 1865).

2. HI 48 (John B. Helm, June 20, 1865) (Helm admitted also that poverty would have precluded the cost of school for Lincoln.)

3. Indiana Territory became the State of Indiana on December 18, 1816. The Lincolns crossed the Ohio River within a few weeks before that date. Spencer County hosted no public school before one run by Crawford beginning in the winter of 1820.

4. 3 C.W. 511 (Lincoln to Jesse W. Fell, December 20, 1859).

5. HI 41 (Dennis Hanks, June 13, 1865); Atkinson, 26.

6. 3 C.W. 511 (Lincoln to Jesse W. Fell, December 20, 1859).

7. See HI 123 (William Wood, September 15, 1865).

8. HI 104 (Dennis Hanks, September 8, 1865).

9. HI 40 (Dennis Hanks, June 13, 1865); Atkinson, 19.

10. HI 113 (Nathaniel Grigsby, September 12, 1865).

11. HI 109 (Matilda Johnson Moore, September 8, 1865).

12. HI 145. (Original: "a vary tall Woman Straight as an Indian, fair Complection and was when I first remember her vary handsome, Sprightly talkative and proud wore her Hair Curled till Gray...")

13. HI 107–08 (Sarah Bush Lincoln, September 8, 1865) ("Abe never gave me a cross word or look and never refused in fact, or even in appearance, to do anything I requested him."); See HI 87 (Presley Nevil Haycraft, July 19, 1865) (Tom Lincoln "had courted Sarah Johnson before his first marriage but she had preferred Johnson.") Although Sarah is sometimes depicted as a saintly, sweet old lady, on the contrary, the most candid "snapshot" of her is of a querulous, opinionated woman. In 1861, Dennis Hanks and John J. Hall, the son of Lincoln's stepsister, Matilda Johnston Hall, argued over the responsibility for caring for Sarah. From Washington, Lincoln sent Hanks $50. In acknowledging the money, Hanks said that Sarah was a "mity childish heep of truble to us." Atkinson, 23.

14. Kaplan, 22–23, projects that Lincoln attended Andrew Crawford's school in the winter of 1820/21, James Swaney's, the following winter and Azel Dorsey's, 1824/1825. I believe that Crawford was first, followed by Azel Dorsey, with minor time spent with Dorsey's young ward and successor, James Swaney. Accepting Dennis Hanks as correct that Lincoln wrote fluently beginning in 1821, that would likely be a consequence of resuming school at about age 12. John Hanks, who arrived at the Lincolns' Indiana home in 1824, recalled little time away from school (probably Swaney's). The chronology would be Crawford in 1821, Dorsey in 1822 or 1823, and only a few weeks with Swaney in 1824. See Appendix B.

15. On these points, see chapter 2 and Atkinson; also, 1 C.W. 456 (Lincoln to Solomon Lincoln, March 6, 1848) (Tom Lincoln was not the wind in his son's educational sails. Lincoln did not look to his father even for his family history).

16. LL 195 (WHH to Jesse W. Weik, January 10, 1886) ("He was no *Conversationalist* as I understand that word. Mr. Lincoln was a poor listener.")

17. 1 C.W. 276 (Lincoln's "Temperance Address," February 22, 1842).

18. John Locke Scripps, *Life of Abraham Lincoln*, Roy P. Basler and Lloyd A. Dunlap, eds. (Bloomington: Indiana University Press, 1961), 29. The editors' note on point states, "The questions of when, where, and from whom Lincoln learned to read and write can be answered only from evidence based on confusing, and often conflicting, recollections. It is possible, of course, that Lincoln told Scripps of his accomplishment, but his reluctance to dwell on the details of his early life and the fact that he did not review the manuscript make it unlikely."

19. HI 40 (Dennis Hanks, June 13, 1865) (Lincoln "learned to write so that we could understand it in 1821."); Fred Kaplan recently made the same guess. After analyzing the total body of relevant evidence, Kaplan was satisfied that Lincoln began to write at about the age of 12, possibly a year before Lincoln again had a schoolmaster. Given evidence from Sarah that the unschooled boy was only up to a crude signature when he was 10 or 11, Kaplan's estimate is about as early as any reasonable person might suggest.

20. HI 123 (William Wood, September 15, 1865).

21. *Ibid.*

22. HI 124 (William Wood, September 15, 1865).

23. *Ibid.*

24. 1 C.W. 282–83 (Lincoln to Joshua Speed, March 27, 1842).

25. Atkinson, 24–25.

26. HI 43 (John Hanks, June 13, 1865).

27. *Ibid.*

28. HI 41 (Dennis Hanks, c. June 1860) ("Abe's father often said, 'I had to pull the old sow up to the trough,' when speaking of Abe's reading...")

29. HI 105 (Dennis Hanks, September 8, 1865).

30. Brian Danoff, "Lincoln and the 'Necessity' of Tolerating Slavery before the Civil War," online, 77 Cambridge Core, Vol. 1 (Winter, 2015), pp. 47–71. (Eventually, Lincoln parted company from Thomas Jefferson and Henry Clay, sliding toward emancipation.) See also an unsent letter in response to Charles Fisher's book on territorial slavery, at 4 C.W. 101 (Lincoln's unfinished letter to Charles H. Fisher, August 27, 1860).

31. Kaplan covers this book and visualizes how Lincoln may have read it.

32. HI 125 (Elizabeth Crawford, September 16, 1865).
33. *Ibid.*, 126.
34. *Ibid.*
35. *Ibid.*
36. *Ibid.*, 127.
37. *Ibid.*
38. HI 79 (J. W. Wartmann, July 21, 1865).
39. Lowell H. Harrison, *Lincoln in Kentucky* (Lexington: University Press of Kentucky, 2000), 17.
40. 3 C.W. 511 (Lincoln to Jesse W. Fell, December 20, 1859).
41. Speed's offer or suggestion followed Lincoln's month-long on-site pleasant introduction to farming life by seven months, namely, his stay on the Speed family plantation outside Louisville in August, 1841. During his stay, Lincoln had an enslaved valet assigned personally to him. Lincoln had been pursuing whatever education was necessary in order to become a thinking, intellectual, cultured gentleman. He was not going to claim to own people and run a farm or plantation like his grandfather. He was going to be his grandfather's intellectual equal, but he was not tempted to replicate his grandfather in farming or in romance. His view of people in bondage during his trip to Speed's plantation only raised feelings of compassion. When he saw Blacks strung together "like mackerel on a trot line," as he described them, the sight scorched his conscience. (NOTE: Contradictions existed within him, however. What Lincoln eschewed personally he did not mind encouraging state-wide or nationally. In 1840, Lincoln was positively proud of a new farmland distribution scheme that he sent his old law partner and proxy-in-Congress, John Stuart. Along with a copy of land resolutions he had authored and shepherded through both houses in Illinois, he asked Stuart, "Will you show them to Mr. Calhoun, informing him of the fact of their passage through our Legislature?")

"Calhoun" was John Calhoun, the Senator from South Carolina, of whom Lincoln said, "Mr. Calhoun suggested a similar proposition last winter; and perhaps, if he finds himself backed by one of the states, he may be induced to take it up again. You will see by the resolutions, that you and the others of our delegation in Congress are instructed to go for them." Nothing thereafter is documented. Senator Calhoun is infamous, of course, for affirming that slavery was a "positive good." No partnership evolved after all between Lincoln and Calhoun to create farms. One is stunned to think that some of those farms, so sponsored and carved out by the Federal government, would have been operated only via the labor, knowledge and skills stolen from the enslaved.

42. 1 C.W. 456 (Lincoln to Solomon Lincoln, March 6, 1848).
43. HI 124 (William Wood, September 15, 1865); 1 C.W. 280 (Lincoln to Joshua Speed, February 25, 1842).
44. 4 C.W. 63 (Lincoln to John L. Scripps, c. 1860).

Chapter 12

1. When the Lincolns moved to Indiana, then the newest state in the Union, it as yet had no public schools. Because the first one-room school near the Lincoln home opened only in the winter of 1820, Lincoln's mother was his teacher by default as long as she lived.
2. Atkinson, 17–18.
3. Miller, 87.
4. 4 C.W. 63 (Lincoln to John L. Scripps, c. June 1860).
5. Miller, 99.
6. John Locke Scripps, *Life of Abraham Lincoln*, Roy P. Basler and Lloyd A, Dunlap, eds. (Bloomington: Indiana University Press, 1961), 50.
7. 4 C.W. 63 (Lincoln to John L. Scripps, c. June 1860).
8. Miller, 98–99; Albert Beveridge, *Abraham Lincoln, 1809–1858*, Vol. 1 (Boston: Houghton Mifflin Co., 1928), 104–05.
9. Aleksandr Solzhenitsyn, *One Day in the Life of Ivan Denisovich* (1962); an author intimately familiar with cold, doubted that a man who is warm can ever understand one who is freezing.
10. John W. Smith, *History of Macon County* (Unknown, 1876), 144, 295–96.

11. Tom Emery, *Jacksonville Journal-Courier* (December 25, 2016; updated February 9, 2018); available online at https://www.myjournalcourier.com/news/article/ Year. Accessed January 30, 2012.

12. Roy P. Basler, ed., *The Collected Works of Abraham Lincoln* (New Brunswick, NJ: Rutgers University Press) (1953) (hereafter, "C.W."), Vol. 4, 63.

13. *Ibid.*, 63–64. Richard Lawrence Miller, *Lincoln and His World, The Early Years: Birth to Illinois Legislature* (Mechanicsburg, PA: Stackpole Books) (2006) (hereafter, "Miller"), 98–101.

14. *Ibid.*, 63.

15. HI 9 (Mentor Graham, May 29, 1865) ("an unsteady—noisy—fussy—rattle brained man, wild & unprovidential"); HI 13 (Hardin Bale, May 29, 1865) ("a gassy—windy—brain rattling man"), HI 18 (William G. Greene, May 30, 1865) ("a wild—reckless—careless man—a kind of wandering horse tamer.")

16. 4 C.W. 64 (Lincoln's autobiography to John L. Scripps, c. June 1860).

17. See 4 C.W. 60–63. Those whom Lincoln mentioned in his autobiographical outline up to age 21 were his father (mentioned seven times), his mother (once, saying she died), his stepmother (three times), her children (twice), his three teachers in Indiana, Allen Gentry (called the "son of the owner" of the flatboat they both took to New Orleans), and, on the occasion of that flatboat trip, seven violent "negroes" he fought, whom he mentioned in two lines. By inference, the universe in which Lincoln moved up until age 21 was occupied memorably by fewer than twenty people.

18. 1 C.W. 8 (Lincoln's "Communication to the People of Sangamon County," March 9, 1832).

19. See 1 C.W. 5, note 1. No copy of the handbill itself (vouched for in Hay and Nicolay's Lincoln biography) has been discovered; the text is taken from the newspaper.

20. 1 C.W. 509–10 (Lincoln speech in House of Representatives, July 27, 1848); 4 C.W. 62, 64 (Lincoln autobiography to John L. Scripps, c. June 1860).

21. HI, 10 (Mentor Graham, May 29, 1865).

Chapter 13

1. HI 779, Appendix, "Brief Outline of the Joseph Hanks Family," by Paul H. Verduin.

2. Louis Austin Warren, *Lincoln's Parentage & Childhood, A History of the Kentucky Lincolns Supported by Documentary Evidence* (New York: The Century Co., 1926), 33.

3. Arthur W. Frank, *Letting Stories Breathe* (Chicago: University of Chicago Press, 2010) (hereafter "Frank"), 145.

4. Some ten years later, when those future hopes were on the cusp of realization, Lincoln invoked God's blessing again. "In *giving* freedom to the *slave*, we *assure* freedom to the *free*—honorable alike in what we give, and what we preserve. We shall nobly save, or meanly lose, the last best, hope of earth. Other means may succeed; this could not fail. The way is plain, peaceful, generous, just—a way which, if followed, the world will forever applaud, and God must forever bless." 5 C.W. 537 (Lincoln's message to Congress, December 1, 1862).

5. Frank, 2.

6. LL 311 (WHH to Jesse W. Weik, January 23, 1890); 316 (WHH to Jesse W. Weik, July 23, 1890); HI 350 (Judge David Davis interview, September 20, 1866) (punctuation modernized).

7. 1 C.W. 94 (Lincoln to Mary S. Owens, August 16, 1837); 1 C.W. 289 (Lincoln to Joshua Speed, July 4, 1842).

8. Lincoln in New Salem was skittish around women. His first job, at the mill by the river, was a virtual male enclave for fishing, nude swimming and shooting the breeze as grain ground into flour. Lincoln made friends with men like Jack Kelso, Mentor Graham and "Slicky Bill" Greene.

9. See John Evangelist Walsh, *The Shadows Rise: Abraham Lincoln and the Ann Rutledge Legend* (Chicago: University of Illinois Press, 2008).

10. I C.W. 94 (Lincoln to Mary Owens, August 16, 1837).

11. Interestingly, Lincoln associated Mary Owens with his *mother*. Not as prepossessing, lovely or charming, but as intelligent, Mary made him think of his mother, he said. When Lincoln wrote

Mrs. Orville Browning about his difficulty, he used the W-word but the image of "woman" he verbalized was physically a revoltingly gross and distorted, fat, and old body. Nobody else ever saw Nancy Hanks as her son wrote of her in this letter. His supposed description in his comic letter accordingly needs very careful handling in determining how much truth his letter contains, just how close it comes to being about his mother. In defense of its potential accuracy, Nancy Hanks Lincoln was medically under siege for some time before she died. Although she died at age 34 (or 35 or 36, as her birth year is uncertain), she may have finally appeared to her son more like a grandmother than a mother. He was age nine. Perhaps she seemed not only sickly but old. She may have met death afflicted by edema, swollen and in crippling circulatory distress, as well as losing her teeth, lying low with fatigue and haggard. This is Lincoln, supposedly describing his mother to Mrs. Browning:

> When I beheld her, I could not for my life avoid thinking of my mother; and this, not from withered features, for her skin was too full of fat, to permit its contracting in to wrinkles; but from her want of teeth, weather-beaten appearance in general, and from a kind of notion that ran in my head, that nothing could have commenced at the size of infancy, and reached her present bulk in less than thirty-five or forty years.

His caricature contradicts other descriptions of Nancy. For example, only two brothers maintained that Nancy Hanks was more than amply fleshed. Samuel Haycraft wrote that Nancy Hanks was a "heavy built squatty woman," HI 84, but he apparently confused Lincoln's mother with another Nancy Hanks. Lincoln once sent a letter to Haycraft in which he said that Haycraft was "wrong" about his mother, although the letter to which Lincoln replied has not survived to clarify exactly what Lincoln denied. CW Samuel's brother, Presley Nevil Haycraft, likewise said that Nancy Hanks "was of good size." HI 87. Everyone else recalled Nancy as a slim woman.

12. 1 C.W. 118 (Lincoln to Mrs. Elizabeth Browning, April 1, 1838).

13. *Ibid.*
14. *Ibid.*
15. *Ibid.*
16. 1 C.W. 78 (Lincoln to Mary Owens, May 7, 1837).
17. HI 664 (Sarah Rickard Barret, August 3, 1888).
18. The reverse may clinch the case. Lincoln's reaction when discussing a woman who was going to renounce her matrimonial vow and leave her marital bed was extraordinary. (In context, Lincoln used "married lady" in describing Parthenia Hill, the one who introduced him to Mary Owens, and "widow lady," which he used for the woman who kept house for him when he and Mary Todd Lincoln were newlyweds. When Lincoln wrote Joshua Speed, he spoke of his "lady," Fanny, too. In a published account of one of his trials, Lincoln mentioned what the "prosecution also proved by a respectable lady," while in another letter he directed "the result to Ebenezer Stout, the lady's husband.") While we do not know the exact circumstances behind Lincoln's response, if it were spoken rather than written, it would have been uttered through clenched teeth. Lincoln did not apply the word "lady" to her. In the context of a request from a fellow attorney that he file a divorce action, "lady" disappeared. Lincoln responded gracelessly and namelessly regarding "the woman."

Chapter 14

1. Anita E. Kelly, *The Psychology of Secrets*, 2nd ed. (New York: Springer, 2002).
2. 2 C.W. 320 (Abraham Lincoln to Joshua Speed, August 24, 1855).
3. LL 94 (WHH to Ward Hill Lamon, March 3, 1870). Many similar references may be found, including his interview with Mary Todd Lincoln, LL 113 (WHH to *Daily State Journal*, January 12, 1874), in which she quoted her husband's basic philosophy in the couplet, "Mr. Lincoln's maxim and philosophy was, 'What is to be will be,/And no cares (prayers) of ours can arrest the decree.'"
4. 1 C.W. 378 (Lincoln to Andrew

Johnston, April 18, 1846). Lincoln never knew the author (newspapers commonly printed poems anonymously). The poem's author was British poet John Knox.

5. 1 C.W. 1 (Lincoln's copybook verses, c. 1824–26).

6. 1 C.W. 378 (Lincoln to Andrew Johnston, April 18, 1846).

7. Frank, 159.

Chapter 15

1. 4 C.W. 63–64 (Lincoln's autobiography for John L. Scripps, c. June 1860).

2. 1 C.W. 282 (Lincoln to Joshua Speed, March 27, 1842).

3. "Planter" and "farmer" were synonymous for plantation owners, as was "farm" for slave plantations. (For example, Abraham wrote a letter in 1841 referring to a gentleman who "had purchased twelve negroes in different parts of Kentucky and was taking them to a farm in the South. They were chained six and six together." Abraham Lincoln to Mary Speed, Sept. 27, 1841 (1 CW 260); Roy P. Basler, ed., *The Collected Works of Abraham Lincoln* (New Brunswick, N.J.: Rutgers University Press) (1953). See, however, Chapter 14, this book.

4. 2 C.W. 146 (Lincoln's speech to the Springfield Scott Club, August 26, 1852).

5. 2 C.W. 239 (Lincoln's speech at Bloomington, Illinois, September 26, 1854).

6. 2 C.W. 281 (Lincoln's speech at Peoria, Illinois, October 16, 1854).

7. 2 C.W. 493–94 (Lincoln's speech at Chicago, Illinois, July 10, 1858). In his debates with Douglas in 1858, he used "plant" eight times more, similarly.

8. 3 C.W. 480–81 (Lincoln's address to the Wisconsin State Agricultural Society, September 30, 1859).

9. *Ibid.*, 480.

10. 3 C.W. 477–80 (Lincoln's address to the Wisconsin State Agricultural Society, September 30, 1859).

11. *Ibid.*, 480. He also told the huge crowd of farm folk around him, "I know of nothing so pleasant to the mind, as the discovery of anything which is at once new and valuable—nothing which

so lightens and sweetens toil, as the hopeful pursuit of such discovery. And how vast, and how varied a field is agriculture, for such discovery. The mind, already trained to thought, in the country school, or higher school, cannot fail to find there an exhaust less source of profitable enjoyment."

12. Ward Hill Lamon, *Recollections of Abraham Lincoln*, 14–15.

13. *Ibid.*, 15.

14. *Ibid.*

Chapter 16

1. Brookhiser made nothing of Lincoln's grandfather, the Virginia planter, whom he categorized as fantasy.

2. Strozier, 120; 1 C.W. 465 (Lincoln to Mary Todd Lincoln, April 16, 1848).

3. 2 C.W. 255 (Lincoln's speech at Peoria, October 16, 1854); 3 C.W. 78–79 (Lincoln's speech at Carlinville, August 31, 1858) (Apart from a "self-made" Tennessee politician, Hugh L. White, Lincoln's choices for President—Henry Clay, William Henry Harrison, Zachary Taylor and Winfield Scott—were all descendants [sons] of Virginia planters, to any of whom he may have been [and felt] biologically akin.) (In this speech, he asked the crowd, "I can express all my views on the slavery question by quotations from Henry Clay. Doesn't this look like we are akin?").

4. 2 C.W. 255 (Lincoln's speech at Peoria, October 16, 1854).

5. *Ibid.*

6. *Ibid.*, 256.

7. *Ibid.*, 256.

8. 3 C.W. 140 (Douglas's speech during debate at Jonesboro, Illinois, September 15, 1858).

9. LL 284 (WHH to Joseph Fowler, October 30, 1888).

10. "Hear what Mr. Clay said: 'And what is the foundation of this appeal to me in Indiana, to liberate the slaves under my care in Kentucky? It is a general declaration in the act announcing to the world the independence of the thirteen American colonies, that all men are created equal. Now, as an abstract principle,

there is no doubt of the truth of that declaration; and it is desirable in the original construction of society, and in organized societies, to keep it in view as a great fundamental principle. But, then, I apprehend that in no society that ever did exist, or ever shall be formed, was or can the equality asserted among the members of the human race be practically enforced and carried out. There are portions, large portions, women, minors, insane, culprits, transient sojourners, that will always probably remain subject to the government of another portion of the community. That declaration whatever may be the extent of its import, was made by the delegations of the thirteen States. In most of them slavery existed, and had long existed, and was established by law. It was introduced and forced upon the colonies by the paramount law of England. Do you believe, that in making that Declaration the States that concurred in it intended that it should be tortured into a virtual emancipation of all the slaves within their respective limits? Would Virginia and other Southern States have ever united in a declaration which was to be interpreted into an abolition of slavery among them? Did any one of the thirteen colonies entertain such a design or expectation? To impute such a secret and unavowed purpose would be to charge a political fraud upon the noblest band of patriots that ever assembled in council; a fraud upon the confederacy of the Revolution; a fraud upon the union of those States whose constitution not only recognized the lawfulness of slavery but permitted the importation of slaves from Africa until the year 1808. This is the entire quotation brought forward to prove that somebody previous to three years ago had said the negro was not included in the term "all men" in the Declaration. How does it do so? In what way has it a tendency to prove that? Mr. Clay says it is true as an abstract principle that all men are created equal, but that we cannot practically apply it in all cases. He illustrates this by bringing forward the cases of females, minors and insane persons with whom it cannot be enforced; but he says it is true as

an abstract principle in the organization of society as well as in organized society, and it should be kept in view as a fundamental principle. Let me read a few words more before I add some comments of my own. Mr. Clay says a little further on: "I desire no concealment of my opinions in regard to the institution of slavery. I look upon it as a great evil; and deeply lament that we have derived it from the parental government; and from our ancestors. But here they are and the question is, how can they be best dealt with? If a state of nature existed and we were about to lay the foundations of society, no man would be more strongly opposed than I should be, to incorporating the institution of slavery among its elements."

Now here in this same book—in this same speech—is this same extract brought forward to prove that Mr. Clay held that the negro was not included in the Declaration of Independence—no such statement on his part, but the declaration that it is a great fundamental truth, which should be constantly kept in view in the organization of society and in societies already organized."

11. Douglas may have wooed Mary Todd, but it did not go far. In any case, Lincoln won the woman (and lived to regret it). Douglas may have hurt his friend, Simeon Francis, the local Whig editor. Douglas also became rich feeding in the public trough, raking in large fees as Lincoln labored for far less. In the race of life, Lincoln had been flat failure. Did Douglas ever say anything? Yes. That Lincoln served alcohol in grocery. Lincoln batted charges back like flies. The only one Lincoln could have brooded over he left unanswered at the time.

12. 2 C.W. 544 (Lincoln speech at Bath, Illinois, August 16, 1858); 2 C.W. 545 (Lincoln's speech at Lewistown, Illinois, August 17, 1858).

13. 2 C.W. 545 (Lincoln's speech at Lewistown, Illinois, August 17, 1858).

14. Speaking of that generation, he said, "They grasped not only the whole race of man then living, but they reached forward and seized upon the farthest posterity. They erected a beacon to guide their children and their children's

children, and the countless myriads who should inhabit the earth in other ages. Wise statesmen as they were, they knew the tendency of prosperity to breed tyrants, and so they established these great self-evident truths, that when in the distant future some man, some faction, some interest, should set up the doctrine that none but rich men, or none but white men, were entitled to life, liberty and the pursuit of happiness, their posterity might look up again to the Declaration of Independence and take courage to renew the battle which their fathers began—so that truth, and justice, and mercy, and all the humane and Christian virtues might not be extinguished from the land; so that no man would hereafter dare to limit and circumscribe the great principles on which the temple of liberty was being built." *Ibid.*, 546–47.

15. *Ibid.*, 547.

16. *Ibid.*, 547. A reporter present noted the "tremendous directness" with which Lincoln spoke. HI 4 (Horace White, May 17, 1865).

17. 3 C.W. 413. (Abraham Lincoln address in Ohio, September 16, 1859).

18. The strategy of recruiting Revolutionary allies went back to Lincoln's first years in public life. 1 C.W. 170 (Lincoln's "Sub-Treasury Speech," December 26, 1839) (when Lincoln defended the constitutionality of a national bank, saying, "We have often heretofore shown, and therefore need not in detail do so again, that a majority of the Revolutionary patriarchs, whoever acted officially upon the question, commencing with Gen. Washington and embracing Gen. Jackson, the larger number of the signers of the Declaration, and of the framers of the Constitution, who were in the Congress of 1791, have decided upon their oaths that such a bank is constitutional."

19. 3 C.W. 533 (Lincoln's address at Cooper Union, February 27, 1860).

20. Richard Brookhiser, *Founder's Son* (New York: Basic Books, 2014), 34.

Chapter 17

1. 4 C.W. 235 (Lincoln's address to the New Jersey Senate, February 21, 1861).

2. *Ibid.*, 236.

3. British victories and draws were the common result of battles during the Revolution. Passing over the British evacuation of Boston (a victory, but not a battle), and the desperate but successful holding action at Harlem Heights, covering a general retreat, Lincoln chose the aggressive and successful battles around Trenton as the staple of his earliest "book reading."

4. 1 C.W. 8 (Lincoln to the people of Sangamon County, March 9, 1832).

5. LL 173 (WHH to editor of the *Religio-Philosophical Journal*, December 4, 1885).

6. See a short YouTube produced by the Library of Congress. https://youtu. be/qnux4tPiNMI (accessed 11/13/20); Eleanor Atkinson, *The Boyhood of Lincoln* (1908), 18.

7. 4 C.W. 61 (Lincoln's autobiography to John L. Scripps, *c.* June 1860); besides photographs, an amazing amount of detail about the baby and the small tombstone is available online at the Abraham Lincoln Research Site, https://www. rogerjnorton.com/Lincoln2.html (accessed 3/29/21).

8. 4 C.W. 235–36.

9. LL 100 (WHH to Ward Hill Lamon, March 6, 1870).

Afterword

1. Lincoln's elevation of the male grandparent over the female is unfair but documented. Lincoln celebrated her as the successful "thief" of the best genetics available in the neighborhood of her youth. Unlike his maternal grandfather, his maternal grandmother Lincoln did not figure into his development, his mind, or hopes.

2. Atkinson, 23. (In Lincoln's family Bible, in his own handwriting, the date of Nancy Hanks's birth is noted as February 5, 1784, and the date of death August 8, 1818. Scholars who doubt the accuracy of the birthdate hold that she was born earlier, around 1782.)

3. HI 454 (John Hanks interview with Herndon, 1865–66).

4. Atkinson, 23.

5. David Herbert Donald, *Lincoln* (New York: Simon & Schuster, 1995), 19.

6. 1 C.W. 279 (Lincoln's "Temperance Address") (Lincoln deferred eulogizing Washington in favor of honoring his name only); 3 C.W. 376 (Lincoln to Henry L. Pierce, April 6, 1859) ("All honor to Jefferson"); Each quality Lincoln expressed to Herndon in chapter 5, section 5, is consistent with the qualities of Jefferson, as his admirers saw Jefferson.

7. The Virginia planter's "broad mindedness" cannot be explored now while the founders' attitudes varied among one another and changed in time. The debate over whether the founders in fact meant to end or to continue slavery is ongoing. Independent of that controversy, Lincoln's singular impression of his grandfather is taken to reflect his own inclinations, to accept the Constitution but to work for the goal of equality as promised in the Declaration of Independence, which approach Lincoln viewed to be consistent with Jefferson, the founders, and, implicitly from that, his grandfather.

8. As I researched this one, a new book appeared written by an expert in Revolutionary era figures who tried his hand at researching and writing about Lincoln. Richard Brookhiser's insightful and highly original composite of close readings of primary documents, substantiates Lincoln's celebration of the men of '76 and especially of the Declaration of Independence. However, although his *Founders' Son* included a paragraph about the secret ancestor Lincoln disclosed to Herndon, Brookhiser dismissed Lincoln's remark and stories as so much fantasy. I gratefully direct readers to Brookhiser's work for a complete tour of Lincoln's identification with the men of '76, but I note that he disagrees on the reality of "the Virginia planter" whom I posit to stand behind Lincoln's disclosures and use of the founders in lieu of his grandfather.

9. Others have worked with genealogical charts of the First Families of Virginia. Across from the Capitol, in Arlington, Virginia, was the plantation of Robert E. Lee. In an article entitled "Is Lincoln among the Aristocrats?"

by William E. Barton, Journal of the Illinois State Historical Society, Vol. 22, No. 1 (April, 1929), 65–78, www.jstor.org/stable/40187611, accessed 2/25/2018, Barton said, "I confess to some pride in this discovery. If any man notable in Southern history represents aristocratic birth and breeding, it is Robert E. Lee. If any American is accepted as standing for democracy and humble antecedents it is Abraham Lincoln. This is the first time any suggestion has been made that they were blood relations."

Appendix A

1. C.W. 114, (Lincoln's speech to the Lyceum, January 27, 1838). (Lincoln called the battles "scenes," as in a story. During the Black Hawk War, Lincoln witnessed scenes of carnage but was in no combat action. Perhaps self-consciously, he served, as it were, behind the scenes.) (This speech marks the only time that Lincoln used the phrase "nearly every adult male" or anything broadly like it.)

2. J. L. Hochschild and Brenna M. Powell, "Racial Reorganization and the United States census 1850–1930: Mulattoes, Half-Breeds, Mixed Parentage, Hindoos, and the Mexican Race," Studies in American Political Development, 2008; 22(1):59-96. https://scholar.harvard.edu/jlhochschild/publications/recial-reorganization-and-united-states-census-mulattoes-half-br Accessed 2/28/20.

3. 3 C.W. 84, (Lincoln's reply to Douglas, September 2, 1858).

4. C.W. unnumbered first pages, (twenty pages from "Lincoln's Sum Book"); HI 12, (William G. Greene to Herndon, May 29, 1865), 426, (Robert B. Rutledge to Herndon, November 30, 1866); LL 159, (WHH to Jesse Weik, October 28, 1885), 188, (WHH to Jesse Weik, January 7, 1886).

5. C.W. 222-23, (Lincoln, fragment of approximately July 1, 1854) (Lincoln's direct line expired with Robert Todd Lincoln Beckwith, who died in 1985. Lincoln's relatives are now strictly collateral. Lincoln's *projected* closest living relatives would, ironically, be the descendants of

enslaved mothers who were raped by his rogue grandfather.)

6. C.W. 320, (Lincoln to Joshua Speed, August 24, 1855) ("I confess I hate to see the poor creatures hunted down, and caught, and carried back to their stripes, and unrewarded toils; but I bite my lip and keep quiet.")

7. See above note. The terms "certainty" and "certain" are used not in a historical sense but personally to Lincoln, alluding to Lincoln's inner or apparent certainty.

Bibliography

Books

Anonymous. *History Book of Shelby County*, 1885 (est.).

Atkinson, Eleanor. *The Boyhood of Lincoln*. New York: Doubleday, Page & Co., 1908.

Barton, William E. *The Life of Abraham Lincoln*. Milwaukee: Bobbs Merrill, 1925.

Basler, Roy P., ed. *Abraham Lincoln: His Speeches and Writings*. New York: The World Publishing Co., 1946.

_____. *The Collected Works of Abraham Lincoln*. New Brunswick, NJ: Rutgers University Press, 1953.

Beveridge, Albert. *Abraham Lincoln, 1809–1858*, Vol. 1. Boston: Houghton Mifflin Co., 1928.

Blackburn, Joyce. *George Wythe of Williamsburg*. New York: Harper & Row, 1975.

Bloom, Harold. *The Anxiety of Influence: A Theory of Poetry*. New York: Oxford University Press, 1973, 2nd ed., 1997.

Bray, Robert. *Reading with Lincoln*. Carbondale: Southern Illinois University Press, 2010.

Brookhiser, Richard. *Founder's Son*. New York: Basic Books, 2014.

Burlingame, Michael. *The Inner World of Lincoln*. Chicago: University of Illinois Press, 1997.

_____, ed. *Lincoln's Journalist: John Hay's Anonymous Writings for the Press, 1860–1864*. Carbondale: Southern Illinois University Press, 1998.

_____. *Abraham Lincoln: A Life*. Baltimore: Johns Hopkins University Press, 2009.

Carpenter, F.B. *Six Months in the White House*. New York: Current Literature Publishing Co., 1907.

Donald, David Herbert. *Lincoln*. New York: Simon & Schuster, 1995.

_____. *Lincoln's Herndon*. New York: Alfred A. Knopf, 1948.

Foner, Eric. *Thomas Paine and Revolutionary America*. Oxford University Press, 2nd edition, 2005.

Frank, Arthur W. *Letting Stories Breathe*. Chicago: University of Chicago Press, 2010.

Harrison, Lowell H. *Lincoln of Kentucky*. Lexington: University Press of Kentucky, 2009.

Herndon, William H., and Jesse W. Weik. *Life of Lincoln: The True Story of a Great American Life*. Chicago: Belton, Clark & Co., 1889.

_____ (Douglas L. Wilson and Rodney O. Davis, eds.). *Herndon's Lincoln*. Chicago: University of Illinois Press, 2016.

Hochschild, J. L., and Brenna M. Powell. "Racial Reorganization and the United States Census 1850–1930: Mulattoes, Half-Breeds, Mixed Parentage, Hindoos, and the Mexican Race." *Studies in American Political Development* 22(1), 2008, pp. 59–96.

Holzer, Harold, Craig L. Symonds, and Frank J. Williams, eds. *Exploring Lincoln: Great Historians Reappraise Our Greatest President*. New York: Fordham University Press, 2015.

Kaplan, Fred. *Lincoln: The Biography of a Writer*. New York: HarperCollins, 2008.

Kelly, Anita E. *The Psychology of Secrets*. New York: Springer, 2nd ed., 2002.

Bibliography

Lamon, Ward Hill. *Recollections of Abraham Lincoln, 1847–1865*. Lincoln: University of Nebraska, reprint, 1994.

Miller, Richard Lawrence. *Lincoln and His World: The Early Years, Birth to Illinois Legislature*. Mechanicsville, PA: Stackpole Books, 2006.

Paine, Thomas. *Common Sense*, 1776.

_____. *The Rights of Man*, 1791.

Scripps, John Locke. *Life of Abraham Lincoln*. Bloomington: Indiana University Press, 1961.

Smith, John W. *History of Macon County*. Unknown, 1876.

Solzhenitsyn, Alexandr. *One Day in the Life of Ivan Denisovich*, 1962.

Strozier, Charles B. *Lincoln and the Quest for Union: Public and Private Meanings*. Chicago: University of Illinois Press, 1982; Philadelphia, Paul Dry Books, 2nd ed., 2001.

Warren, Louis Austin. *Lincoln's Parentage & Childhood: A History of the Kentucky Lincolns Supported by Documentary Evidence*. New York: The Century Co., 1926.

Wead, Doug. *The Raising of a President: The Mothers and Fathers of Our Nation's Leaders*. New York: Simony & Schuster, 2005.

Wilson, Douglas L., and Rodney O. Davis, eds. *Herndon on Lincoln: Letters*. Chicago: University of Illinois Press, 2006.

_____. *Herndon's Informant: Letters, Interviews, and Statements about Abraham Lincoln*. Chicago: University of Illinois Press, 1998.

Articles

Barnhart, John D. "The Southern Influence in the Formation of Indiana," *Indiana Magazine of History*, Vol. 3 (September, 1937).

Barton, William E. "Is Lincoln Among the Aristocrats?" *Journal of the Illinois State Historical Society*, Vol. 22, No. 1 (April, 1929).

Child, Christopher Challender. "The Maternal Ancestry of Abraham Lincoln: The Origins of Nancy (Hanks) Lincoln; A Study in Appalachian Geneaology," *New England Ancestors*, Vol. 4, No. 1 (Winter, 2003).

Danoff, Brian. "Lincoln and the 'Necessity' of Tolerating Slavery before the Civil War," *Cambridge Core* online (Winter, 2015).

Emery, Tom. "The Winter of the Deep Snow." *Jacksonville Journal Courier* (December 25, 2016).

Gordon-Reed, Annette. "Rebellious History," *New York Review of Books* (October 22, 2020).

Havlik, Robert. "Some Influences of Thomas Paine's Age of Reason Upon Abraham Lincoln," *Lincoln Herald* (Summer, 2002).

Jukic, A.M., D.D. Baird, C.R. Weinberg, D.R. McConnaughey, and A.J. Wilcox. "Length of Human Pregnancy and Contributors to Its Natural Variation," *Human Reproduction*, Vol. 28, Issue 10, 2848–55 (October, 2013).

Warren, Louis A. "Mr. and Mrs. Thomas Lincoln at Home," *Lincoln Lore* (June 12, 1950).

Wilson, Douglas L. "Keeping Lincoln's Secrets," *The Atlantic* (May 2000).

Index

Index